DISCARD

Science Fiction Criticism
An Annotated Checklist

Science Fiction Criticism

An Annotated Checklist

By Thomas Clareson

The College of Wooster

The Kent State University Press

The Serif Series
Bibliographies and Checklists, Number 23
William White, General Editor
Wayne State University

Contents

Introduction vii

I. SF: General Studies 1

II. SF: Literary Studies 27

III. SF: Book Reviews 107

IV. SF: The Visual Arts 139

V. SF: Futurology, Utopia, and Dystopia . . . 155

VI. SF: Classroom and Library 167

VII. SF: Publishing 181

VIII. SF: Specialist Bibliographies, Checklists,
and Indices 189

IX. SF: The Contemporary Scene 199

Author Index of Entries 209

Index of Authors Mentioned 219

Introduction

Within the past year alone, many teachers, both at the high school and college-university levels, faced with the need to prepare a course in science fiction and modern fantasy for immediate presentation, have asked *Extrapolation* to help them obtain critical materials in the field. That is why it has seemed a particularly appropriate time to issue this checklist of science fiction criticism.

Science Fiction Criticism: *An Annotated Checklist* is an expansion of the list published in *Extrapolation* between May 1970 and May 1971. Several hundred items, particularly book reviews, have been added, and while the earlier bibliography was confined to a listing by author only, here special categories have been introduced to facilitate the handling of the approximately eight hundred entries. While not definitive, it does gather together for the first time from widely diverse sources those critical materials which are needed by the student of the genre and which have thus far made up the reaction to, and evaluation of, science fiction in the general and scholarly press.

From the beginning of the project, two criteria have governed the inclusion of any item. First it must have been available for annotation since mere lists of titles can be both frustrating and misleading. Second, with few exceptions, the author must explicitly discuss science fiction or, at least, make serious reference to it. Thus, for example, many articles whose titles indicated that they concerned themselves with science and literature have been omitted because they did not address themselves to the genre; amusingly in 1971, some of these articles repeated, essentially, the same arguments which fostered such fierce debate around the turn of the century under the impact of the "new science." Obviously many of them will be of interest to the student of science fiction, but reference to them is available in generally accessible bibliographies, and if they ever are brought together, it should be in a volume of their own.

In compiling this checklist, I have tried to recognize that the genre is not only a subject for literary study, but is of interest to a number of groups and disciplines. Thus, the categories established for this bibliography are as follows:

I. *SF: General Studies.* Although content and expression can never be separated, by and large these entries emphasize the content of science fiction and its place in the intellectual milieu, with no more than casual or incidental attention to it as an art form. In a sense they could be called *interdisciplinary* studies, for in each case the author has used the fiction to illuminate some aspect of the contemporary scene. They range from a study of the genre's relationship to science and technology to a consideration of its ethical, religious, and political themes and their implications. For example, those items which explore its mythic nature as well as those which reveal how psychologists have used it to analyze the public state-of-mind are included here.

II. *SF: Literary Studies.* Whether focusing upon an individual author, title, motif, or the genre as a whole, these entries do essentially one of two things. Either they consider the relationship of science fiction to the literary tradition in terms of literary history, literary criticism, and language, or they focus upon the characteristics of the *modern* genre and try to evaluate it as a form of popular literature. (I use *modern* to designate that body of science fiction which has appeared in the so-called "specialist" magazines, beginning in 1926, a quirk of publishing history that has had much to do with the critical and popular reception of the genre.)

III. *SF: Book Reviews.* Because of projects now being undertaken by such individuals as H. W. Hall (see category VIII), I have not tried to do more than include a wide sampling of British and American reviews which would give something of the flavor of the *popular* critical reception of the genre over the past twenty years or so. To do this, I have emphasized three areas: (1) representative reviews from *The Library Journal*, the London *Times Literary Supplement, New Statesman*, the *New York Times Book Review*, and *Saturday Review*; (2) certain crucial books which have gained wide attention; and (3) certain continuing review columns/reviewers. Beyond these criteria, I have made a random selection from other reviews, choosing them for their writers' attitudes toward a given book or the genre as a whole.

As might be expected, these three categories comprise some two-thirds of the present volume. In addition, however, several special-interest categories seemed necessary.

IV. *SF: The Visual Arts.* This category includes those items which deal with science fiction both in the cinema and on TV and radio as well as those yet infrequent titles giving attention to the history of science fiction magazine illustration or to the relationship of the genre to the fine arts.

V. *SF: Futurology, Utopia, and Dystopia.* Although attention has long been given the role of prophecy in science fiction, only comparatively recently has the genre become linked with the field of futurological studies. This category includes those titles dealing with science fiction as a means of prediction or as a medium by which to construct alternative futures;

in other words, as a tool in the methodology of futuristic studies. The inclusion of utopian and dystopian materials needs little explanation, for it is this changing motif that has, fundamentally, given the futurologists the science fiction materials they work with.

VI. *SF*: *Classroom and Library*. All articles concerned with the advisability of including science fiction in the curriculum or in a library's holdings as well as those reporting the actual use of such materials in class are included here. In addition, those which enumerate specific lists of recommended books for library or school use are included.

VII. *SF*: *Publishing*. This is the smallest of the categories, primarily because except for a few years in the early 1950's—often called the "boom" or "boomlet"—little attention has been paid to this aspect of the field. As a result, most of the articles are concerned either with the criteria set up by the editors in accepting stories or with advice given to young or would-be writers.

VIII. *SF*: *Specialist Bibliographies, Checklists, and Indices*. Perhaps the greatest problem facing students wishing to work with the field of science fiction has been that many of the bibliographical tools needed have been issued in small, often privately-sponsored editions. A few have received attention and have gained recognition as standard works, but many have become unavailable and may be irretrievably lost. Others simply are not known to the general public. Because their compilers have completed work that the individual student might well have to undertake for himself—beginning, oftentimes, from scratch—the standard works and those now available have been included here. There are undoubtedly others; but they have not been available for annotation.

IX. *SF*: *The Contemporary Scene*. Under its seemingly catch-all label, this category focuses upon the published biographical and autobiographical sketches of authors, editors, and personalities affiliated with the field; upon interviews; and finally upon the scattered published accounts of the activities of science-fiction enthusiasts.

In a number of instances, entries have been listed in more than one category, with appropriate cross-references to the main listing. An additional reference tool is the index, in which two listings have been included: one giving the authors of the entries, the other giving the authors focused upon. In the first case, articles have been listed by title when their authors are unknown.

The nine categories, as noted, attempt to recognize the widely differing approaches to the genre which will be of value to different students. Some individuals may regard them as too inclusive; others, too exclusive. But one aim has been kept in mind throughout the volume: to document the reception of the genre in the popular and scholarly press during approximately the past twenty years.

In addition to the requirement that entries in *Science Fiction Criticism* address themselves specifically to the genre, certain other criteria governing inclusion have been set up. One has been that the bibliography bring together materials not previously gathered. Another has been the exclusion of any comprehensive listing of titles dealing with such figures as Poe, Verne, and Wells because they are included in readily available sources such as the *Poe Newsletter*, the annual PMLA bibliography, and *American Literature*. Nor, for example, is there a comprehensive listing of materials dealing with Utopia. Such deliberate exclusions will undoubtedly draw some criticism; however, the sheer bulk of such material, much of it unrelated to science fiction, has precluded it from a volume having a specialized focus.

Two arbitrary exclusions do, however, require further

xii

explanation. In the May 1970 issue of *Extrapolation* some
European titles were listed, and the promise was made that
the bibliography would give attention to foreign language
materials. That has proved impossible at this time, largely
because of the unavailability of the material for annotation.
Quantitatively, the attention given to science fiction in Europe
equals, if it does not exceed, the attention given it in the
United States and Great Britain. An annotated bibliography
of European titles will be prepared and published in *Extrapolation* and, hopefully, in the Serif Series, but it will require a
separate volume to do it justice. On the other hand, many
European titles that have been published in the English
language are annotated here.

Secondly, with few exceptions, determined by various factors,
no material from the magazines specializing in science fiction,
from the so-called "fanzines," nor from the legions of anthologies has been included in *Science Fiction Criticism*, unless
it has been published in book form and is generally available.
This area also merits a separate volume, but whether or not
it can ever be realized remains in question, for a great deal
of the material seemingly has already vanished so that chances
of complete coverage are slight.

To the degree that *Science Fiction Criticism* has achieved
its goal, I am indebted to numerous individuals. Many editors
have provided me with copies of out-of-print articles. Among
the individuals who have referred me to specific titles or
have themselves provided annotations are Professor Dick Allen,
Miss Ruth Berman, Miss Joanne Burger, Professor J. R.
Christopher, Mr. Fred Lerner, Professor Dennis Livingston,
Professor Willis E. McNelly, Professor Richard D. Mullen,
Professor Robert Plank, Professor Ivor Rogers, Professor Glenn
Sadler, Professor David Samuelson, and Mr. Donald Wollheim.
In a few cases when I have not read the article, the individual

sending me the annotation has been named in brackets. I should also like to thank the staffs of the libraries at Case-Western Reserve University, The College of Wooster, Kent State University, Oberlin College, and the Ohio State University, as well as the Cleveland Public Library and the Wayne County Public Library. Most of all, of course, I am indebted to Alice Super Clareson, who did a great many things very well.

Cape May, New Jersey
October, 1971

I. SF: General Studies

1 Abernethy, Francis E. "The Case for and against Science Fiction," *Clearing House*, 34 (April 1960), 474–477.

Sees sf as a new mythology, with the Unknown as God, the scientist as priest, and the new planet as the promised land. Yet it remains a "long enduring fad that has not yet achieved the stature of Literature." Perhaps it can serve as a stimulant to those who do not like to read, "who might then read further in science."

2 Adams, J. Donald. "Speaking of Books," *New York Times Book Review*, 13 September 1953, p. 2.

Believes sf deserves serious attention: it is not only an escape literature but also a form "deeply concerned with mankind's present plight and its problematical future." Singles out Bradbury and Clarke for praise.

3 Appel, Benjamin. *The Fantastic Mirror: Science Fiction Across the Ages*. New York: Random House, 1969.

Fine illustrations from early works. Introduction repeats clichés about the 20th-century "wonder story" which "reflects scientific thought." Crowded with excerpts across the ages, from Lucian onward.

4 Ascher, M. "Computers in Science Fiction," *Harvard Business Review*, 41 (November-December 1963), 40–42.

In section called "Keeping Informed." Executives follow sf to measure public reaction to computer revolution. Among earliest sf themes: (1) machines develop consciousness and turn on masters, and (2) through misusing technology, man destroys himself. Sf emphasizes "moral responsibility" that accompanies "technological development." Stresses that man's creativity cannot be delegated to machines.

5 Asimov, Isaac. "The By-Products of S-F," *Chemical and Engineering News*, 13 August 1956, pp. 3882–3886.

"Science and intelligence" are represented "sympathetically" in sf. "Scientific research is presented, almost invariably," as an exciting process; its usual ends are "both good for themselves and for mankind."

6 ————. "Fact Catches Up with Fiction," *New York Times Magazine*, 19 November 1961, p. 34.

Scientific achievements have destroyed such sf plots as the flight to the moon. At its best sf "resembles the mainstream novel at its most thoughtful," for it is not the function of sf to "predict the next gadget"; it is instead to explore serious questions regarding the consequences of scientific development.

7 ————. "Science Fiction, an Aid to Science, Foresees the Future," *Smithsonian*, 1 (May 1970), 41–47.

One of the fullest statements of Asimov's familiar themes regarding sf as prophecy and as "a recruiting ground" for science writers, scientists, and even scientific concepts.

8 Barron, A. S. "Why Do Scientists Read Science Fiction?" *Bulletin of Atomic Scientists*, 13 (February 1957), 62–65.

"Viewed as literature," sf is of only "moderate interest"; viewed sociologically, "of extreme interest." Scientists read it because

it "serves at least three personal functions for them": (1) it
glamorizes them; (2) it expresses their "protests against the use
of [scientific] knowledge for antihuman ends"; and (3) it
"reaffirms the basic humanistic values of the scientist's creed." (See
Asimov, II, 12)

9 Bernabeu, Ednita. "Science Fiction: A New Mythos," *Psycho-
analytical Quarterly,* 26 (October 1957), 527–535.

The "fantasies" of sf are "vehicles for expression of far greater
anxieties and more deeply repressed defenses than even those
which evoked the demigods, devils, and witches of other times."
Specifically, for example, women, even as mothers, are rejected,
while the language of space travel "is suspiciously reminiscent
of expulsion at birth." Widely influential, without naming a title
or author.

10 Bishop, Claire Huchet. "Children and Science Fiction,"
Commonweal, 15 November 1955, pp. 172–174.

Almost exclusively Verne; no contemporary titles. In Verne
science and technology were not ends in themselves; they expressed
"realization of the age-old aspirations of mankind": freedom
from war, tyranny, colonization, slavery. His works reflected the
freedom of the "communiterrean" city, not a technocratic
totalitarianism.

11 Campbell, John W., Jr. "Science of Science Fiction,"
Atlantic, 181 (May 1948), 97–98.

In "Accent on Living" section. The genre, a "form of prophecy,"
fills "that gap" between laboratory discovery and its application
in engineering. Suggests that engineers "read gratefully" because
sf suggests possible solutions to problems; "when we want something badly enough," sooner or later we get it.

4

12 ———. "Value of Science Fiction," in *Science Marches On*,
ed. James Stokley. New York: Ives Washburn, 1951,
pp. 43–47.

Discussion of sf incidental to his appraisal of the scientific scene
at the time of World War II and in 1951. Asserts that sf is "based
on natural law and research laboratory operations in discovering
new facts" about nature. It has its chief value as "a relaxation
literature for the amusement of technically trained people."

13 Clarke, Arthur C. "In Defense of Science Fiction," *UNESCO
Courier*, 15 (November 1962), 14–17.

Excerpt from his speech of 27 September when he accepted the
Kalinga prize in New Delhi. In praising sf, he notes that its value
is inspirational rather than educational, that it should be accurate
although accuracy should not be a "fetish," and that its "cultural
impact" has never been measured. It "helps us face the strange
realities of the universe in which we live." It is "a literature of
change," whereas " 'mainstream literature' usually paints a
static picture of society—a snapshot, frozen at one moment of
time."

14 ———. "When Earthman and Alien Meet," *Playboy*, 15
(January 1968), 118.

Although encounter with alien intelligence is one of the "oldest
and most hackneyed themes" in sf, there have been "few serious
factual discussions" of it. Discovery of another intelligent race
might have greatest importance in that "we would no longer feel
so alone in an apparently hostile universe." It would also show
that other races have survived their entries into the nuclear age.
Refers to such writers as Stapledon.

15 Conklin, Groff. "Science in Science Fiction," *Science Illustrated*, 1 (July 1946), 44–45, 109.

Calls sf "bizarre and untrammeled by-product of the amazing
forward march of science in the 20th century." It "stretches the

imagination. It suggests the richness of worlds yet undiscovered, of inventions yet unmade." Suggests that "today" the scientists are "taking over" the genre.

16 Deasy, Philip. "God, Space, and C. S. Lewis," *Commonweal*, 1 August 1958, pp. 421–423.

Recounts plots of Ransom trilogy and refers to his own article, "Will We Lose God in Outer Space," in *Christian Herald*. Wonders "whether the vast astronomical distances may not be God's quarantine precautions. They prevent the spiritual infection of a fallen race from spreading."

17 deCamp, L. Sprague and Willy Ley. *Lands Beyond*. New York and Toronto: Rinehart, 1952.

A scholarly account of those travellers and mythical kingdoms which have eluded man from classical times onward: Atlantis, Odysseus, Sinbad, Prester John, the Lost Tribes, *Terra Australis Incognita*, and the Amazons.

18 deCamp, L. Sprague. *Lost Continents: The Atlantis Theme in History, Science, and Literature*. New York: Gnome Press, 1954.

One of the most readable accounts of Atlantis and Lemuria, having particular value because it helps to explain the impact of those kingdoms upon 19th- and 20th-century imaginations and thus upon fantasy and sf. Well documented, with an excellent bibliography.

19 deFord, Miriam Allen. "Science Fiction Comes of Age," *Humanist*, 17 (November-December 1957), 323.

Brief, general introduction to three articles. Agrees that the genre encompasses "social aspects of future life."

6

20 DeVoto, Bernard. "Doom Beyond Jupiter," *Harpers*, 179 (September 1939), 445–448.

Highly critical of the genre, emphasizing the catastrophe motif. "It is as if a race drifting hopelessly to destruction found itself able to drift more tranquilly" by knowing the inevitability of such disaster on other worlds in other times. Does not see how sf could interest scientists. Finds it only pessimistic, without literary quality to compensate.

21 deWohl, Louis. "Religion, Philosophy, and Outer Space," *America*, 24 July 1954, pp. 420–421.

"In the wrong hands [sf] can and will introduce new heresies and revive old ones. In the right hands it can be one more instrument to glorify God." If sf suggests that Christ, Buddha, and others came to earth from far planets, this could introduce polytheism and imply that God is far distant from us. Mentions Lewis, Williams, and Werfel. Objects to portrayal of all aliens as "malignant" because we cannot be certain all races have fallen from grace.

22 Egoff, Sheila A. "Tomorrow Plus X: Some Thoughts on Science Fiction," *Ontario Library Review*, 45 (May 1961), 77–80.

Relies on Crispin's definition to argue that a "disturbance" in the moral order, in the normal structure of society, or in the normal behavior of human beings is as "valid" a basis for sf as is technology. Suspects that such practitioners as Christopher, C. S. Lewis, and Wyndham "are forging a branch, and an important one, of the mainstream of fiction."

23 Finer, S.E. "Profile of Science Fiction," *Sociological Review*, n.s. 2 (December 1964), 239–246.

From a sampling of 2000 based upon Campbell's questionnaire, he characterizes sf readers: 80% under 35, 93.3% male, and the majority either scientists or technicians. It is a "new look" romanticism "without permanent literary or social value."

24 Finkelstein, Sidney. "World of Science Fiction," *Masses and Mainstream*, 8 (April 1955), 48–57.

Begins as a general critique of sf, whose "social significance far excels its artistic merit." Its central strength lies in its treatment of significant themes. "And since it cannot deal with them realistically and rationally, it must take them up in a fantastic and irrational manner." Becomes an extended discussion of Bradbury, praised for his "deep honesty [and] his courage in making so explicit and unmistakable a criticism of the destructive forces he sees about him in his own land."

25 Franklin, H. Bruce. "Science Fiction as an Index to Popular Attitudes Toward Science: A Danger, Some Problems, and Two Possible Solutions," *Extrapolation*, 6 (May 1965), 23–31.

Derived from 1964 MLA Seminar. Speaks of sf as "unconscious revelation" of attitudes toward science; analyzes stories by Hawthorne to show how they attempt to make "a coherent statement *about* popular attitudes." To find the perfect future is at once a central function of sf "and one of its principal dangers."

26 Fuller, Florence. "Is God Science Fiction?" *Colloquy*, 4 (May 1971), 26–27.

Tape of an interview between the author and four boys, aged five to seven, about sf. The title is derived from a question directly asked the boys.

27 Giffin, S. F. "On Reading Science Fiction," *Alabama Librarian*, 8 (January 1957), 2–3.

Introduces three papers at a Maxwell AFB panel on sf during Book Week. Stresses the importance of story in sf and insists that the genre deal with the "scientifically possible or plausible." Yet while it "relies on a basis of scientific truth, it does not forward the cause of natural or physical science in anyway whatever," for its "inventions are those of dreams." Ends on the point of man's loneliness in "our almost limitless universe" as explanation for the interest in sf and in space travel. (See Lambert, II, 180; Field, VI, 14.)

28 Glass, Bentley. "The Scientist in Contemporary Fiction," *Scientific Monthly*, 85 (December 1957), 288–293.

After dismissing most sf because the scientist is merely a device to move the plot, he concentrates upon portraits of scientists given by Wells and by Lewis in *Arrowsmith*. Nowhere in modern fiction, however, does there "appear to be any profound understanding of science itself" or of the scientist. Valuable for the breadth of examples from both British and American fiction.

29 Hartley, Margaret L. "Is Science Fiction Subversive?" *Southwest Review*, 38 (Summer 1953), 244–250.

Groups investigating un-American activities would find sf subversive. "The idea that difference from the American norm in appearance and customs does not necessarily mean inferiority is sometimes carried so far as to include the inhabitants of other planets." Names Bradbury, Brown, Poul Anderson, among others, but concentrates upon such British writers as Huxley, Orwell, and C. S. Lewis.

30 Highet, Gilbert. "From World to World," in *People, Places, and Books*. New York: Oxford, 1953, pp. 130–137.

"Most of us rather despise science fiction . . . most of it is despicable . . . sometimes frightening." Condemns it roundly for its "lack of moral and intellectual content." Reveals intense subjectivity of his position when he asks: If there are "intelligent beings on other planets, many races of them, then what is their knowledge of God?" Like ours? The idea of "a universe empty of everything except ourselves and a few chemical or physical reactions" appalls him.

31 ———. "Perchance to Dream," in *The Clerk of Oxenford*. New York: Oxford University Press, 1954, pp. 3–10.

Having now read more sf, as letters advised, he retracts his 1953 attack. Finds a "surprising number" of stories "far better conceived and more interestingly written than many of the dull realistic novels and machine-made historical romances that pour off the printing press." Still finds little science; "there is only dreaming." Judges sf to be a form of fantasy and, therefore, myth.

32 Hillegas, Mark. "Science Fiction and the Idea of Progress," *Extrapolation*, 1 (May 1960), 25–28.

Early sf reflected a belief in progress; while more recently it has become critical of society and objects to science because of its "quantification" of human problems.

33 ———. "Cosmic Pessimism in H. G. Wells's Scientific Romances," *Papers of the Michigan Academy of Science, Arts, and Letters*, 46 (1961), 655–663.

In his five scientific romances, Wells "set about to jolt the English-speaking world out of its complacency, and his efforts took the form of imaginative presentation of T. H. Huxley's pessimism about the outcome of the cosmic or evolutionary processes." Analyzes each novel in turn. When Wells became a reformer and educator, his writings lost their "vitality of imagination and depth of meaning."

34 ———. "Science Fiction as a Cultural Phenomenon: A Re-evaluation," *Extrapolation*, 4 (May 1963), 26–33.

Derived from ASA session at 1962 MLA. Basic to sf are the beliefs that by "systematic investigation" man can learn the secrets of the universe and improve his condition, but that, by nature, the universe is a machine lacking a purpose and thus indifferent to man. Illustrates how a "plausible other world" can be used as the basis for social criticism. (Reprinted in Clareson, *SF. The Other Side of Realism*, II, 71.)

35 Hirsch, Walter. "Image of the Scientist in Science Fiction,"
American Journal of Sociology, 43 (March 1958),
506–512.

Based upon a sampling from Day's 1926–1950 *Index,* this remains
one of the most frequently cited articles. Finds that during that
period the adulation of the scientist declined in sf. The scientist
was replaced by three patterns: (1) "application of social science
(or natural and social science combined)"; (2) "the magical
or charismatic powers of human beings"; (3) "the intervention of
aliens." *Bête noire* of sf during period seems to have been the
businessman. Hirsch refers to his dissertation, "American SF
1926–1950: A Content Analysis." (See Day, VIII, 14.)

36 ———. "Science Fiction: A Study," *Scope,* 13
(October 1959), 12.

Prophecy is one of the chief functions of sf. Writers support a
democratic society, but do not indicate how democratic ideals can
be preserved in technological society. Scientists are generally
presented as a favored elite in future societies. Refers to his
dissertation. (See I, 35.)

37 Hurley, Neil P. "Coming of the Humanoids," *Commonweal,*
5 December 1969, pp. 297–300.

In the field of bio-engineering sf provides a number of stories
permitting "us in the early stages of thinking machines to ponder
the social and ethical implications" of "mannikins" — humanoids.
Suggests "ethicians, philosophers, moral theologians, and
behavioral scientists" should take sf more seriously before
androids/humanoids become a *fait accompli.*

38 Huxley, Aldous. *Literature and Science.* New York:
Harper & Row, 1963.

Huxley cannot accept either "the bland scientism" of *The Two
Cultures* or the one-track, moralistic literalism of Leavis's
Richmond Lecture, which he finds violent and ill-mannered.
Calls for an end to the false dichotomy because neither is adequate
alone.

39 Johnson, William B. and Thomas D. Clareson. "The
Interplay of Science and Fiction: the Canals of Mars,"
Extrapolation, 5 (May 1964), 37–48.

Brief discussion of the controversy precipitated by Schiaparelli's
discovery in 1877 of the "canali" of Mars, followed by an annotated
checklist of 37 articles, with references to 14 others.

40 Kelly, R. Gordon. "Ideology in Some Modern Science
Fiction Novels," *Journal of Popular Culture*, 2 (Fall 1968),
211–227.

Asserts that sf "soothes and reassures" because its basic premise
is that "rational intelligence can preserve the future and make it a
better, fuller life for all men." Thus, instead of confronting
"accelerating change," it looks "backward to a future that will
never be." Suggests that scientists read it "as a symbolic affirmation
or rationalization" of their participation "in the corporate
organization of science"; it may also involve a working out "of
the author's anxieties over the morally ambiguous position of the
scientist in society and the ultimate value of science."

41 Kenkel, William F. "Marriage and the Family in Modern
Science Fiction," *Journal of Marriage and the Family*,
31 (February 1969), 6–14.

Kenkel's 1968 presidental address. He examines sf for its
treatment of (1) "the childbearing function"; (2) "the socializa-
tion function"; and (3) "love and marriage." The sf references
serve as a frame for his own speculations on such problems as
over-population, organ-transplanting, euthanasia, and the
"exclusive landlord" concept of man's role on earth.

42 Lantero, Erminie Huntress. "What Is Man? Theological
Aspects of Contemporary Science Fiction," *Religion in Life*,
38 (Summer 1969), 242–255.

Describes the attitudes toward theology in a number of sf stories,
emphasizing James Blish, particularly *Black Easter*. Rather than

orthodoxy, she finds "principally . . . an overall concern for human values and relationships and celebrations of the human character at its best." If God is seldom dwelt upon in sf, there is "frequent mention" of a covenant of man to man or man to nature.

43 Lear, John. "Let's Put Some Science in Science Fiction," *Popular Science Monthly*, 165 (August 1954), 135–137, 244–248.

Eulogizes Gernback's *Ralph 124C 41+* and Heinlein. Asks for a fiction "bearing some relation to science as it is practiced on earth," with detail "authentic enough to allow" it to be assigned as out-of-class reading for science students. Since "creative literature" imitates life, "its reason for existence is to mirror man's accomplishments, hopes, and fears."

44 Luckiesh, M. "A Scientific Fortune Teller," *North American Review*, 233 (May 1932), 438–444.

Peripheral reference to sf, especially Verne. Obsessed with idea of a "super telescope" which permits us to see into past history. Such observation would dwarf "a mere physical trip to Mars."

45 McDonnell, Thomas P. "The Cult of Science Fiction," *Catholic World*, 178 (October 1953), 15–18.

Morals, ethics, philosophy, and even religious beliefs "are bandied about" sf with a "complete disregard for their real uses and meanings." The presence of "Scientism" in sf affirms the "supremacy of natural law, and refutes the belief in the supernatural" at a time when the imagination of Western man "has moved from the traditional center," the human heart, to technology. Heinlein as the "Papa Hemingway" of the genre; *Astounding* rebuked for asserting that the "great" development of evolution "has been the mind."

46 Mandel, Siegfried and Peter Fungesten. "The Myth of
Science Fiction," *Saturday Review*, 27 August 1955, pp. 7–8.

Genre expresses man's desire to escape all confinement—political,
sociological, and personal reality—and to find a place/condition
where "all is simple machines and clean space." Its mythology is a
counterpart to that of primitive man; it contains "little overt
sexuality" because it "emphasizes intellectual feeling à la Plato."
Humanistic values permeate sf, in which there has been a point
by point exchange of old religious ideas for modern concepts.

47 Manser, A. R. "Science in S.F.: Alien Sociology,"
Listener, 14 January 1965, pp. 56–58.

Identifying characteristic of sf is "a general law or set of scientific
facts" known by author and reader to be "untrue," so that some
important element of story is "quite different from anything in our
normal experience." The sub-class, "sociological fiction," creates
a "fictional society in all its details." Aliens are "rarely pleasant"
and their societies "seldom credible." Yet they make us "more
aware of our own social organizations." Argues against societies of
social insects or telepaths.

48 Marple, Allen. "Off the Cuff," *Writer*, 69 (May 1956),
147–148.

On Vonnegut, Bradbury, and Heinlein. Pretends horror at "un-
American" themes of best sf, but wonders why "these bright
people" must disguise their satire in sf. Believes sf satirizes
effectively.

49 Marshak, Alexander. "How Kids Get Interested in Science,"
Library Journal, 15 April 1958, pp. 1253–1255.

Calls Verne, Wells, and older magazines "false psychologically
and inept scientifically." Laments that in U.S. all great achievements
are "portrayed as Horatio Alger successes." Even in sf "an

emotional relevance is created not for science, but for the extraordinary personal success." Must emphasize science as "discovery of the unknown," the author's task being to make it relevant to the whole.

50 Medd, H. J. "The Scientist in Fiction," *Ontario Library Review*, 46 (May 1962), 81–83.

Draws upon no sf in discussing 19 novels, mostly written since World War II, which portray scientists and use the realistic mode. They emphasize "problems of political bias and social responsibility." Balchin and Snow alone have more than one title.

51 Menzel, Donald H. "Space—The New Frontier," *PMLA*, 77 (May 1962), 10–17.

Dr. Menzel's speech to MLA on 28 December 1961. Laments the division between the sciences and humanities, asserting that they must work together "to make this space age a real success." Suggests sf merits "serious consideration" by students of literature and is "delighted" that MLA sponsors the Seminar.

52 Menzies, Ian S. "The Changing Dream," *New Scientist*, 22 December 1966, pp. 190–194.

Writers of sf are "bedeviled" by the closing of the "gap between speculation and fact."

53 Mercer, Derwent. "Science in S.F.: Alien Communication," *Listener*, 7 January 1965, pp. 13–15.

Explores the possibility and methods of communication with aliens. Introduces such problems as (1) our use of pictures assumes "eyes"; (2) our use of diagrams assumes their use of the same kind(s) of diagrams. Wonders whether aliens technologically superior to us would be interested in us. Yet man must keep listening for signals.

54 Michaelson, L. W. "Social Criticism in Science Fiction," *Antioch Review*, 14 (December 1954), 502–508.

The best writers have used the genre as a vehicle for social protest. Notes the recent unfavorable reactions of the critics to the pessimism of these stories. Cites Campbell's division of the genre into three types of story. (See Campbell, II, 61.)

55 ———. "Science Fiction, Censorship, and Pie in the Sky," *Western Humanities Review*, 13 (1959), 409–413.

Updates earlier article, emphasizing the social criticism and, "since 1951," a tendency to "ban 'pessimistic' or critical" sf. Refers to articles and introductions to anthologies to support the idea of the ban.

56 ———. "Science Fiction and the Rate of Social Change," *Extrapolation*, 11 (December 1969), 25–27.

Although sf is concerned with prediction, he is uncertain how much it or any literary form has effected reform. Does not, however, dismiss its influence upon bringing about change.

57 Muller, Herbert J. "Science Fiction as an Escape," *Humanist*, 17 (1957), 33–37.

Denounces concept of duality and treatment of evolution in sf. "We sorely need its speculations, but these should be genuine. We have had enough of the phantasms dreamed up by our forefathers."

58 ———. "A Note on Utopia," in *The Children of Frankenstein: A Primer on Modern Technology and Human Values*. Bloomington & London: Indiana University Press, 1970, pp. 369–384.

"Industrialism by no means requires the elimination of traditional cultures." Discussion of sf confined to one chapter, mentioning Wells, Huxley, Orwell; most detailed commentary is on Skinner's *Walden Two*. The book helps fix the context in which sf evolved.

59 Murphy, Carol. "The Theology of Science Fiction,"
Approach, no. 23, (Spring 1957), pp. 2–7.

Theologians would judge sf as 'negative witness' because it "merely
points to the mystery of life without giving a Christian answer."
Yet they should not expect a "thoroughgoing positive answer . . .
within the bounds of a jet-propelled morality play."

60 Norton, Andre. "Living in 1980+," *Library Journal*, 15
September 1952, pp. 1463–1464.

Science in fiction leads to science in fact. Up until 15 years ago
gadgets and space opera dominated the genre. Names Heinlein,
Hal Clement, Malcolm Jameson, and Raymond Jones among
the best current writers.

61 O'Brien, Robert C. "Telepsyche: The Meeting of Minds,"
Holiday, 41 (February 1967), 8.

Believes telepathy is the "end product" of contemporary sf, and
so discusses what he believes the "Age of Telepsyche" will be
like. Although, "with certain exceptions," sf cannot be taken
seriously as "literature," as prophecy "it has rarely failed us." No
titles or authors named.

62 Patrouch, Joseph. "The Unpopularity of Science Fiction,"
Focus on the University of Dayton, 4 (January 1971),
14–17.

Emphasizes the concept of the two cultures, suggesting that the
majority of readers belong to the "eighteenth century, non-
technological world." As a result sf writers gain little prestige and
no monetary reward. Its authors also face special problems
intrinsic to the genre. All of this deprives sf of recognition and
readers because it is "out of tune" with the many persons disliking
science and technology.

63 Phelan, J. M. "Men and Morals in Space," *America*,
113 (1965), 405–407.

Discounting such exceptions as Bradbury and Heinlein, sf, as
fiction, is merely another adventure story; as science, "it is often
not fictional at all." Praises C. S. Lewis for basing his universe
"on a fusion of Christian angelology and theology with the more
generalized insights of later Greek philosophy and mythology."
Lewis gives truths "a fresher and more concrete reality." Asserts
that nature, man, and God are real and objective; "they are
realities."

64 Pierce, John R. "Science and Literature," *Science*, 20
April 1951, pp. 431–434.

In its maturity sf goes beyond gadgets to study their effects upon
man. He finds a noticeable lack of scientific ideas in current stories,
but feels this "merely reflects the lack of science in the public
mind." Praises *Arrowsmith* for its treatment of science and the
scientist.

65 Pilgrim, John. "Science Fiction and Anarchism," *Anarchy*,
3 (December 1963), 361–375.

Since sf contains "most of the genuinely subversive thought of our
time," it has no need of "the kind of academic respectability
Amis would wish on it." One of the basic premises of sf is that
established laws, taboos, morals, and customs are not eternally
true constants, but are a "part of a planetary culture that may be
good or bad." The genre combines a "genuine sympathy for the
condition of man" with a skepticism of "man's view of himself
as 'Lord of the Universe.' " Its constant examination of moral,
ethical, and social questions is what makes it "so important in
popular literature." Attacks Heinlein's views as atypical. Because
of its many specific examples, both British and American, this
must be regarded as one of the fullest and most effective statements
from the leftist critics.

66 Plank, Robert. "Communication in Science Fiction," *Etc*, 11 (Fall 1953), 16–20.

Works like Raymond Jones's *Discontinuity* and L. Ron Hubbard's "fictitious science" point up the inadequacy of present methods of communication. Some attention to telepathy. (Reprinted in S. I. Hayakawa, ed., *Our Language and Our World*. New York: Harper, 1959, pp. 272–278.)

67 ———. "The Reproduction of Psychosis in Science Fiction," *International Record of Medicine*, 167 (July 1954), 407–421.

To a "greater degree than other literature," sf is morphologically "similar to schizophrenic manifestations." Explores three motifs— space travel, survival after catastrophe, and the "influencing" machine. Sf thus reflects "a growing discomfort" in a "technological civilization."

68 ———. "Portraits of Fictitious Psychiatrists," *American Imago*, 13 (1956), 259–268.

Since an sf writer is not bound to verisimilitude, his works may reveal his feelings more fully than do other forms of literature. Surveys the ambivalent and frequent reference to psychiatry and psychiatrists in sf, suggesting they show both a "discontent with civilization" and many writers' unsuccessful experiences with psychiatrists.

69 ———. "Lighter Than Air, But Heavy As Hate: An Essay in Space Travel," *Partisan Review*, 24 (Winter 1957), 106–116.

The configurations of space travel literature are "remarkably similar to certain configurations of psychotic fantasies." Notes the absence of love and sexuality. Sees instead a yearning to escape, thus leaving the genre to "brash young men in the service of super-imperial schemes" and "devouring clashes between civilizations." (Reprinted in Leslie Fiedler, ed., *The Art of the Essay*. New York: Thomas Y. Crowell, 1958.)

70 ————. "Orthopsychiatric Observations on Patterns of
Literature in Today's Milieu: Science Fiction," *American
Journal of Orthopsychiatry*, 24 (October 1960), 799–810.

Today's sf is "less expressive of our aggression and more of our
anxiety." In addition to the absence of love and sexuality, there is
no "true and complete father figure" and very little family life
in the genre. The grandiosity of its hero "bears a close resemblance
to a phenomenon we know from our clinical work: the child's
fantasy of his omnipotence." In contrast to sf, the utopia has
provided Western civilization with "a voice of conscience"; he
hopes that the utopic element will give sf "maturity" and "balance
its tendency to regression."

71 ————. "The Longing for Space Travel," *Air Force and
Space Digest*, 46 (August 1963), 43–45.

Suggests the interest in space travel lies in our desire to answer
the question: Is man alone in the universe? Mentions three types
of stories involving aliens, giving most attention to the "guardians
of man" ideas as expressing our anxieties over problems and
possible catastrophes.

72 ————. *The Emotional Significance of Imaginary Beings:
A Study of the Interaction Between Psychotherapy,
Literature, and Reality in the Modern World*. Springfield,
Ill.: Charles C. Thomas, 1968.

Deals with one of the basic areas of myth, concentrating upon
the most recent of man's inventions: the extraterrestrial alien who
is, by consensus, superior to man. The encounter with such an alien
is paradoxical in that "any event that seems to push the final
epochal meeting with alien life into greater remoteness is greeted
with disappointment; any event that brings it closer, with joy."
Plank sets himself the problem of trying to find out why; he
reaches his final level of symbolism in a chapter entitled "Hamlet
and Prospero."

73 Pohl, Fred. "Long John Nebel and the Woodlouse,"
Library Journal, 1 November 1956, pp. 4704–4708.

Incidental reference to sf in discussion of prediction and information retrieval.

74 "Pop Theology: Those Gods from Outer Space," *Time*,
5 September 1969, p. 64.

Discusses Erich von Daniken's *Chariots of God*, which suggests
that aliens visited earth sometime in the past and became prototypes
of the gods of various mythologies. Writers of sf "have long
enjoyed developing similar themes"; cites stories by Nelson Bond,
C. S. Lewis, Bradbury, del Rey, and Farmer as well as an episode
from *Star Trek*.

75 Priestley, J. B. "They Came from Outer Space," *New
Statesman*, 5 December 1953, pp. 712–714.

Both sf and the flying saucer legend "show us what is happening
in men's minds." They are "myths and characteristic dreams of
our age, and far more important than our more rational accounts
of ourselves." (Reprinted in J. B. Priestley, *Thoughts in the
Wilderness*. New York: Harper; London: Heinemann, 1957,
pp. 20–26.)

76 Rhodes, Carolyn H. "Intelligence Testing in Utopia,"
Extrapolation, 13 (December 1971), 25–47.

Examines the use of the techniques of modern psychology,
particularly intelligence testing, by such writers as Victor Rousseau,
Kurt Vonnegut, Michael Young, John Hersey, H. G. Wells, and
J. T. M'Intosh. Close analysis of individual novels. The writers
vary in their reaction to psychotechnology: dystopians "concede the
accuracy of the tests [but] fear that the power to gauge intelligence will be misused." Utopian writers "assume that the
potentialities of psychotechnology will be beneficially developed."
Their reactions turn upon their attitudes toward the ideas of
selecting an intellectual elite and of thereby basing the society upon
false (or incorrect) values.

77 Riley, Robert B. "Dreams of Tomorrow," *Architectural Forum*, 126 (April 1967), 66–67, 112–113.

The architectural dreams of sf tell us three things: (1) "that technological advance may not produce better living conditions"; (2) "that architecture has great potential for immediate sensual satisfaction"; and (3) "that architectural dreaming can be a positive force." Contrasts Le Corbusier's vision of the *Ville Radieuse* and the supercity of sf which "becomes one monstrous building." Frames discussion with attack upon modern architecture for looking backward, not forward.

78 Robinson, Guy S. "Science in S.F.: Hypertravel," *Listener*, 17 December 1964, pp. 976–977.

Argues against the probability/plausibility of either time travel or the idea of hyperspace and faster-than-light travel. But does not object that sf uses such ideas. "One of the chief points of science fiction in a literal-minded and sceptical age is to loosen the hobbles that have been put on our imaginations by the scientific attitude itself."

79 Rongione, Louis A. "The Psychological Aspects of Science Fiction Can Contribute Much to Bibliotherapy," *Catholic Library World*, 36 (October 1964), 96–99.

The concern of sf with outer space "compensates for our disappointment in a shrinking world," while its attention to scientific techniques (space travel) "restores or revives our confidence in American know-how." It also provides "solace from frustrations" arising from "so many seemingly unsolvable problems" because sf "solves all problems." Thus, "carefully selected titles" can have "therapeutic effect," but only "philosophy and theology" can keep us from "plunging the world into the Icarian sea of total destruction."

80 Rose, Carl. "Europe Instantly," *Atlantic*, 195 (February 1955), 88–89.

In "Accent on Living" department, a reply to Charles W. Morton's column in the January 1955 issue (pp. 88–89) concerning the speed of aerial transportation to Europe. Derisive; makes fun of sf.

81 Rose, Lois and Stephen. *The Shattered Ring: Science Fiction and the Quest for Meaning*. Richmond, Va.: John Knox, 1970.

The quest is for personal meaning in this naughty world, with occasional, incidental asides, assertions, and long quotations about sf. Of no value to the study of sf, and of little value to an understanding of the contemporary scene.

82 "Science Fiction Presents a Strange Picture of Science," *Science Newsletter*, 10 May 1958, p. 296.

Reports the conclusions reached by Walter Hirsh in his study of sf. Not a review. (See Hirsch, I, 35.)

83 "Science in Science Fiction," *Advancement of Science*, 26 (August 1965), 195–207.

Reprint of the four articles originally published in *The Listener* (December 1964–January 1965), derived from a symposium given at the meeting of the British Association at Southampton in 1964. Articles by A. R. Manser, D. M. A. Mercer, G. S. Robinson, and W. T. Williams. (See I, 47, 53, 78, 93.)

84 Searls, Hank. "The Astronaut, the Novelist, and Cadwalder Glotz," *Writer*, 78 (September 1965), 24–25.

The typical reader/man-in-the-street ("Glotz") fears the technological tidal wave, while scientific documentation and sf bore him. Yet Searls feels that a novelist "sensitive to technology and people" can act as an effective filter for scientific information.

85 Shaftel, Oscar. "The Social Content of Science Fiction,"
   Science and Society, 17 (Spring 1953), 97–118.

   A distinct tradition and subject matter set sf "apart from the great
   bulk of pulp writing." It has a high potentiality for serious social
   speculation through which "a healthy humanistic spirit can speak
   out." It is a "dynamic relationship between technological
   innovation and human readjustment" that occasionally raises sf
   above the pulp pattern.

86 Simon, Frank. "Plot for an Epoch," *Saturday Review of
   Literature*, 31 December 1949, p. 23.

   Refers to an editorial of 3 December (p. 24) which proposes a
   novel that would solve the problems of society and the threat of the
   A-bomb by providing a "substitute outlet." This letter cites those
   sf stories which employ the theme of "a common enemy to unite
   the world." A period of danger makes possible the formation of a
   world government.

87 Stumpf, Edna. "Why It's All Right Now," *Colloquy*,
   4 (May 1971), 10–12.

   Personalized attempt to explain changing attitudes toward sf
   during the past generation. Speaks of "speculative fabulation"
   and refers to Robert Scholes, *The Fabulators*.

88 Sussman, Herbert L. *Victorians and the Machine*: *The
   Literary Response to Technology*. Cambridge, Mass.:
   Harvard University Press, 1968.

   Concentrates upon Carlyle, Dickens, Ruskin, Morris, Butler,
   Wells, and Kipling. Emphasizes the "deep-seated confusion about
   the aesthetic value of the machine that runs through all of the
   Victorian arts." Explores the attempt to find "a literary language
   derived from the new technology" and to break down the
   antithesis between intellect and emotion, science and art. "The
   antimachine feeling in Victorian literature" found the machine a
   symbol "for what may best be called the scientific habit of

mind, the desire to reduce the complex operations of the natural world, of society, and of the psyche to a few simple, quantitative laws." Provides an essential part of the context necessary to understand the rise of sf and the subsequent critical attitudes toward it.

89 Sutton, Thomas C. and Marilyn. "Science Fiction as Mythology," *Western Folklore*, 28 (October 1969), 230–237.

Since myth "cannot be simply a representation of contemporary reality," it must view the present "in relation to a transcendent order." Substituting the concept of space for the older cosmos, sf "is not formulated primarily to advance technological knowledge" but "operates on a visionary, mythopoeic level." Cites Herbert and Blish, but gives most extended attention to Clarke's "The Star" as an example of how an sf author mingles religion, psychology, and science to "develop a mythopoeic vision . . . [a] mythology concocted for the delight of technological man."

90 Tomlin, R. J. "Mr. Priestley's Gynaeolatry," *New Statesman*, 19 December 1953, p. 798.

Letter replying to Priestley's article on sf, objecting to his suggestion of matriarchy, calling it the "last and fatal heresy of our civilization." The flying saucer fantasy is "the nearest approach to a matriarchy the world has ever seen." In 2 January 1954 issue (p. 16), Priestley replies, saying he really spoke of masculine and feminine "principles" and "opposing sets of values." Wishes to do an article; will Tomlin wait? (See II, 244.)

91 Vandenberg, Stephen C. "Great Expectations, or, The Future of Psychology as Seen in Science Fiction," *American Psychologist*, 11 (July 1956), 339–342.

In sf little psychology is taught as a science and profession, but there is much emphasis upon its wide use in public health. Much experimental psychology, but little developmental. Stories concentrate upon reaction between individuals and social institutions. The genre does open up parapsychology for exploration.

92 West, Robert H. "Science Fiction and Its Ideas," *Georgia Review*, 15 (Fall 1961), 276–280.

"Science fiction is too wildly hypothetical, too much shaped by the needs of its adventure fiction to preserve more than a distant illusion of being like science." Asserts that "true" sf would keep "science and its results in the center of its focus." This is not to say that sf is not "penetrating enough or persuasive enough in itself to influence the masses decisively for change."

93 Williams, W. T. "Science in S.F.: Alien Biology," *Listener*, 24 December 1964, pp. 1003–1004.

Rejects as "fantasy" both insect-like creatures with high intelligence (because of brain size) and "plant-animal mixtures" (because such creatures could not survive evolutionary "pressure"). Will accept any portrait of an alien so long as three "basic requirements" without which intelligent life cannot exist are observed: (1) "most vital . . . some compound sufficiently complex and ordered to carry hereditary information"; (2) some liquid must be present in which such changes as energy-transfer can take place; (3) some "permanently ordered framework" to allow for memory must be present.

II. SF: Literary Studies

1 Aldiss, Brian. "One That Could Control the Moon: Science Fiction Plain and Coloured," in *International Literary Annual*, ed. Arthur Boyars and Pamela Lyon. London: John Calder, 1961. 3: 176–189.

Excellent brief commentary on some 30 sf titles published within the year. Relying upon Crispin's definition, he asserts that "Ever since Shakespeare's day, fantasies and speculations based on new discoveries have appeared unceasingly in most European countries." Such "speculations are generally the ones of the moment—discoveries of new races or cancer cures—something with novelty enough to catch the writer's inner eye and so the more likely to be outmoded."

2 ———. "Judgment at Jonbar," *SF Horizons*, 1 (1964), 13–37.

Uses review of Jack Williamson's *Legion of Time* as departure for consideration of sf as whole. "While its virtues belong to Williamson, its defects belong to science fiction," which he regards as the "most difficult of all contemporary prose media in which to write." The genre has not yet "established its canons." Sf critic's task to discover purpose, judge worth, criticize technique. "Satire must never" be the "only standard" by which sf is judged.

3 ———. "British Science Fiction Now," *SF Horizons*,
2 (1965), 13–37.

Considers works by Lan Wright, Donald Malcolm, and J. G.
Ballard, with most attention to Ballard, whom he judges an
experimenter capable of producing outstanding fiction. (The
section on Ballard has been reprinted in Clareson, *SF*: *The Other
Side of Realism*, II, 71.)

4 Allen, D. C. "Science and Invention in Greene's Prose,"
PMLA, 53 (December 1938), 1007–1018.

"Of all the Euphuists Greene was the one most fascinated by the
rhetorical possibilities provided for literature by science." In his
works this is best represented by the way he fuses science and
his own imagination in treatment of birds.

5 Allen, Dick. "The Poet Looks at Space—Inner and Outer,"
Arts in Society, 6 (Summer–Fall 1969), 185–193.

Surveys "attitudes of contemporary poets to space exploration,"
citing Lowell, Eberhart, and Auden. Most attention to those who
have embraced sf, such as Vosnesensky, Ginsburg, Kumin, and
D. M. Thomas. Also notices Edward Fields, whose poetry uses
old horror films as a point of departure.

6 ———. "Science Space Speculative Fantasy Fiction,"
Yale Alumni Magazine, January 1971, pp. 7–12.

Stresses the diversity of the modern genre and makes the crucial
point that its critical recognition was long delayed by the New
Criticism, which concerns itself with language and structure
rather than idea.

7 Allot, Kenneth. *Jules Verne*. London: Crescent Press, 1940.

"Primarily a study of the relationship of Verne's work to romanticism and to scientific and technological advances." Significant
"for its understanding of the impact of science and technology on
the nineteenth century imagination." (For a bibliography devoted
to critical studies of Verne, see Hillegas, VIII, 22.)

8 Amis, Kingsley. *New Maps of Hell: A Survey of Science Fiction.* New York: Harcourt, Brace, 1960.

This study gave direction to current criticism of science fiction by emphasizing its role "as an instrument of social diagnosis and warning."

9 ———. "Science Fiction: A Practical Nightmare," *Holiday*, 37 (February 1965), 8.

Seems obsessed with garish covers. Praises Wells, Verne. Genre applies "realism not only to what is wonderful but also to what is disturbing, dismaying, frightening." It stimulates "fancy without bypassing intellect."

10 ———. "The Situation Today," in *The Art of the Essay*, ed. Leslie Fiedler. New York: Thomas Y. Crowell, 1969 (2nd ed.), pp. 297–313.

The second chapter of *New Maps of Hell.* (It replaced Isaac Asimov's "Other Worlds to Conquer," included in the 1958 ed.)

11 Appel, Alfred, Jr. "Vladimir Nabakov," *Contemporary Literature*, 9 (Spring 1968), 236–245.

Begins as criticism of Andrew Field's study of Nabakov; sf references pp. 241–244. Nabakov, who as a boy read Poe, Wells, and Verne, has employed many of the modes, conventions, and themes of sf in such stories as "Visit to a Museum" and "Lance." If future setting identifies sf, then *Invitation to a Beheading* is another example.

12 Asimov, Isaac. "Letter to Editor," *Bulletin of Atomic Scientists*, 13 (May 1957), inside back cover.

Objects to Barron's attack upon the quality of sf. Some are "as well written as many 'mainstream' novels"; Heinlein, Clarke, Sturgeon. It is a "highly-specialized art-form, perhaps the most specialized in the field of fiction, and it has certain standards of excellence beyond those it holds with all writing in general." (See Barron, I, 8.)

13 ———. "Escape into Reality," *Humanist*, 17 (November-December 1957), 326–332.

The "most modern" literary form, sf is the "one literary response to problems peculiar to our own day and no other." While the 'mainstream' concerns itself with character, there are three "specialized" forms in which "background or setting has as little relation to reality as do the characters themselves": fantasy (ghost story, folklore), satire (More, Swift), and science fiction (where background is "dealt with for its own sake, not for its moral application"). Sf stories "represent the eyes of humanity turned for the first time outward in a blind and agonized contemplation of the exciting and dangerous future, not to the individual, but to the human race in general."

14 Atheling, William, Jr. [pseud. for James Blish]. *The Issue at Hand*. Chicago: Advent, 1964.

Collected reviews of American sf from 1952 to 1963, this remains one of the most successful volumes of its type because of Blish's critical insight. (2nd ed., 1967.)

15 ———. *More Issues at Hand*. Chicago: Advent, 1970.

Derived from reviews and talks between 1965 and 1970. Begins with his desire for "the technical critic" whose work "usually takes the form of an *explication du texte*, or what used to be called the New Criticism," and ends with his talk to the 1970 BSFA meeting, at which he agreed there had been a "revolution" in sf, though most of its works had failed and its advocates been in error. Praises Aldiss highly.

16 Atwood, Margaret. "Superwoman Drawn and Quartered: The Early Forms of *She*," *Alphabet*, no. 10 (July 1965), pp. 65–82.

"The problematical themes and patterns of *She* had been present in [Haggard's] work since the writing of his first work of fiction." As a "gigantic allegory," the novel falters because it reads "like

a *Faerie Queen* from which the supporting technological and
political substructures have been removed: the emblematic
topography and the stylized figures are present but they have no
specific referents." Ayesha remains ambiguous because, as an
amplification of patterns in his earlier novels, "she is a combination of the Ideal and the Dark Sorceress types." *She* may be
Haggard's attempt to dramatize "some of the central conflicts of
his society."

17 Bailey, J. O. "An Early American Utopian Fiction,"
    American Literature, 14 (1942–1943), 285–293.

A discussion of Captain Adam Seaborn's *Symzonia* (1820) as
the first American utopian fiction, giving attention to the characteristics of the society.

18 ———. *Pilgrims Through Space and Time*. New York:
    Argus Books, 1947.

Of paramount importance as the first historical analysis of the
genre as a whole. Particularly strong in its treatment of British
and American writers through Wells. (2nd ed., 1972.)

19 ———. "Is Science Fiction Art? A Look at H. G. Wells,"
    Extrapolation, 2 (December 1960), 17–19.

If one drops "the demand that imagined items correspond one
for one with probable realities," and reads "the items as symbols
and the stories as allegories," then Wells's early scientific
romances may achieve an " 'art' superior to that of *Lewisham,
Kipps, and Mr. Polly*."

20 ———, ed. *Symzonia: A Voyage of Discovery (1820)*.
    Gainesville, Fla.: Scholars' Facsimiles and Reprints, 1965.

Makes available for first time a fine reproduction of the utopian
novel which advanced Symmes's theory of the hollow earth,
influenced Poe, and provided the 'lost race' motif with one of its
most popular settings.

21 Baring-Gould, William S. "Little Superman, What Now?" *Harpers*, 193 (September 1946), 283–288.

Although sf faces a crisis because "fact" is catching up, he feels that this will produce better writing. Greater part given over to description of fan meetings and the "Shaver Mystery" in *Amazing Stories*; feels these represent the poorer quality of sf.

22 Barthell, Robert J. "SF: A Literature of Ideas," *Extrapolation*, 13 (December 1971), 56–63.

Attacks the trend to criticize sf in literary terms by defending the concept of the genre as something very different from other fiction. "In this literature the traditional humanistic and aesthetic goal of the writer is dispensed with. . . . Science fiction extrapolating from scientific concepts is 'idea' literature. No other field of the arts displays such experimentation by the conscious mind. [It] becomes an art form that is rationalistic and abstract" and does not demand the close association of other fiction. Perhaps the fullest recent statement of this view.

23 Bass, Ralph. "Mark Twain: Science Writer," *Science Digest*, 54 (August 1963), 47.

In a story in *Century Magazine*, November 1898, Twain used a "telelectroscope," a form of world-wide TV, to save the life of a man wrongly accused of murder.

24 Beck, Clyde F. *Hammer and Tongs*. Lakeport, Calif.: The Futile Press, 1937.

Small volume (xiii, 20) of reviews taken from *The Science Fiction Critic*; important as perhaps the first 'book' of sf criticism and for its "Author's Preface." Beck denies term science fiction as "self contradictory" and inadequately defining the mode. The first to emphasize sf as "modern mode" of obtaining "a semblance of truth" sufficient to bring about a willing suspension of disbelief. Ties sf to main literary traditions.

25 Becker, Mary Lamberton. "Pseudo-scientific Fiction," *Saturday Review of Literature*, 26 July 1930, p. 13.

In "Readers Guide" section. Letter from Lee Road Library, Cleveland, offers titles in response to a request of 24 May signed J.O.B.; asks for an updated listing for the library; and refers to a recent article in *New Statesman* by Edward Shanks about *Amazing Stories*. (See Shanks, II, 267.)

26 Bennett, Michael Alan. "The Theme of Responsibility in Miller's *A Canticle for Leibowitz*," *English Journal*, 59 (April 1970), 484–489.

Each part of the novel focuses upon a single character—Brother Francis, Thon Taddeo, or the Defense Minister—who fails to take on "individual responsibility" and oppose evil. Brother Joshua, Benjamin, Dom Paulo, and Abbot Zerchi assume it, with Zerchi expressing the identity of all men: "Thee me Adam Man we."

27 Bergonzi, Bernard. "The Publication of *The Time Machine 1894–1895*," *Review of English Studies*, n.s. 11 (1960), 42–51.

Discusses variant forms: *New Review*, January–May, 1895; New York: Henry Holt, early May, 1895; and Heinemann, late May, 1895. It is a "finer artistic and imaginative achievement than any of his later fiction." Study of successive versions also shows "an artistic scrupulosity almost rivalling that of James himself." (Reprinted in Clareson, *SF: The Other Side of Realism*, II, 71.)

28 ———. "*The Time Machine*: An Ironic Myth," *Critical Quarterly*, 2 (1960), 293–305.

Excellent analysis of *The Time Machine*'s embodiment of "the tensions and dilemmas" of the *fin de siècle*. One may interpret the Eloi and Morlocks to represent not only the class struggle but also the "opposition" between aestheticism and utilitarianism, pastoralism and technology, contemplation and action, beauty and ugliness. Since the tensions are imaginatively and not intellectually resolved, irony increasingly enters; "the story is a skillfully wrought imaginative whole, a single image."

29 ———. *The Early H. G. Wells: A Study of the Scientific Romances*. Toronto: University of Toronto Press, 1961.

Definitive study of Wells as a myth-maker and a spokesman for the turn of the century. Special emphasis upon *The Time Machine* and *The War of the Worlds*, although all work covered.

30 ———. *"The Battle of Dorking,"* Notes & Queries, 206 (September 1961), 346–347.

Corrects Eric Solomon's assertion that *The Battle of Dorking* was written by a "Mrs. Brown." (See Solomon, II, 276.)

31 Bester, Alfred. "Gourmet Dining in Outer Space," *Holiday*, 27 (May 1960), 30.

Before taking up "serious business of cooking in space," he notes that in sf of the 1920's, characters dined on pills; in the 1930's, on extraterrestrial menus; in the 1940's, in a "valiant attempt at realism," on food from hydroponic tanks.

32 Billam, E. R. "Science Fiction," *New Statesman*, 27 March 1954, p. 406.

Letter replies to Lovell. Acknowledges "literary attainment" of sf "not so high as to class it as good literature," but dislikes any "peremptory dismissal" of the genre. Praises *Astounding* and Bradbury. (See Lovell, II, 187.)

33 Birchby, Sid. "Sexual Symbolism in W. H. Hodgson," *Riverside Quarterly*, 1 (November 1964), 70–71.

Brief note that while Hodgson's *House on the Borderland* ostensibly "lays on a wash of courtly love," the swine-like creatures from underground besieging the protagonist are described amid "images of carnality, foulness, and female genitalia."

34 Blank, E. W. "Alchemy and Chemistry in Literature,"
   School Science and Mathematics, 42 (June 1952), 550-557.

Last sections consider the "development of the Modern Scientific
Novel" and "Chemical Novels of the 20th Century." Begins
with Verne, who covered "all areas of science," and notes that
the scientific novel has "become popular and kept apace" of the
advances in science. The brief coverage includes R. C. Sherrif,
Sinclair Lewis, Bulwer-Lytton, and Arthur Machen. No explicit
reference to sf by name.

35 Blish, James. "Is This Thinking?" *SF Horizons*,
   1 (1964), 54–57.

Beginning with Wells and American sf of the 1940's, he distinguishes between "hard sf" and a new "science fantasy." Article
becomes a denunciation of those writers who "have utterly
rejected Wells's respect for the facts themselves" and so forfeit
any claim "on the respect of the reader." Singles out Ray Bradbury,
with his "indifference to accuracy of even the most minimal
sort." Uses Aldiss as second example, though milder. Insists that
if sf is to have any value other than as "an exercise in self
expression, I think it ought to be believable." Brief, incisive,
important because he knows the field so well.

36 ———. "S.F.: The Critical Literature," *SF Horizons*,
   2 (1965), 38–50.

Examines such critics as Knight, Moskowitz, and Amis; finds
Knight's reviews initiated the end of the "mutual admiration
society," but essentially points out the limitations of all book length
studies thus far done. Calls Amis's *New Maps of Hell* the "only
existing serious study of any weight . . . by an outsider." Thinks
most highly of it and de Camp's *Handbook*. (See Amis, II, 8;
de Camp, II, 95.)

37 ———. "On Science Fiction Criticism," *Riverside Quarterly*, 3 (August 1968), 214–217.

Directly replies to Butor's "Notes on Science Fiction: the Crisis of Its Growth." Attacks non-specialist critics who speak of the genre's weakness although they do not have a command of the material, often seeming unacquainted with living authors. (See Butor, II, 59. Reprinted in Clareson, *The Other Side of Realism*, II, 71.)

38 ———. "The Tale That Wags the Dog: The Function of Science Fiction," *American Libraries*, 1 (December 1970), 1029–1033.

Highly provocative analysis of the history and criticism of sf. At the end of the 19th century, sf "was considered to be a normal and legitimate interest for any writer or reader of fiction." The specialized magazine produced a "segregation" that has been harmful to the field. At present sf "is the only art form which appeals to the mythopoeic side of the human psyche," achieving its success because it fuses together both our operational and affective experience.

39 ———. See William Atheling, Jr. [pseud. for James Blish], II, 14, 15.

40 Boggs, W. Arthur. "*Looking Backward* at the Utopian Novel, 1888–1900," *Bulletin of the New York Public Library*, 64 (June 1960), 329–336.

Analysis of the influence of Bellamy's *Looking Backward*: 55 titles in America, five in Germany, two in Britain. Most opposed his views at least to some extent. Six types can be identified; most have no literary value, but he influenced Donnelly, Morris, Wells, London, and Howells.

41 Boucher, Anthony. "Letter to Editor," *Saturday Review*, 16 June 1956, p. 29.

Says that Campbell's article (12 May) describes one type of story making up "a good deal less than half" the stories in *Astounding* and "none elsewhere." Campbell does not consider Bradbury, Judith Merril, Ward Moore, or Sturgeon, who make sf "a part of the mainstream," nor does he mention Huxley and Orwell, who made the "mainstream part of" sf. (See Campbell, II, 62.)

42 ———. "Science Fiction Still Leads Science Fact," *New York Times Magazine*, 1 December 1957, p. 56.

Uses Sputnik as a point of departure. Prophecies of sf have been too conservative; yet the field at present deals less frequently with "detailed, specific prophecies" because technological possibilities have been so thoroughly explored. Instead, it deals, "to be blunt, with the impossible." Character study receives emphasis instead of scientific hardware.

43 Bowen, John. "The Virtues of Science Fiction," *Listener*, 31 December 1964, p. 1063.

The genre has "taken over territory which most serious novelists have (in my view mistakenly) abandoned." Modern novel has lost interest in "what happens" in favor of "exploration of character, with the complex interplay of invented people." In sf something must happen. It is uninterested in "moral ambiguities," but does have "moral concern."

44 Bradbury, Ray. "Day After Tomorrow: Why Science Fiction?" *Nation*, 2 May 1953, pp. 364–367.

Briefly lists "Best of Recent SF." Contends sf only contemporary form in which philosophy, sociology, psychology, and history may be "played with" without ruining the work as literature. It creates "outsize images" of problems facing society, as well as trying to "avoid the tyranny" of either the far left or the far right.

45 ———. "At What Temperature Do Books Burn?" *Writer*, 80 (July 1967), 18–20.

Reprint of the introduction to Simon and Schuster edition of *Fahrenheit 451* (1967). Speaks of genesis of such short stories as "The Pedestrian" and "The Veldt" as well as *451*. Traces all to some event or attitude in his own life, such as his love of libraries or the fire at his grandmother's house.

46 Bradley, Marion Zimmer. "Two Worlds of Fantasy," *Haunted: Studies in Gothic Fiction*, 1 (June 1968), 82–85.

Tends to dismiss influence of Poe on Lovecraft; similarly, dismisses the influence of Robert Chambers, despite such borrowings as place names, because Chambers' world held "valor, heroism, and beauty." The pervasive influence, the source of the Cthulhu Mythos, was Arthur Machen.

47 Brady, Charles A. "Lunatics and Selenophiles," *America*, 26 July 1958, pp. 448–449.

Discussion of influence of moon on literature, with attention to the early moon-voyages from Kepler to Poe, Verne, Wells.

48 Brandis, Eugeni and Vladimir Dmitrevsky. "In the Land of Science Fiction," *Soviet Literature*, no. 5 (1968), pp. 145–150.

A survey of Soviet sf, focusing on Ivan Yefremov. "Soviet science fiction is an embodiment of mankind's hopes and anxieties."

49 Bretnor, Reginald, ed. *Modern Science Fiction: Its Meaning and Future*. New York: Coward-McCann, 1953.

A collection of essays by such editors and writers as Campbell and Asimov, it has its value in presenting the views of these men during the first period of intense interest in sf after World War II. It concerns itself primarily with the genre's themes.

50 ———. "On Taking Science Fiction Seriously," *Science
Fiction Advertiser*, 7 (Winter 1954), 3–8.

In an era when the average man increasingly declines to give
attention to materials demanding serious consideration and
independent thought, sf is equated with the vanishing personal
essay. Regardless of its artistic merit, sf must maintain a "serious
speculative content" or lose its identity.

51 Brien, Alan. "Adam Beyond the Stars," *Spectator*,
19 September 1958, p. 379.

"Now that the boom is over," we will learn whether sf is more
than "just Mickey Spillane among the planets or Wyatt Earp
lopin' along the trail of the galactic frontiers." It is the "most
erudite branch of popular literature ever published."

52 Brophy, Liam. "Grave New Worlds," *Catholic World*,
17 (April 1954), 40–43.

Refers to Koestler controversy in England. General sketch limited
to such earlier writers as Wells, Bellamy, Bulwer-Lytton. Praises
Alfred Noyes's *Last Man*. Chief benefit of sf "lies in making
us reconciled with our time and place."

53 Brown, Harcourt. "A Duty to the Devil: Some Suggestions
for a Humanistic History," *French Review*, 25
(May 1952), 437–443.

Some of "most important works of the age" extrapolate
"beyond the present situation of man." Mentions Verne; emphasizes the use of non-human societies. The genre is "not frequently
cultivated" by French writers.

54 Brunner, John. "The Genesis of *Stand on Zanzibar*, and
Digressions into the Remainder of Its Pentateuch,"
Extrapolation, 11 (May 1970), 34–43.

Derived from the 1969 MLA Seminar at Denver. Brunner begins
with some of the ideas that went into the novel and ends with a
discussion of the "New Wave," citing Aldiss's *Barefoot in the
Head*.

55 Bryan, C. D. B. "Kurt Vonnegut on Target," *New Republic*, 8 October 1966, pp. 21–26.

Although naming Vonnegut's first four novels, this becomes a discussion of *Mother Night* and *God Bless You, Mr. Rosewater*, with much plot summary, several lengthy quotes. Bryan judges him a fine ironist, but decides early that he "lacks the anger and impatience which great satire demands."

56 Bufkin, E. C. "The Ironic Art of William Golding's *The Inheritors*," *Texas Studies in Language and Literature*, 9 (Winter 1968), 567–578.

Acknowledges Golding's theme as "the evil that intelligence brings," and undertakes a close structural analysis to show how irony provides the "over-all" pattern of the book. Finds the shift in point of view necessary to the final irony: man's transfer of his own characteristics to the Neanderthals, whom he regards as devilish.

57 Burgum, Edwin Berry. "Freud and Fantasy in Contemporary Fiction," *Science and Society*, 29 (Spring 1965), 224–231.

"The rise of the novel of fantasy is the most noteworthy innovation in fiction throughout the western world" because it discards the novel's dominant tradition: namely, the idea of "the objective existence of society as a common point of reference" between writer and reader. Observes two patterns in fantasy: as in *Don Quixote* or *Catch 22*, one type uses "the preposterous" to convey "a tenable interpretation of the social reality external to the subjectivity of the individual"; as in Kafka, the other blurs the distinction "between the real and plausible and the distorted and implausible, to leave the reader in a troubled state of ambiguity about fact and fancy whatever his conception of reality may be." Although sf is not mentioned explicitly, this essay has particular importance in suggesting its role in modern fiction and its potential for development.

58 Butor, Michel. "Growing Pains in Science Fiction," *Carleton Miscellany*, 4 (Summer 1963), 113–120.

Finds sf "a fantasy framed by a realism." Differs from other fantasies directly in proportion to the "solid scientific elements" its writers introduce. If sf "could limit and unify itself," it would "be capable of acquiring over the individual imagination a constraining power comparable to any classical mythology."

59 ———. "Notes on Science Fiction: The Crisis of Its Growth," *Partisan Review*, 34 (Fall 1967), 595–602.

Somewhat revised version of the essay in *Carleton Miscellany*. (See II, 58; also Blish, II, 37. Reprinted in Clareson, *The Other Side of Realism*, II, 71.)

60 Callahan, Patrick J. "The Two Gardens in C. S. Lewis's *That Hideous Strength*," in *SF: The Other Side of Realism*, ed. Thomas D. Clareson. Bowling Green, Ohio: Bowling Green University Popular Press, 1971, pp. 147–156.

To illustrate that Lewis "renders his morality into the image, symbol, and dramatic situation of art," Callahan undertakes an analysis of the significance of the gardens of St. Anne's and Belbury. St. Anne's "suggests a harmonious order of nature, an order in terms of which man must live if he is to be human."

61 Campbell, John W., Jr. "Concerning Science Fiction," *Writer*, 59 (1946), 149–150.

Divides sf into three types of stories: prophecy, philosophical, adventure. It is *not* pseudo-science, but "makes no pretense of being truth." Asserts that "top authors" in field are, "in general, technicians of one sort or another," who write not only as a hobby but also to "place before other keen and interested minds the ideas, suggestions, and problems they themselves have encountered."

62 ————. "Science-Fiction and the Opinion of the Unwise,"
Saturday Review, 12 May 1956, pp. 9–10.

Feels we must judge sf as a literature of prophecy. Gives much
attention to Steve Cartmill's "Deadline" (1944), dealing with
atom bomb. To Reisman's three types of characters he adds a
fourth: universe-directed man, dominated by scientific facts of
universe. Discusses characterization in this light. The seemingly
emotionless, authoritarian sf character acts "as the messenger of
the Universe." Concludes that "the total difference in objective . . .
renders irrelevant and fatuous the 'literary criticism' " of sf by
anyone "himself not primarily a science-fictioneer." (See Boucher,
II, 41.)

63 Carter, Everett. "The Scientist as the New Hero," in
Howells and the Age of Realism. New York-Philadelphia:
J. B. Lippincott, 1950, pp. 91–94.

Points out that "the admiration for the scientist became a
commonplace of realistic fiction." Rejecting both transcendentalism
and Calvinism, such writers as DeForest, Howells, Twain, and
Holmes turned to empiricism. "Howells' generation was one
in which science, both theoretical and applied, was either
capturing or oppressing the imagination of creative artists."

64 Cerf, Bennett. "Trade Winds: The Literary Scene,"
Saturday Review, 27 January 1951, p. 4.

Quotes Christopher Isherwood, in *Tomorrow*, as praising sf not
only as a literature of escape, "for while the realistic action story
is going through a phase of imaginative bankruptcy, the science-
fiction story grows more prodigious, more ideologically daring."

65 Chambers, John. "The Cult of Science Fiction," *Dalhousie
Review*, 40 (1960–1961), 78–86.

A sketch of the development of sf, tracing it to such sources as
Lucian of Samosata, and emphasizing in particular the "space
travel" and "worlds of if" motifs. Although much of it has little

value, it does provide "a remarkably rich and unique idiom" as well as "a unique vehicle for symbolic expression." Finds in an account of a spaceman battling aliens on another planet a "re-phrasing of those intimations which caused the Anglo-Saxons to create Beowulf battling against non-human monsters in the meres of Denmark."

66 Clareson, Thomas D. "A Note on Voltaire's *Micromegas*," *Extrapolation*, 2 (December 1960), 4.

Cites Bentley Glass's assertion that Pierre Louis Moreau de Maupertuis is the object of Voltaire's personal attack.

67 ———. "The Classic: Aldous Huxley's *Brave New World*," *Extrapolation*, 2 (May 1961), 33–40.

Emphasizes three techniques used by Huxley: extrapolation, parody and juxtaposition of detail, and sharply contrasting points of view. These help him "dramatize several of the conflicts that have haunted western civilization."

68 ———. "The Scientist as Hero in American Science Fiction 1880–1915," *Extrapolation*, 7 (December 1965), 18–28.

Point of departure is Carter's discussion in *Howells and the Age of Realism*. Describes appearances of the scientist/inventor in sf motifs and suggests that in them he achieved mythic proportion. (See Carter, II, 63.)

69 ———, ed. "Science Fiction: The New Mythology," *Extrapolation*, 10 (May 1969), 69–115.

The tape of the papers and ensuing discussion at the MLA Forum on sf 29 December 1968. Professor Bruce Franklin served as moderator; speakers were Professor Darko Suvin, Isaac Asimov, and Fred Pohl.

44

70 ———. "Science Fiction and Literary Tradition," in *Nebula Awards 6*, ed. Clifford Simak. New York: Doubleday, 1971, pp. xi–xxvii.

Analysis of the novels and stories nominated by the members of SFWA for the 1970 awards. Stresses Burgum and Stevenson in suggesting that sf belongs to the continuing tradition of fantasy, noting that more and more writers are turning from realism and naturalism to "novels of fantasy." Questions the widely assumed premise that sf must be scientifically plausible and/or probable. (See Burgum, II, 57; Stevenson, II, 283.)

71 ———, ed. *SF: The Other Side of Realism*. Bowling Green, Ohio: Bowling Green University Popular Press, 1971.

The first anthology of sf criticism, 25 essays, drawing upon original materials as well as reprints from *Extrapolation* and other journals. Critics from eight countries are represented, as well as a variety of disciplines, both academic and popular. Stresses the diverse approaches possible to the study of sf, but emphasizes its relationship to the main literary traditions.

72 ———. "SF: The Other Side of Realism," in *SF: The Other Side of Realism*. Bowling Green, Ohio: Bowling Green University Popular Press, 1971, pp. 1–28.

Primarily historical, the essay suggests that literary realism-naturalism and science fiction were twin responses to the intellectual milieu of the last third of the 19th century. Except as both have attained metaphorical level, they have trapped themselves in *cul-de-sacs*: realism, in the "here-and-now" of the dramatic scene and psychological probing; sf, in the projection of a narrowly linear future that was only an extension of the present day, particularly when it was the instrument of didacticism in the utopias and dystopias. Because it creates unreal worlds, sf has the freedom and potential to explore significantly the human condition.

73 ———, ed. *A Spectrum of Worlds*. New York: Doubleday, 1972.

An anthology including fourteen stories, a lengthy introduction, and critical analyses of each story. The stories range from Bierce, Wells, and London to Simak, Ballard, Delany, and Silverberg. Suggests that fantasy and science fiction allow the author the greatest freedom in creating model worlds capable of sustaining metaphorical statement; emphasizes that literary quality has been inferior primarily when sf was used as a vehicle of didacticism.

74 Clarke, I. F. "Science Fiction Past and Present," *Quarterly Review*, 295 (1957), 260–270.

Cites forerunners of Wells as early as *The Last Man* (1806) and *The Mummy* (1827). "The science romance seems to be the natural literary product of a time of crisis." Only general mention of contemporary period.

75 ———. "Shape of Wars to Come," *History Today*, 15 (February 1965), 108–116.

A discussion of the novels during the period 1900–1914 which portrayed an impending world war. Finds these novels "among the first fruits of the new technologies and the new primary schools." Shows how novels reflected actual events. (Reprinted in Clareson, *SF: The Other Side of Realism*, II, 71.)

76 ———. "The Battle of Dorking 1871–1914," *Victorian Studies*, 8 (June 1965), 308–328.

Materials essentially incorporated into chapter 2 of *Voices Prophesying War*. (See II, 77.)

77 ———. *Voices Prophesying War 1763–1984*. New York & London: Oxford University Press, 1966.

Definitive study of the "future war" motif as developed in Europe, and as such may serve as a model for the intensive studies of motif so badly needed. Particularly strong in showing how literary expression resulted from political tensions and technologies from 1870 onward. Four bibliographies. (Panther Arts paperback ed., 1970.)

78 ———. "*Voices Prophesying War*: Problems in Research," *Extrapolation*, 9 (May 1968), 26–32.

Derived from 1967 MLA Seminar. Asks for close investigation of popular literature for the insight it can give into the intellectual milieu of a period. Asks also for bibliographies of fiction and critical materials so that further work may be accomplished.

79 ———. "Forecasts of Future Wars, 1871–1914," *Futures*, December 1969, pp. 553–557.

By the 1870's the tale of the future had become established "as the most effective means of describing the pattern of probabilities." This concentrates on the "future war" motif.

80 Collins, Christopher. "Zamyatin, Wells and the Utopian Literary Tradition," *Slavonic and East European Review*, 44 (1965–1966), 351–360.

Argues effectively that Wells provided the primary literary influence upon Zamyatin's *We*, although introducing Plato and the tradition of the 17th and 18th centuries. Zamyatin's principal contribution to the tradition lies in his making the revolt against "rationalism, collectivism and alienation . . . primarily a battle of the self." He introduced the "first split protagonist in the manner of Dostoyevsky" in that to Wells's "entire amalgam" he added "psychology and [the] existential revolt of Dostoyevsky, as well as his own brand of 20th century expressionistic style." Denies that *We* is specifically anti-Soviet.

81 Colquitt, Betsy Feagan. "Orwell: Traditionalist in Wonderland," *Discourse*, 8 (1965), 370–383.

Orwell's writings came to focus upon an anti-utopian world "in which the accepted, traditional views not only can be put down, but more frighteningly can be obliterated from the minds of men." His writing has a political orientation, concentrating upon the totalitarian state to find a symbol for "a world gone mad."

82 Conklin, Groff. "What Good Is Science Fiction?" *Library Journal*, 15 April 1958, pp. 1256–1258.

Dates "modern" sf from "the last few years of the 1930's." Its "greatest boost" was the A-bomb. Stories extrapolate to "see how much fun the author and reader can have exploring the imaginary outer limits of a given idea's potentialities." Emphasizes that even satires do not have a "momentary reality," although they all embody "ethical or critical or sociological lessons." For the best sf, follow the anthologies, not the magazines.

83 Conquest, Robert. "Science Fiction," *New Statesman*, 20 March 1954, p. 358.

Replies to Lovell. Attacks him for his insistence upon literary quality. The greatest prose writers since Defoe have not had this "Paterish attitude." (See Lovell, II, 187.)

84 ———. "Science Fiction and Literature," *Critical Quarterly*, 5 (Winter 1963), 355–367.

One of the best discussions of the relationship and differences between sf and so-called mainstream literature. Stresses the domination of the novel of character over 200 years and "the acceptance of conventions implicit in this." Uses sf to provide "illumination" of "the nature of our literary habits." Says it "makes a fairly clean break with the principles taken for granted in a novel," in part at least because it is "interested more in environmental changes."

85 ———. "Beyond the Moon," *Encounter*, 32 (June 1969), 48–50.

Because sf has existed so long he cannot understand why anyone is surprised at space travel, which he defends. As for the "New

Wave" writers in sf: they employ "the same material as its
equivalent in mainstream fiction—pornography tempered by
incomprehensibility."

86 "Controversy over Ideology in Science Fiction Works,"
Current Digest of the Soviet Press, 2 March 1966,
pp. 16–20.

Reprints three articles: (1) Yefremov, "The Billions of Facets
of the Future"; (2) Brandis and Dmitrevsky, "Fantasy Writers
Write for Everyone"; and (3) Federovich, "Not Only Entertaining Reading." The controversy focuses upon the purpose and
future of sf: whether it is merely "prophetic preview" and
"entertaining popularization of science" or whether it deals and
should deal with "social-psychological, esthetic, and philosophical
problems." The controversy turns upon various criticisms of the
novels by the brothers Strugatsky.

87 Cox, Arthur Jean. "A Question of Identity," *Riverside
Quarterly*, 1 (February 1965), 88–110.

Follows two images, the head (intellect) and the face (identity),
through Harry Bates's fiction to show how he develops a favorite
theme: "bringing a person face to face with himself . . . confronts
in the most direct way possible the question of what constitutes
that person's identity." Dwells upon entrance into a closed
chamber as another recurrent device. Concludes that Bates rejects
pure intellect.

88 Crichton, J. Michael. "Sci-Fi and Vonnegut," *New Republic*,
26 April 1969, pp. 33–35.

There is "no explanation of the ineptitude of sf as fiction"; it
remains, by and large, "as pulpy, and as awful, as ever." Vonnegut
"is too cute, precious, silly." Yet he notes that Vonnegut has
attacked our "deepest fears . . . our deepest political guilts, our
fiercest hatreds and loves." Declares "ultimate difficulty" with
Vonnegut is that "he refuses to say who is wrong." (This is the
author of *The Andromeda Strain*.)

89 Crispin, Edmund. "Science Fiction," *Times Literary Supplement*, 25 October 1963, p. 865.

Both science and the future are incidental to sf, whose real subject matter is "the present seen against the perspectives of history." Calls it *"Origin-of-the Species"* fiction because individuals "count for very little" since its "basic valuation of man is as just one of the horde of different animals sharing the same planet." The genre's "popular image" emphasizes its utopian vision; in that context, there exists "remarkably little" sf at present. He has not here judged it "simply as literature. This in any case would be difficult: achievement can hardly be judged except by reference to intention—and the intentions of sf differ so radically from the intentions of, say, *The Music of Time*, that no sensible critic would dream of attempting to apply the same yardstick to both."

90 Cruse, Amy. "Science and Romance," in *After the Victorians*. London: Allyn and Unwin, 1938, pp. 163–173.

Significant for date, this glances at writers who used scientific materials: Kipling, Wells, Robert Eustace, Mrs. L. T. Meade, Rider Haggard, duMaurier.

91 Dane, Clemence. "American Fairy Tale," *North American Review*, 242 (Autumn 1936), 143–152.

Whereas Britain looks to the past for its fairy tales, America looks to the future; sf, therefore, is "nothing but America's fairy tale." At best its stories are no more than "nonsense," but they do stimulate imagination. He discusses *Astounding*, *Weird Tales*, and *Wonder Stories*.

92 Davenport, Basil. *Inquiry into Science Fiction*. New York & London: Longmans, 1955.

An 87-page sketch of the history, method, and "mystique" of sf, as well as sketches of personalities, this now has little but historical value.

93 ———, ed. *The Science Fiction Novel: Imagination and Social Criticism.* Chicago: Advent, 1959.

Four essays based on lectures given at the University of Chicago: Robert Heinlein, C. M. Kornbluth, Alfred Bester, and Robert Bloch. The unevenness is perhaps compensated for by the divergent views of the four writers. Now primarily of historical value.

94 Davies, H. Neville. "*Symzonia* and *The Man in the Moone*," *Notes & Queries*, 213 (September 1968), 342–345.

Suggests a close modelling of incident and structure between the two books, thereby suggesting that *Symzonia* "shows a concern with the techniques of fiction hitherto not noticed in its author."

95 deCamp, L. Sprague. *Science Fiction Handbook.* New York: Hermitage House, 1953.

The first three chapters provide one of the best discussions of the history of sf, while chapter 6 has continued value for its biographical sketches of contemporary writers.

96 Deisch, Noel. "The Navigation of Space in Early Speculation and in Modern Research," *Popular Astronomy*, 38 (January 1930), 73–88.

A survey of literary speculations from Lucian and Francis Godwin to Poe. Brief mention of novels at the turn of the century by such men as Simon Newcomb, ending with a consideration of the research and theories of Professors Robert H. Goddard and Hermann Oberth.

97 Delany, Samuel R. "About Five Thousand One Hundred and Seventy Five Words," *Extrapolation*, 10 (May 1969), 52–66.

Derived from the 1968 MLA Seminar meeting. Delany here gives a most useful and entertaining account of the process of writing. The importance of the word: "any serious discussion of speculative fiction must get away from the distracting concept of sf content and examine precisely what sort of word-beast sits before us." [Reprinted in Dick Geis, *SFReview*, no. 32 (August 1969), pp. 8–14; George Hay, *The Disappearing Future*, pp. 73–84; and Clareson, *SF: The Other Side of Realism*, II, 71.]

98 ———. "Critical Methods: Speculative Fiction," in *Quark / 1*. New York: Paperback Library, 1970, pp. 182–195.

This essay establishes Delany as one of the major popular critics, with a fine knowledge of mainstream literary traditions. Two Victorian views—that of orderly progress and that of the universality of human nature—did much to shape and limit sf. Only with the editorship of Gold (*Galaxy*) did "whole new systems and syndromes of behavior" appear, with writers neither praising nor condemning (i.e., taking a utopian-dystopian bias) but exploring "both the worlds and their behaviors for the sake of exploration . . . an aim closer to poetry than to any sociological brand of fiction." Introduces four images as typifying the variant myths of the world—Arcadia, The Land of Flies, Brave New World, and the New Jerusalem; would like to have sf criticism examine "how all four of these mystic visions sit in concert in given books," not praising or blaming a book because it does or does not "reflect any one."

99 Denney, Reuel. "Reactors of the Imagination," *Bulletin of Atomic Scientists*, 9 (July 1953), 206–210.

Discusses sf as literature, stressing elements of catharsis and shock. Suggests it expresses an essentially metaphysical symbolism. Emphasis on Bradbury and Frederic Brown as best of current writers.

100 Derleth, August. "Contemporary Science Fiction," *College English*, 13 (January 1952), 187–193.

Calls sf "a development of fantasy" paralleling "supernatural fiction . . . Dunsanian whimsey . . . a cousin of the tall story . . .

the legendary of the atomic age." Modern sf has little relationship to its forebears save in theme. Mentions Heinlein, but suggests that Charles Fort "did more to stimulate imaginations of writers and readers alike" than anyone else. "Literary merit but a recent goal."

101 Devoe, Alan. "Scientifiction," *American Mercury*, 77 (August 1953), 26–29.

A discussion focusing upon Heard, Bradbury, and C. S. Lewis introduces a tribute to Ernest Thompson Seton. At its best sf "may open out fresh magics for creative energy and imagination." Scientists and clergymen detest it for unspecified reasons; it appeals, as in the case of Seton, to "nobody but the people."

102 Doherty, G. H. "Use of Language in Science Fiction," *SF Horizons*, 1 (1964), 43–53.

The worlds of technology and science are increasingly becoming a part of popular culture so that the images and themes of sf are therefore more viable. The language of sf, like that of any other fiction, must either be "poetry or nothing."

103 Donovan, Richard. "Morals from Mars," *Reporter*, 26 June 1951, pp. 38–40.

Extended analysis of Ray Bradbury, with biographical data. Emphasizes Bradbury's opposition to "machinery in almost any form." His fiction is symbolic; "his subject is always man." He wishes to "maintain a foothold for the old-style natural man."

104 Ducharme, Edward. "A Canticle for Miller," *English Journal*, 55 (November 1966), 1042–1044.

Miller's achievement in *Canticle for Leibowitz* "lies in [a] skillful handling of thought-provoking ideas." Despite "sensational plot materials . . . he has placed most of his emphasis on the moral issues of Man's way—his life and survival." Suggests approaches for classroom use.

105 Egoff, Sheila A. "Tomorrow Plus X: Some Thoughts
on Science Fiction," *Ontario Library Review*, 45
(May 1961), 77–80. (See I, 22.)

106 Ellik, Ron and Bill Evans. *The Universes of E. E. Smith*.
Chicago: Advent, 1968.

A concordance of the "Lensman" and "Skylark" novels, with a
good bibliography. Recreates the worlds of the first "space
operas," still regarded by some as the best of their kind.

107 Ellis, H. F. "Queen of Viscerotonia," *New Yorker*,
27 December 1969, pp. 54–56.

Attempts quietly to satirize the sf theme of the invasion of earth
by disguised aliens; provides a cast of characters and a passage
from an imagined novel. The success of the satire rests upon the
classifications of characters established and upon the blending
of a preposterous style with inane detail from the novel.

108 Emmons, Winfred S., Jr. "H. P. Lovecraft as a Mythmaker,"
Extrapolation, 1 (May 1960), 35–37.

Brief exploration of the Cthulhu mythos.

109 Fadiman, Clifton. "Party of One," *Holiday*, 11
(June 1952), 14, 16.

He notes that sf has "mushroomed" into a new popular, mass
entertainment. "However crude," it attempts "to cope in popular
terms with our rejection of the past." He notes Conant's warning
"against a naive acceptance" of the genre as a "true picture of
the possibilities of technology," but concludes: "like all visions,
it does not explain or instruct. It is a form incorporating the fears,
the hopes, and the bewilderments of the unconscious."

110 ———. "Wild Child," in *Party of One: Selected Writings
of Clifton Fadiman*. Cleveland and New York:
World, 1955, pp. 324–333.

Revision of "Party of One" from *Holiday*. (See II, 109.)

111 Fenton, Robert W. *The Big Swingers*. Englewood Cliffs, N. J.: Prentice-Hall, 1967.

An amateurish hodge-podge of information on the life of Burroughs, his work, and the Tarzan movies. [Mullen]

112 Fiedler, Leslie A. "The Divine Stupidity of Kurt Vonnegut," *Esquire*, 74 (September 1970), 195–204.

Discusses Vonnegut's fiction in the context of the death of the "Old Art Novel"—the product of "Modernism"—and the "New Pop." Vonnegut has made use of the mythology of the future, and his books "tend to temper irony with sentimentality and to dissolve both in wonder." His works have also explored the potentials of sf. Each novel is given attention, but this is noteworthy for its (rare) concern with *Mother Night* and *The Sirens of Titan*. Vonnegut has been a writer of fantasy rather than of analysis.

113 Fishwick, Marshall. "Evolution of Monsters: Adapted from *Faust Revisited*." *Saturday Review*, 14 September 1963, pp. 23,63.

"Pseudoscientific tale of horror or wonder probably appeals to the same kind of personality that endorsed diabolism or witchcraft in ages past." Spends most time on *Brave New World* and *1984*. Mentions Bradbury's *Fahrenheit 451* and Knight's *Country of the Kind*. Unless it answered some "deep psychic need," sf would not be read.

114 Fison, Peter. "That Thing from Another World," *Twentieth Century*, 158 (September 1955), 280–288.

Laments the loss in sf of the potential for "high adventure which used to be the novel's birthright in Dumas." The genre takes itself too seriously; certain narrow categories and pessimistic themes are now stylish. Praises Bradbury as literary artist and deCamp as humorist.

115 Forbes, Allyn B. "The Literary Quest for Utopia, 1880–1900," *Social Forces*, 6 (December 1927), 179–189.

Brief but acute analysis of the forces producing the flood of utopian literature in late 19th-century America when industrialization "first reached such large dimensions as to be the greatest single determining factor in all phases of American life." All of the novels reflect idea that "problems of society" are economic. Includes a listing of 48 titles, arranged by date of publication.

116 Frank, Stanley. "Out of This World," *Nation's Business*, 40 (March 1952), 40–42.

Hasty, name-dropping survey of the field from Lucian to L. Ron Hubbard. Stresses prophecy and gadgets. Most interesting for its anecdote of Cartmill's "Deadline," which brought about the FBI investigation of *Astounding* because the story dealt with the A-bomb in 1944. "To have *stopped* running such stories . . . would have been as much of a tip-off."

117 Franklin, H. Bruce. *Future Perfect*: *American Science Fiction of the Nineteenth Century*. New York: Oxford University Press, 1966.

Excellent selection of stories from Poe and Hawthorne to Twain. Although the critical essays seem brief, they are uniformly provocative. Remains the soundest study of sf as it emerged in American literature.

118 ———. "Fiction of the Future," *Stanford Today*, Summer 1966, pp. 28–30.

This is one of his earliest discussions of Soviet sf, where reader and writer are in "general agreement about what will happen to man." Stresses didactic role of sf.

119 "From Icarus to Arthur Clarke," *Forbes*, 1 July 1968, pp. 112–114.

Sympathetic and well-illustrated general sketch of the field. Discusses Clarke, but draws no other examples later than the 1920's.

120 Fuson, Ben W. "A Poetic Precursor of Bellamy's *Looking Backward*," *Extrapolation*, 5 (May 1964), 31–36.

Reprint of Paxton's "A Century Hence," first published in 1880. (Reprinted in Clareson, *SF: The Other Side of Realism*, II, 71.)

121 ———. "Three Kansas Utopian Novels of 1890," *Extrapolation*, 12 (December 1970), 7–24.

Examines C. C. Dail's *Willmoth the Wanderer; or, The Man from Saturn*, Alvarado Fuller's *A.D. 2000*, and Cyrus Cole's *Auroraphone*, emphasizing their plot lines and themes. They are unique in Kansan literary history, no other utopias being published for several decades afterward. One infers they react, at least in part, to Bellamy's *Looking Backward*.

122 "Future Indefinite," *Times Literary Supplement*, 2 August 1963, p. 593.

Critical analysis of sf as "a new form of the Gothic," intended to be "horrid in precisely the late 18th-century sense." It "underlines and heavily black-borders the death of the 19th-century belief in progress, as well as the confidence in the religious significance of man." Judges Ballard's stories of a "high order" reminiscent of Kafka.

123 Gallant, Joseph. "A Proposal for the Reading of 'Scientific Fiction,'" *High Points*, 33 (April 1951), 20–27.

Asks for a new classification, "scientific fiction," which would include both the "conventionalized" sf from pulps and such older stories as those by London or Burroughs, now best represented in kind by the fiction of George Stewart. It would "satisfy the desire for fantasy and escapism within the framework of the ideology of an industrial, scientific culture without importing foreign or archaic mythologies." It should deal with the "basic social and historical problems of our times."

124 Gardner, Martin. "Humorous Science Fiction," *The Writer*, 62 (1949), 148–151.

Suggests that humor in sf is not based on "funny dialogue or funny scenes" but is "built around situations fundamentally absurd." Refers to de Camp, Padgett, Leinster, and Tenn as "four of the leading humorists in the field."

125 Gehman, Richard B. "Imagination Runs Wild," *New Republic*, 17 January 1949, pp. 16–18.

Notes expansion within last three years of "science and fantasy." Reviews history of genre, giving attention to J. O. Bailey's study. Emphasis on Wells and Lovecraft as "first notable modern" sf writers in America. Speaks of fantasies of the past becoming realities and of the present authors as "prophets of doom" who will "live to see their prophecies come true." (See Bailey, II, 18.)

126 Gibbs, Angelica. "Onward and Upward with the Arts: Inertium, Neutronium, Chromalogy, P-P-P-Proot!" *New Yorker*, 13 February 1943, p. 36.

Unfavorable survey of the field, with attention to fan conventions and low prices paid authors. Finds a "touching rapport" between readers and writers, as evidenced by selected letters to editors. Focuses upon Gernsback and Burroughs, but mentions Leinster and such early magazines as *Argosy* and *Munsey*.

127 Gilmore, Maeve. *A World Away*. London: Gollancz, 1970.

The widow of Mervyn Peake (the *Titus Groan* trilogy) gives her personal memoir of her husband's life and art. She records, with deep feeling and perception, his early life in China, sudden love and marriage, early struggles as an artist and illustrator, conflicting days in the army when he wrote *Titus Groan*, his rising fame and courageous fight with his final illness. It is an indispensable insight into Peake's life and striking career. [Sadler]

128 Glicksohn, Susan. "A City of Which the Stars Are Suburbs," in *SF: The Other Side of Realism*, ed. Thomas D. Clareson. Bowling Green, Ohio: Bowling Green University Popular Press, 1971, pp. 334–347.

Examines Olaf Stapledon's *Last and First Men* and Isaac Asimov's *Foundation* to show how, both literally and figuratively, they reach toward Northrop Frye's concept of the "limit of the imagination." Both "attempt to depict, not a single theme or the lives of individual men, but a concept of human life. . . ."

129 Golding, William. "Androids All," *Spectator*, 24 February 1961, pp. 263–264.

Ostensibly a review of Amis, but more a general discussion of the characteristics of sf. It is the "province" of a "privileged class" that "can afford to take less interest in people than in things." Says that to read sf "is to pass the time" with an "ingenious paradox, a mild satire . . . to be entertained without either edification or delight." The genre avoids "profound experiences and emotions." But he praises Bradbury, who "always get his focal point dead right."

130 ———. "Astronaut by Gaslight," *Spectator*, 9 June 1961, pp. 841–842.

Verne's talent was not spurred by a love of pure science, but by technology. His books are the "imaginative counterpart of the Great Eastern, the Tay Bridge, or the Great Steam Flying Machine." Yet they attract today because of the "charms of his nineteenth century interiors." Notes almost total absence of women from the books. "His heroes, too, are a pattern of what the twelve-year-old boy considers a proper adult pattern—they are tough, sexless, casually brave, resourceful, *and making something big.*"

131 ———. *The Hot Gates.* New York: Harcourt, Brace & World, 1966.

Several selections, such as "Fable," are pertinent to fantasy and sf, but the most explicit discussion occurs in "Astronaut by Gaslight," pp. 111–115, reprinted from the 1961 *Spectator.* (See II, 130.)

132 Goldsmith, Maurice. "Soviet Science Fiction," *Spectator*, 21 August 1959, pp. 226–227.

Distinguishes between "Science in Fiction" (SiF) and SF, the latter of which involves "complete accuracy," while SiF "fills the reader with an awful sense of doom—death and destruction, and a belief in authoritarianism." After praising John Campbell, he turns to Alexander Malinovski's *Red Star* (1908), portraying a coming Socialist world on Mars. Notes Lenin's interest in the genre. "After 1929" in sf "the official party line dominated." Discusses in detail Alexander Belyayev's *Leap into Nothing*, A. Kazantsev's *Circle of the Winds*, and Ivan Yefremov's *Heart of the Dragon.*

133 Gove, Philip Babcock. *The Imaginary Voyage in Prose Fiction.* New York: Columbia University Press, 1941.

Analysis of the manner in which the imaginary voyage motif seized upon 18th-century literary and popular imaginations to become the vehicle both for a sense of wonder resulting from exploration and for social criticism. It gives modern idiom to the voyage motif, which remains the most pervasive framework and myth behind sf.

134 Green, Martin. "Distaste for the Contemporary," *Nation*, 21 May 1960, pp. 451–452.

Begins as review of Golding's *Free Fall*, but becomes a general statement on his novels. Points out how much *Lord of the Flies* relies upon a reversal of conventions and devices of the "well known Victorian boys' book, R. M. Ballantyne's *Coral Island*." Calls *The Inheritors* "a tour de force technically" because we share consciousness of nonhuman creatures. In *Free Fall*, notes the "repeated discovery of meanness and nastiness in others and in oneself." Thinks all books show that we have "rediscovered man's essential savagery" and thus help "corroborate" C. P. Snow's assertion concerning the hostility between the two cultures.

135 ———. "Science and Sensibility," *Kenyon Review*, 25 (Autumn 1963), 713–728. Article in two parts: (1) "Science for the Layman"; (2) "Science Fiction."

He believes that sf "brings with it an atmosphere of literary possibility which a writer can find hardly anywhere else today." Nevertheless, he feels it "cannot develop into forms which engage major talents and deliver major meanings, though it can reinvigorate the forms of conventional literature by merging into them." He does not regard it as a genre.

136 ———. "Two Surveys of the Literature of Science," in *Science and the Shabby Curate of Poetry*. New York: W. W. Norton, 1965, pp. 120–156.

This reworks the materials appearing in *Kenyon Review*. (See II, 135.)

137 Green, Roger Lancelyn. *Into Other Worlds: Space Flight in Fiction from Lucian to C. S. Lewis*. New York and London: Abelard Schuman, 1958.

At Oxford, Green's tutor was C. S. Lewis; book dedicated to him. Green prefers Lewis-type story and cannot hide dislike of Wells. His own preferences lead him to rank E. R. Burroughs with *Perelandra*.

138 Grennan, Margaret R. "The Lewis Trilogy: A Scholar's Holiday," *Catholic World*, 167 (July 1948), 337–344.

During a general introduction to the trilogy, this essay emphasizes how Ransom on Malacandra often resembles Gulliver defending men to the emperor of Brobdingnag, how Perelandra parallels the "Celtic paradise of many ancient *imrama*," and how in the last book Ransom resembles "Anfortas—even to an incurable wound." [Christopher]

139 Haight, Gordon. "H. G. Wells: 'The Man of the Year Million,'" *Nineteenth Century Fiction*, 12 (March 1958), 323–326.

Presents details of Wells's reference in Book 2, chapter 2, of *War of the Worlds* to *Pall Mall*, November-December, 1893, in which a writer, actually himself, forecast a man of Martian-like structure. *Puck* caricatured it, 16 November 1893, as did *Punch*, 25 November.

140 Hamilton, John B. "Notes Toward a Definition of Science Fiction," *Extrapolation*, 4 (December 1962), 2–13.

Uses as a basis for his analysis 19th century fiction by/about medical men. Suggests two criteria: (1) "to what degree does a scientific concept determine the nature of the work as well as help reveal the meaning"; (2) does the work have "a meaning on the adult level?"

141 Harrison, Harry. "We Are Sitting on Our . . . ," *SF Horizons*, 1 (1964), 39–42.

Suggests censorship and lack of maturity exclude sex and profanity from American sf, though not from British.

142 ———. "With a Piece of Twisted Wire," *SF Horizons*, 2 (1965), 55–63.

Stresses awe of science and naivete of sf during the 1930's. Cites F. L. Wallace's *Address: Centauri* for hilarious errors in simple

science, involving the heroine's digestive tract (a car disemboweled
her without hurting her in any other way) and her twenty-year
thirst. The author shows his ignorance of (or ignoring of)
"*contemporary* medical knowledge," thereby destroying "our
sense of involvement."

143 Hart, Lyn. "Science Fiction," *Booklist*, 1 November 1949,
pp. 73–75.

Thinks sf "to the fore" because it is "an inevitable product of
our time." It falls under the "general classification of fantasy."
Cites J. O. Bailey and Bleiler's *Checklist*. (See II, 18 and VIII, 2.)

144 Heinlein, Robert. "Ray Guns and Rocket Ships," *Library
Journal*, 78 (July 1953), 1188–1191.

First published in the School Library Association of California
Bulletin in November 1952, pp. 11–15. Suggests whole field be
called "speculative fiction," with sf as a subdivision. In defining
sf, he remarks, "The result can be extremely fantastic in content,
but it is not fantasy; it is legitimate—and often very tightly
reasoned—speculation about the possibilities of the real world."
Asks that critics do not apply too hastily as a test of quality of
sf "what are merely the conventions of better known fields" of
literature. Stresses as criteria: (1) entertainment value, (2) a
moral sense, (3) literary quality, and (4) authenticity. (This seems
the first time the term *speculative fiction* was used.)

145 Henighan, Tom. "Tarzan and Rima, The Myth and the
Message," *Riverside Quarterly*, 3 (March 1969), 256–265.

In the growing urban culture of the early 20th century, W. H.
Hudson's *Green Mansions* and Burrough's *Tarzan of the Apes*
most successfully crystalized "the longings of urban man for
the primitive, the natural, the animal self." Analysis of the
'Darwinian' world in both as well as their "coinages of the central
myth of recovered integrity."

146 Hicks, Granville. "From Out of This World: Contemporary Scene," *Saturday Review*, 20 August 1966, pp. 23–24.

Article responds to request of Damon Knight, then president SFWA, that sf receive more serious attention. Hicks surprised at how much sf writers "distrust science—or, at any rate, technology." Sf more varied than he had supposed, and a certain amount "stands up well when judged by the standards by which we judge literature."

147 Highet, Gilbert. "Perchance to Dream," in *The Clerk of Oxenford*. New York: Oxford University Press, 1954, pp. 3–10. (See I, 31.)

148 Hillegas, Mark. "The First Invasions from Mars," *Michigan Alumnus Quarterly Review*, February 1960, pp. 107–112.

Discussion of both Kurd Lasswitz's *Auf Zwei Planeten* and Wells's *War of the Worlds*. Credits impetus for interest in Mars to Schiaparelli's announcement in 1877 of his discovery of the *canali* of Mars.

149 ———, ed. *The Mysterious Island*, by Jules Verne. New York: Scholastic Book Services, 1964.

Excellent edition of one of Verne's most provocative novels.

150 ———. *The Future as Nightmare: H. G. Wells and the Anti-Utopians*. New York: Oxford, 1967.

Somewhat briefer than one might wish, but it remains the most acute analysis of Wells's "cosmic pessimism" and its influence upon Forster, Huxley, Zamyatin, C. S. Lewis, and Orwell.

151 ———, ed. *A Modern Utopia*, by H. G. Wells. Lincoln, Neb.: University of Nebraska Press, 1967.

Reproduces the text of the 1905 edition, including Wells's own footnotes and his Appendix, "Skepticism of the Instrument." Brief but sound introduction.

152 ———, ed. *Shadows of Imagination*: *The Fantasies of C. S. Lewis, J. R. R. Tolkien, and Charles Williams.* Carbondale, Ill.: Southern Illinois University Press, 1969.

Most important recent volume on these writers; balancing all three equally shows how pervasive is "the longing for some myth to bring meaning again to the universe and human existence." Their relationship to the dystopian tradition also emphasized. (The idea of the book grew out of the 1966 MLA Seminar on Science Fiction.)

153 ———. "Martians and Mythmakers: 1877–1938," in *Challenges in American Culture*, ed. Ray B. Browne, Larry N. Landrum, and William K. Bottorff. Bowling Green, Ohio: Bowling Green University Popular Press, 1970, pp. 150–177.

The most comprehensive and penetrating analysis of the "myth of the superior Martians and their invasion of earth," which followed Schiaparelli's discovery of the *canali* of Mars. The myth was given shape by Percival Lowell's *Mars* (1895), Kurd Lasswitz's *Auf Zwei Planeten* (1897), and Wells's *War of the Worlds* (1897). Wells made the most "imaginative use of the conventions of the Martian myth." Detailed discussion of Burroughs and C. S. Lewis, as well as a climactic discussion of the manner in which the Martian myth itself has disappeared from literature since 1938.

154 Hilton-Young, Wayland. "The Contented Christian," *Cambridge Journal*, 10 (July 1952), 603–612.

An allegorical interpretation of the Ransom trilogy which sees (1) in *Out of the Silent Planet*, "the three communities of inhabitants" of Mars as "the three parts of man": the *hrossa*, emotion; the *seroni*, reason; the *pfifltriggi*, will; (2) in the latter two novels, the myths of the beginning and ending of the human race, and the Creation and prelude to the Second Coming. Ends by comparing Lewis to other modern religious novelists. [Christopher]

155 Hipolito, Jane. *"The Last* and First *Starship from Earth,"*
in *SF: The Other Side of Realism,* ed. Thomas D. Clareson.
Bowling Green, Ohio: Bowling Green University
Popular Press, 1971, pp. 186–192.

Analyzes John Boyd's novel, suggesting that while it is a criticism
of contemporary society, more importantly it shows that "the
human mind must forever return to its primitive beginnings for
inspiration. And man's history, like man's mind, is patterned. . . .
Boyd restates emphatically the enigmatic question of the Sphinx:
what is man? And he answers the question with a Joycean
affirmative."

156 Hobana, Ion. "A Survey of Romanian Science Fiction,"
Romanian Review, 22 (1968), 46–51.

Sketches the history of Romanian sf, in part to disprove critical
assertion that sf is "an exclusively Anglo-Saxon creation." Henri
Stahl's *Romanian in the Moon* (1914) is cited as the first title,
while Felix Aderca's *Submerged Towns* (1935) "can vie with the
best foreign works." Introduces "anticipatory fiction" as a
possible generic name.

157 Holcomb, Claire. "Science-Fiction Phenomenon in
Literature," *Saturday Review of Literature,* 28 May 1949,
pp. 9–10.

Presents historical sketch going back to 17th century and
emphasizing Wells and Verne. Mentions recent "philosophical"
sf, citing Huxley and Stapledon. Genre is "tonic to imagination,"
preparing "hearts and minds to accept . . . whatever answers
there may be."

158 Howe, Irving. "Orwell: History as Nightmare,"
American Scholar, 25 (Spring 1956), 193–207.

Praises *1984* for the terror of its nightmare, "particular to our
century," suggesting that it cannot be "valued simply by resorting
to the usual literary categories" because they are no longer

significant. Thus, he defends the characterization on the grounds that "the human relationships taken for granted in a novel" are no longer possible in such a totalitarian state. "Politics has displaced humanity and the state has stifled society." Says Orwell's profoundest insight is that in such a state "man's life is shorn of dynamic possibilities." In *1984* "all political themes reach their final and terrible flowering."

159 Hughes, David Y. "H. G. Wells: Ironic Romancer," *Extrapolation*, 6 (May 1965), 32–38.

Derived from 1963 MLA Seminar. Presentation of sources for Wells's "The Sea Raiders," "Aepyornis Island," and "The Empire of the Ants." All add evidence of Wells's skepticism of any naive concept of progress.

160 Hulme, Hilda M. "*Middlemarch* as Science-Fiction: Notes on Language and Imagery," *Novel*, 1 (Fall 1968), 36–45.

Some will object to the use of sf in the title, but here an accepted definition provides point of departure for an analysis of how "details of scientific theory were to be reflected in many details of the novel's organization, language, and imagery," particularly as Eliot employed the theories of Bichat, the French anatomist and surgeon.

161 Iosefescu, Silvian. "Wanted a Dante," *Romanian Review*, 22 (1968), 52–55.

Finds sf "a form of synthesis between narration and lyricism" built upon the "scientific illusion" that the story corresponds to the real. It "acts with high artistic efficiency when it builds the most daring conjecture on the basis of contemporary knowledge."

162 Janes, Adrian. "Status of Science Fiction as Literature," in *Collecting Science Literature for General Reading*. Champaign: Illinois Graduate School of Library Science, 1961, pp. 171–180.

A general article sketching the characteristics of the genre: it makes the point that sf has not yet achieved the same level of literary quality as most "mainstream" literature.

163 Jones, W. M. "The Iago of *Brave New World*," *Western Humanities Review*, 15 (Summer 1961), 275–278.

Suggests Huxley structured *BNW* on parallels to *Othello*. First, the "feelies" portray a negro kidnapping a blonde; second, the Savage parallels Othello; all else reverses the play. The entire society acts as Iago, poisoning the Savage's mind against Lenina. It is a "tragedy of a man deceived by himself as well as society."

164 Kagarlitski, Julius. *The Life and Thought of H. G. Wells*. London: Sedgwick and Jackson, 1966.

"Biography of Wells the writer" by the editor of the Russian edition of his works in 15 volumes (1964). Wells had "the breadth of vision that our century demands," believing that "science promises mankind a life in the Garden of Eden," but knowing "that Garden concealed a yawning abyss that would destroy mankind" unless the world was transformed. Equal to any modern study of Wells; especially provocative because of Kagarlitski's perspective.

165 ———. "Russian Translations of Foreign Science Fiction," *Soviet Literature*, no. 5 (1968), 159–165.

Two Russian publishers, Mir and Molodaya Gvardia, lead all others in issuing sf. Notices a number of Americans and British, but singles out Stanislaw Lem for extended praise.

166 ———. "Fantasy and Realism," in *SF: The Other Side of Realism*, ed. Thomas D. Clareson. Bowling Green, Ohio: Bowling Green University Popular Press, 1971, pp. 29–52.

Concentrates upon H. G. Wells, showing that his fantasy "was an attempt to return to the image multiplicity of meaning, to raise it by the force of its internal possibilities to the level of a generality. In order to accomplish this task, he turned both to the romanticism scornfully slighted by the naturalists and to everyday, familiar reality the neo-romantics were turning away from." The fusion of the two creates the core of "scientific fantasy"; important to this in Wells's opinion was the concept that only a single speculative premise be introduced into a story.

167 Kagle, Steven Earl. "The Societal Quest," *Extrapolation*, 12 (May 1971), 79–85.

Derived from the 1970 MLA Seminar. Interprets modern sf as a new type of quest pattern, that of the "societal quest," in which a group seeks to achieve an objective beyond the life of an individual man, oftentimes over an extensive timespan or over regions so vast that no unified action is possible. Cites Asimov's *Foundation* trilogy, Clarke's *Childhood's End*, Julius Fast's *League of Grey-Eyed Women*, and Herbert's *Dune*. Its rise as a literary form further reflects the diminution of the individual as hero.

168 Kaufman, V. Milo. "Brave New Impossible Worlds: Critical Notes on Extrapolation as a Mimetic Technique in Science Fiction," *Extrapolation*, 5 (December 1963), 17–24.

Derived from 1962 MLA Seminar. Despite "the realism of its descriptive technique," sf is a "technological fantasy," and its "defining characteristic"—representation of novel worlds— "has certain problems organic to it." Basic problem turns on fact that sf's extrapolated worlds are "an invention whose relationship to the shared human world is tentative to the extreme, whose probability is only the pseudo-probability of author's fiat," with result that appreciation can only be inferior to that of "inventions which conform to real classes and real probability."

169 Ketterer, David A. "New Worlds for Old: The Apocalyptic Imagination, Science Fiction, and American Literature," *Mosaic*, 5 (October 1971), 37–57.

Asks for a literary definition of apocalyptic imagination "in the controlling light of the Book of Revelation," its essential terms thus becoming a preoccupation with the transformation, or transfiguration, of a "limited world of mind" in a context that nullifies and destroys a previous system or makes it part of a larger design. Science fiction provides the "purest expression" of the apocalyptic imagination.

170 Knepper, B. G. "Shaw's Debt to *The Coming Race*," *Journal of Modern Literature*, 1 (March 1971), 339–353.

An analysis of Shaw's adaptation of various elements from Lytton's *Coming Race*, "a respectable specimen of science fiction," to his own ends, most extensively in *Back to Methuselah* but throughout his works. Most important was the vril-force which he transformed to "a product of the will, or the ability to control matter through mental power." Other devices include the Automato and the Ancients as well as the concept of "awe." A number of themes are also similar: the treatment of inferior races, the equality of women, the "responsible anarchy," among others. However Shaw modified his adaptations, "many of the first thoughts were Lytton's. . . ."

171 Knight, Damon. *In Search of Wonder*. Chicago: Advent, 1967 (2nd ed.).

Knight wishes to consider sf in relationship to the mainstream of fiction; this he keeps as his goal, but often the book becomes a delightful collection of anecdotes and details that only a man who has worked so long and so well in the field could preserve. Highly influential revision of review and critical pieces done for the specialist magazines since 1952. Marred only in that unless one is acquainted with the personalities of the field, some portions read like an in-joke. Nonetheless, valuable, because Knight is concerned with sf as literature.

172 Koestler, Arthur. "The Boredom of Fantasy," in *Trail of the Dinosaur and Other Essays*. New York: Macmillan, 1955, pp. 140–147.

From a 1953 BBC broadcast. Sees sf as "typical product of the atomic age," dealing with "new vistas and new nightmares, which art and literature have not yet assimilated. In a crude and fumbling fashion," the genre tries to fill that gap. Yet because "our imagination is limited" and because "we cannot project ourselves into the distant future any more than into the distant past," he rejects fantasy as an effective literary mode.

173 Kostolefsky, Joseph. "Science, Yes—Fiction, Maybe," *Antioch Review*, 13 (June 1953), 236–240.

Refuses to grant sf maturity because it treats grand ideas; demands literary excellence. Its supporters "consider everything but the text—its audience, its place in society, the neurotic drives that make it accepted." Accuses it of being esoteric because every "flight" is an "ascent to the upper reaches of scientific theory." Points out its similarity to proletarian literature of the 1930's in that the environment creates characters. Bradbury, Brown, and Sturgeon are the best, "carrying on their backs" all others. It needs "writers worth reading for what they can do with people, with language, and with ideas."

174 Krueger, John R. "Language and Techniques of Communication as Theme or Tool in Science Fiction," *Linguistics*, no. 39 (May 1968), pp. 68–86.

Bases study on 1,247 stories read since 1964, but concentrates upon one third or so in which "problems of language and communication raise their head, though not always playing a major role." Solutions: (1) some ignore it; (2) aliens learn our language; (3) we learn theirs (time travel especially); (4) translation machines; (5) a convenient *linguae francae*; (6) use of non-speech forms of communication.

175 ———. "Names and Nomenclature in Science Fiction," *Names*, 14 (1968), 203–214.

Descriptive survey of kinds of names given to characters in sf: (1) compound names of diverse origin ("Ryan-Ngana") to suggest such conventions as world government and loss of prejudice; (2) combinations of numbers and syllables ("WA 10 NA 56"); (3) to escape "Earthly limits," euphonious names without ethnic overtones ("Zarth Arn, Vel Quen"); (4) some systematic pattern to indicate such matters as rank and occupation, as in Burroughs.

176 "Kurt Vonnegut, Jr.: A Symposium," *Summary*, 1 (1971), 34–119.

The second number of this new British journal devotes half its issue to Vonnegut, including articles by Robert Scholes, Robert Kiely, David Hayman, Armin Paul Frank, Brian W. Aldiss, Tony Hillman, and Seymour Lawrence. It concludes with "An Account of the Ancestry of Kurt Vonnegut, Jr. by an Ancient Friend of His Family"—possibly Vonnegut himself. Robert Scholes examines Vonnegut's writings for the *Cornell Sun* in the spring and fall of 1941 to show how deeply some of the themes of his books are implanted in him. Aldiss stresses his early titles that were produced as science fiction.

177 Kuttner, Henry. "Science in Fiction," *Science Fiction Advertiser*, 2 (January 1953), 3–6.

Argues for literary quality in sf: ". . . *fiction* is the operative term in *science fiction*. 'Science' deals with part of the content; fiction deals with the form." The science in sf is "primarily *what science means"* to author—i.e., an enemy, way of life, means of escape, and so on. Each requires a different *"quality* of emphasis"; ideally, the result would "move into an area where only the definitions of literature would apply."

178 Kyle, Richard. "Out of Time's Abyss: The Martian Stories of Edgar Rice Burroughs," *Riverside Quarterly,* 4 (January 1970), 110–124.

Suggests that ERB's *Gods of Mars* was the principal, if not the first-planned, novel of the original Barsoom trilogy, and that those novels are heavily indebted to Rider Haggard, particularly to ideas and incidents in *Cleopatra* and *She.* Note the similarity between the Valley of Kor (RH) and Valley of Dor (ERB).

179 LaFleur, Laurence J. "Marvelous Voyages," *Popular Astronomy,* 51 (1943), 76–83, 139–147, 359–362, 434–440.

A series of articles summarizing the plots of Wells's *First Men on the Moon, War of the Worlds,* and *Time Machine,* and pointing out the "errors" in each.

180 Lambert, P. C. "The Wonderful Journey," *Alabama Librarian,* 8 (January 1957), 3–5.

Surveys the "imaginary voyage" motif from Kepler to Garrett P. Serviss. Asserts that two factors caused the increased interest in extraterrestrial voyages: (1) the speculations that other worlds might be inhabited, and (2) the improved knowledge of the earth's surface which "curtailed the unknown places which could be peopled by the fictional beings of imaginative authors." One of the Maxwell AFB papers. (See Giffin, I, 27; Fields, VI, 14.)

181 Leahy, Jack Thomas. "Science Fiction: From Space Opera to Imaginative Literature," *The Trend in Engineering at the University of Washington,* 29 (October 1971), 16–19, 31.

A general survey of the recent changes in sf, aiming at the audience which knows little of the field.

182 Lear, John. "Let's Put Some Science in Science Fiction,"
Popular Science Monthly, 165 (August 1954), 135–137.
(See I, 43.)

183 Leighton, Peter. *Moon Travellers*. London: Oldbourne,
1960.

Reads as though hastily done, but cites and quotes from a number
of the older titles. Praises Verne, but gives little or no attention
to the contemporary scene.

184 Lemire, Eugene D. "H. G. Wells and the World of Science
Fiction," *University of Windsor Review*, 2 (Spring
1967), 59–67.

Wells Centennial issue. Early Wells "still quite unsure" whether
he tells an entertaining story, creates "an ironic reflection of the
'real' world and (like Swift) expose[s] its follies to laughter," or
pressures "an idea like 'natural selection' through an imaginary
setting, with clinical objectivity and absolutely logical consistency."
Acknowledges Wells's early pessimistic element. Left sf for
literary forms "he hoped might more effectively change world."
Imaginative powers were "unabated," but something was lost.

185 Lewis, C. S. "On Science Fiction," in *Of Other Worlds*:
Essays and Stories, ed. Walter Hooper. New York:
Harcourt, Brace, & World, 1966, pp. 59–73.

Concerns himself with the "sub-species" of sf. He dislikes that
type which leaps "a thousand years to find plots and passions
which they could have found at home," but admires a work such
as John Collier's *Tom A-Cold*, which portrays a heroic action
among people fallen to barbarism. Also favors that type which
portrays the "sense experiences and probable emotions and
thoughts" of men visiting a new and strange place; does not
condemn them for any lack of characterization; it "is a fault" if
such characterization exists, because the more unusual the scene
and events, the more typical the characters should be—Everyman,

Anyman. Other sub-species include the "engineers" stories about space travel, those concerned with the "ultimate destiny" of the race, and the "machine" stories. Criticism of all of these should not differ from that given "fantastic or mythopoeic literature in general."

186 Lovecraft, Howard Phillips. *Supernatural Horror in Literature*. New York: Ben Abramson, 1945.

An historical sketch of the development of the "tale of terror," emphasizing in particular the Gothic novel. Valuable for indicating the literary preferences and influences upon the writer whom many regard as the modern master of the "weird" tale. Gives brief descriptions of some 100 titles, emphasizing American contributions. (Reprinted in *Dagon and Other Tales of the Macabre*. Sauk City, Wis.: Arkham House, 1965.)

187 Lovell, A.C.B. "Counterblast to Science Fiction," *New Statesman*, 13 March 1954, pp. 319–320.

Based on 50 novels, mostly American, published in Britain within the year, it savagely attacks sf: "The lunatic fringe of humanity seems to be stimulated by news of Outer Space." Not only dislikes the pessimism of the authors, but finds it "insidiously horrific" and a "protracted reading . . . a nightmare effect." Judges it "a new source of cheap money" in its "exploitations of modern science." (See Conquest, II, 83.)

188 Loveman, Amy. "The Clearing House," *Saturday Review of Literature*, 24 July 1937, p. 2.

A column, with one item entitled "Scientific Novels," which is called an "elastic term." Gives plot lines of some titles from early 20th century.

189 Lundwall, Sam J. *Science Fiction: What It's All About*. New York: Ace Books, 1971.

A survey aimed at the popular audience by a young Swedish fan, its strength lies in a discussion of Heroic Fantasy (said to be unique to the English-speaking countries), a chapter on mass-culture (comics and films), and a brief description of international fan activity. Relies upon popular sources in its discussion of the history of the genre; despite the promise to include European sf, mentions it only at random. Says that Tolkien has come "as close to a Utopia as anything that has been written in the last fifty years." Ignors such writers as Skinner. Most specific references, except the traditional ones, are from the 1960's. Adds nothing new to sf history or criticism.

190 Lupoff, Richard A. *Edgar Rice Burroughs: Master of Adventure*. New York: Canaveral, 1965.

A popular account by an enthusiast who gives too much attention to recapitulating plot-lines, the book nevertheless contains much information regarding such matters as publishing and quotes from ERB's papers. Interesting and brief sketch of "The Descendants of Tarzan" shows the continued influence of ERB. (Reprinted as Ace N-6.)

191 McNelly, Willis E. "Linguistic Relativity in Old High Martian," *CEA Critic*, 30 (March 1968), 4,6.

Uses Heinlein's definitions of "grok" in *Stranger in a Strange Land* to explore the themes of the novel. These include Benjamin Whorf's concept of linguistic relativity, satire of elements of the establishment, love as a unifying power that "will find an identity of expression," and a pervasive religious theme that reaches its climax in the hero's benediction as he is being stoned to death.

192 ———. "The Science Fiction Novel in 1968," in *Nebula Award Stories 4*, ed. Poul Anderson. New York: Doubleday, 1969, pp. xiii-xxv.

Detailed analysis of the novels nominated by members of SFWA as the best sf novel of 1968. Gives particular attention to John Brunner's *Stand on Zanzibar*, James Blish's *Black Easter*, John Boyd's *Last Starship from Earth*, and Robert Silverberg's *Masks of*

Time. Emphasizes how much "involvement or response" the finalists demand of the readers, and asserts that the "gap between so-called mainstream fiction and first-rate science fiction is narrowing." Commends all four for their handling of thematic material and their artistry.

193 Manser, A. R. "Science in S.F.: Alien Sociology," *Listener*, 14 January 1965, pp. 56–58. (See I, 47.)

194 Marshak, Alexander. "Sci Fi—Soviet Style," *Saturday Review*, 2 June 1956, pp. 20–21.

Names first Russian sf as *Ships from the Stars* by I. A. Yefremov. No alien and earthman meeting; "none of the usual interplanetary exchanges of threats, insults, diseases, philosophies, knowledge, or women." No sex, "either of the straight variety or any of the many sci-fi aberrations." He loses those readers for whom "the word 'fiction' has come to be another word for the unrepressed sexual daydream." Instead he unveils a mystery and shows how it serves the growth of the state. Plot summary.

195 "Media Information," *Publishers' Weekly*, 18 July 1953, p. 177.

Refers to Seymour Krim's review of Bretnor's volume, citing his remark that eventually sf will achieve the "highest adult and literary purposes." (See Krim, III, 55.)

196 "Media Information," *Publishers' Weekly*, 16 January 1954, p. 182.

One-paragraph reference to Arthur C. Clarke's discussion of sf at the Publishers' Publicity Circle of England at their December meeting; it was reported in more detail in *Bookseller*. Clarke suggests that British writers have been "foremost" in sf and that it is not "a recent American invention." The best sf is concerned with the problems of today and is far less "fantastic and detached from reality" than the "run-of-the-mill romantic novel."

197 Mercer, Derwent. "Science in S.F.: Alien Communication," *Listener*, 7 January 1965, pp. 13–15. (See I, 53.)

198 Merril, Judith. "What Do You Mean Science? Fiction?" *Extrapolation*, 7 (May 1966), 30–46; 8 (December 1966), 2–19.

One of the fine surveys of the sf field because of her intimate knowledge of it as writer, editor, and reviewer. Moves from the so-called "classic" period of the 1940's to the "New Wave" of the 1960's. (Reprinted in Clareson, *SF: The Other Side of Realism*, II, 71.)

199 Methold, Kenneth. "Science Fiction," *Contemporary Review*, 195 (March 1959), 170–173.

Despite lack of critical attention, the best of sf compares "favourably" with much that is best in contemporary mainstream fiction. At its best sf portrays the reactions of characters to problems which, although projected into the future, portray the relationship of man to his changing environment. Asks that it receive the attention "any serious and competent" fiction deserves.

200 Miesel, Sandra. "Challenge and Response: Poul Anderson's View of Man," *Riverside Quarterly*, 4 (January 1970), 80–95.

Examines Anderson's themes, with plentiful references to specific stories. "Man needs challenge," but he must accept "responsibility for his response." Domestication—i.e., manipulation—is the most heinous crime against rational individuals because it deprives them of freedom.

201 ———. "Samuel R. Delany's Use of Myth in *Nova*," *Extrapolation*, 12 (May 1971), 86–93.

Explores the indebtedness of the novel to the Grail Legend and Indian mythology. Calls Delany "one of the pre-eminent mythopoets in speculative fiction today."

202 Mitchell, Stephen O. "Alien Vision: The Techniques of Science Fiction," *Modern Fiction Studies*, 4 (1958), 346–356.

Science fiction is similar to early realism-naturalism in presenting a vision of an alien universe "that we do not know and would not like." The sf writer must rely on many of the techniques of realism, particularly the massing of detail and creation of a believable framework, so that sf suffers a repetition of the same devices that lead to technical monotony. Names as typical sf Merritt's *The Moon Pool* and Howard's *Conan*.

203 Moorman, Charles. "Space Ship and Grail: The Myths of C. S. Lewis," *College English*, 18 (May 1957), 401–405.

In the first two novels of the Ransom trilogy, Lewis uses an invented mythology which is parallel to Christian doctrine; in the third he dovetails certain aspects of the Arthurian mythology with the cosmic myth of the first two. Moorman adds comments on the function of these myths in the novels, basing them on Lewis's statements about myth. (The essay is nearly identical to the chapter on Lewis in Moorman's *Arthurian Triptych*.) [Christopher]

204 Moskowitz, Sam. *Explorers of the Infinite: Shapers of Science Fiction*. Cleveland and New York: World, 1963.

Sketches of writers from de Bergerac and Poe to Stapledon and Weinbaum originally done as separate pieces for specialist magazines. A protege of Hugo Gernsback, Moskowitz emphasizes the tradition coming from Poe and Verne to the exclusion of utopian-dystopian materials.

205 ———. *Seekers of Tomorrow: Masters of Modern Science Fiction*. Cleveland and New York: World, 1966.

Continues *Explorers* by sketching the biography and works of writers from E. E. Smith to Arthur C. Clarke.

206 ———. *Science Fiction by Gaslight: A History and Anthology of Science Fiction in the Popular Magazines 1891–1911.* Cleveland and New York: World, 1968.

To date this is one of his most valuable works because his long introduction (pp. 15–53) not only traces the development of the cheap, mass-circulation magazines but shows how thoroughly sf had established itself as a popular literary form at the turn of the century.

207 ———. *Under the Moons of Mars: A History and Anthology of "The Scientific Romance" in the Munsey Magazines, 1912–1920.* New York: Holt, Rinehart, and Winston, 1970.

This volume does much to introduce an overlooked period in the evolution of American sf. Emphasizes the influence of Burroughs, who turned sf "from prophecy and sociology to romantic adventure." The stories included capture much of the heroic primitivism that so characterized the "scientific romance" between the periods of utopia and dystopia.

208 Mullen, Richard D. "H. G. Wells and Victor Rousseau Emanuel: *When the Sleeper Wakes* and *The Messiah of the Cylinder*," *Extrapolation*, 8 (May 1967), 31–63.

An analysis of Wells's novel, defending it from apparent earlier neglect. Its theme was "the spiritual impoverishment . . . that had been a concommitant of the material expansion of the industrialized world," thus becoming a satire on capitalism. Suggests horrors of Rousseau's novel come not from socialism but from the eugenics program, and calls it a "sexual fantasy," as well as answering "Futurism" with a "Christian conservatism." Traces Wells's reactions to Rousseau as well as the novel's apparent influence upon Orwell.

209 ———. "Blish, vanVogt, and the Uses of Spengler," *Riverside Quarterly*, 3 (August 1968), 172–186.

Close analysis of Blish's novels in particular, showing how themes, and in some cases actual wording, suggest the direct influence of Spengler. Includes a chart to indicate how the novels extend the "contemporary epochs" of the Spenglerian world.

210 ———. "Edgar Rice Burroughs and The Fate Worse Than Death," *Riverside Quarterly*, 4 (June 1970), 186–191.

In the 24 novels written between 1911 and 1915, Burroughs endangered his heroine's honor no less than 76 times. After speculating upon the lessons a young lady may learn from such escapes, Mullen concludes by noting John Carter's extreme gentility toward those oviparous Martian maidens, Dejah Thoris and Thuvia, who vividly represent that "remarkably beautiful race whose outward appearance is identical with the more god-like race of Earthmen. . . ."

211 ———. "The Undisciplined Imagination: Edgar Rice Burroughs and Lowellian Mars," in *SF: The Other Side of Realism*, ed. Thomas D. Clareson. Bowling Green, Ohio: Bowling Green University Popular Press, 1971, pp. 229–247.

Attacks the popularly held idea that Burroughs patterned the planet Barsoom after Percival Lowell's description of Mars. Instead, he invented as he went along, and a close examination of the novels shows his inconsistencies and contradictions.

212 Neill, Sam. "Report of the Science-fiction Investigation Committee," *Ontario Library Review*, 37 (August 1953), 187–189.

Highly personal, informal tone. Makes a plea for the importance of sf as "the fairy tale of our time," emphasizing its appeal to the "intellectually alert reader." Deplores the state of realistic fiction, and argues that the older novels are too long for modern readers.

213 Nicolson, Marjorie. "Cosmic Voyages," *English Literary History*, 7 (June 1940), 83–107.

One of the first publications of much of the material incorporated into *Voyages to the Moon*. The concentration is upon the appearances of the moon voyages from Lucian to Kepler, "the earliest modern voyage," and John Wilkins.

214 ————. "Kepler, The *Somnium* and John Donne," *Journal of the History of Ideas*, 1 (June 1940), 259–280.

An analysis of *Somnium* followed by a discussion of Donne's *Conclave Ignatii*, in which satire he introduced "important passages concerning the 'new astronomy.' " Suggests on the basis of evidence presented that Donne knew Kepler's manuscript. Concludes with a survey of later authors who were aware of *Somnium*, including Verne and Wells.

215 ————. *Voyages to the Moon*. New York: Macmillan, 1948; Macmillan paperback, 1960.

Sequel to "a small book now out of print," *A World in the Moon* (1935), in which she concerned herself "with the scientific and philosophical backgrounds of the idea of an inhabited moon." Here she turns to the fiction, bringing her discussion to C. S. Lewis. Part of the bibliography lists fiction and non-fiction concerned with "The History of Flight" from 1493 to 1783.

216 ————. *Science and Imagination*. Ithaca, NY.: Cornell University Press, Great Seal Books, 1956.

A study of the impact of the "new astronomy" upon the literary imagination from Kepler through Swift. A final chapter explores the impact of the microscope.

217 Norman, H. L. "The Scientific and the Pseudo-scientific in the Works of Luigi Capuana," *PMLA*, 53 (September 1938), 869–885.

Capuana denies the concept of naturalism; indebted to Wells, Verne, and Poe, but no slavish imitator. In *Conquista dell'aria* (1911), the protagonist, subject to dreams of flight, experimented with his body until he acquired the actual ability to fly.

218 Norwood, W. D. "C. S. Lewis, Owen Barfield, and the Modern Myth," *Midwest Quarterly*, 8 (Spring 1967), 279–291.

In his trilogy Lewis first studies the false myth or superstition (Wells's view of the mechanistic universe) in *Out of the Silent Planet*; then the true myth (Christian heaven, together with the more obvious mythic real-occurrences) in *Perelandra*; and finally, the emergent myth (as the pagan and Jewish myths became reality in Christ, so the romantic fantasies of the first two volumes shift to historical realism in the third) in *That Hideous Strength*. [Christopher]

219 ————. "Unifying Themes in C. S. Lewis's Trilogy," *Critique: Studies in Modern Fiction*, 9 (n.d.), 76–80.

Much briefer on Lewis's treatment of the false, true, and emergent myths. In the archetypal theme, the novels portray a confirmation in Christian experience, a baptism, and a new life, respectively. At this level the novels contain an interlocking system of sub-themes: (1) reason, faith, death; (2) hope and birth; (3) mysticism, love, and choice. [Christopher]

220 O'Connor, Gerard. "Why Tolkien's *The Lord of the Rings* Should *Not* Be Popular Culture," *Extrapolation*, 13 (December 1971), 48–55.

Originally given as a paper at meeting of the Popular Culture Association in 1971, the paper discusses the thematic characteristics of Tolkien's trilogy which should make it unpopular among

today's youth. It "glorifies age and disparages youth"; it is
anti-feminist; it is authoritarian; its society is based upon a caste
(hierarchic) structure; and it advocates a moral and political
absolutism.

221 Olney, Clark. "Edgar Allan Poe—Science Fiction Pioneer,"
The Georgia Review, 12 (Winter 1958), 416–421.

Although Poe was not the first to write sf, he must be recognized
as one of outstanding pioneers because he based his stories
"firmly on a rational kind of extrapolation, avoiding the
supernatural. This has proved to be the underlying convention"
of sf.

222 Panshin, Alexei. "Heinlein in Dimension," *Riverside
Quarterly*, 1 (May–June 1965), 139–164; 2 (January
1966), 35–52; 2 (June 1966), 90–104; 2 (November
1966), 193–209; 2 (March 1967), 284–297.

Successfully evaluates Heinlein's literary artistry, plot patterns,
heroes—called here the "Heinlein individual"—and something of
his influence on the genre. Balanced presentation, for the most
part, of Heinlein's strengths and weaknesses.

223 ———. *Heinlein in Dimension*. Chicago: Advent, 1969.

Book publication of the study appearing in *Riverside Quarterly*.
(See II, 222.)

224 ———. "Science Fiction in Dimension," *Fantastic Stories*,
19 (June 1970), 125–130.

The first of a series of columns in which Panshin tries to explore
and re-define the nature of sf as a literary form. Here he uses
the controversy about the "New Wave" as a point of departure.
Asserts that sf, "as a few have always insisted, is fantasy. What
we are used to thinking of as fantasy is conscious recreation of
myths and symbols that are no longer believed." (Reprinted in
Clareson, *SF: The Other Side of Realism*, II, 71.)

225 ———. "The Nature of Science Fiction," *Fantastic Stories*, 19 (August 1970), 119–122.

Second in the series. Notes widespread discrepancies in definitions of sf and wonders whether the weakness lies in the literature or the definitions. Attacks the concept that sf is either scientific or realistic. "Art is more a game of pattern-making than pattern-testing. It is a metaphorical, discontinuous, and analogical process . . . ."

226 ———. "Unbinding Science Fiction," *Fantastic Stories*, 20 (October 1970), 89–97.

Third in series. Explores how and why the short story, melodrama, and bad writing have limited the potential of sf as it has appeared in the specialist magazines since 1926. Names experimental writers trying to expand the boundaries of the genre.

227 ———. "Science Fiction and Creative Fantasy," *Fantastic Stories*, 20 (December 1970), 124–128.

Fourth in series. Recapitulates by asserting that the old paradigms of sf are "bankrupt" and that new ones are needed. The best of recent titles are "only indications of what is possible, not definitions."

228 ———. "The Nature of Creative Fantasy," *Fantastic Stories*, 20 (February 1971), 100–106.

Fifth in series. Examines the early Gernsback magazines, both editorial blurbs and stories. Instead of scientific content, "the stuff of creative fantasy is distance, whether of time or space, whether taking the form of parable, speculation, nightmare, vision, or myth."

229 ———. "The Short History of Science Fiction," *Fantastic Stories*, 20 (April 1971), 109–115.

Sixth in series. Contends that Gernsback's definition of sf lasted from April 1926 to December 1929—only so long as his view remained dominant and no other editor worked in the field. Again, his definition may never have existed at all in practice because of the stories he selected.

230 ————. "New Perspectives," *Fantastic Stories*, 20 (June 1971), 109–113, 125.

Seventh in series. Suggests two "adjustments" that will help clear away the conflict as to what sf is: (1) abandon the Wellsian insistence upon only one essential difference in each story; and (2) no longer insist that this difference must "be featured at the heart of the story"; focus instead upon its impact upon the character. Sees the key of sf as a change in perspective forcing the reader to look at the world and at ideas in a new way.

231 ————. "A New Paradigm: I," *Fantastic Stories*, 20 (August 1971), 110–113.

Science is "no central and necessary factor, even as atmosphere" in sf. He proposes the name *speculative fantasy*: "a fictional form that uses removed worlds, characterized by distance and difference, as the setting for romantic-and-didactic narrative."

232 ————. "A New Paradigm: II," *Fantastic Stories*, 21 (October 1971), 120–126.

Refers to Scholes and Kellogg's *Nature of Narrative* (1966) and to the three distinct "goals of narrative"—mimesis, didaxis, and romance—to add the final element to his new paradigm. Speculative fantasy uses its removed worlds as the setting for "romantic-and-didactic narrative." It must be judged by the "standard of its ancestors, the best and highest literature that Western man has produced." (These columns suggest something of the scope of Panshin's critical study of contemporary sf, *The World Beyond the Hill*, now being prepared for publication.)

233 ————. "SF and Academia," *Fantastic Stories*, 21 (December 1971), 110–113, 128.

This column is based on a paper given at the Science Fiction Research Association session of Noreascon in Boston, Labor Day weekend 1971. Suggests that the new academic interest is going to be a permanent part of the sf scene. Asks that it not become exclusive ("mandarin") in its approach to the field and to fandom, and believes that it will not because many of the academic persons have long been active in the field.

234 Paris, Bernard J. "George Eliot, Science Fiction, and Fantasy," *Extrapolation*, 5 (May 1964), 26–30.

Derived from 1963 MLA Seminar. Points out that science exists in Eliot's fiction for its "basic principles, fundamental philosophy." Bretnor's characterization of sf as that fiction which is aware of "the nature and importance . . . of scientific method" brings forth a definition that Eliot would accept for her own art. Emphasizes sf's ties to realism and social criticism. But discovers it "self indulgent" in its use of science to "transcend reality"— and thereby to move toward the fairy tale.

235 Parkinson, Robert C. "*Dune*—An Unfinished Tetralogy," *Extrapolation*, 13 (December 1971), 16–24.

Dune Messiah should not be considered a simple sequel to *Dune*, for it continues the as yet unfinished philosophical problems begun by Herbert in the first novel. The two are fused together by an elaborate set of symbols—the ecological systems and religion among them— which center upon the problem of life as a process of change and growth. Thus, complete control or foreknowledge leads to stagnation and death. These ideas oppose each other through the novels and Herbert has not yet resolved them. The last book "surely is Alia's," and the central problem must be whether or not she will avoid "the ultimate corruption of power that doomed Paul."

236 Penzoldt, Peter. "The Supernatural in Science Fiction,"
The Supernatural in Fiction. London: Peter Nevill, 1952,
pp. 49–53.

The volume, which updates Scarborough and Birkhead, concerns
itself with the principal motifs from the ghost to the vampire,
giving individual attention to such writers as LeFanu, M. R. James,
de la Mare, and Blackwood. Treatment of sf is peripheral,
without adequate evidence. Suggests aim of sf is to "give some
probability" to apparently supernatural events, and considers
its "most terrifying convention" to be "the deification of the
machine."

237 Perry, Nick and Roy Wilkie. "Homo Hydrogenesis:
Notes on the Work of J. G. Ballard," *Riverside Quarterly*,
4 (January 1970), 98–107.

Landscape and characters are fundamental to Ballard's works; the
characters' "psychological state is reflected in their environmental
circumstances." The result is that "images of surrealism are the
iconography of inner space." One result: his works provide "an
early warning system for social change."

238 Peterson, Clell T. "Jack London's Sonoma Novels,"
American Book Collector, 9 (October 1958), 15–20.

Incidental mention of *The Iron Heel* as the first novel London
wrote while in the valley. In those works he rejected civilization
and the problems of industrial society in an attempt to return
to nature and freedom.

239 Philmus, Robert M. "*The Time Machine*, or, The Fourth
Dimension as Prophecy," *PMLA*, 84 (May 1969),
530–535.

The Eloi-Morlock sequence prepares for the final vision of the
dying world caught in the solar eclipse. That "vision of man's being
swept away 'into the darkness from which his universe arose.' "—
of life's being "slowly and remorselessly annihilated"—provides

the unifying vision of *The Time Machine*. The Traveler feels compelled to return to resume his journey because his return acts out "the ultimate consequence of his taking a prophetic myth literally." The artistry of *The Time Machine* is comparable to the experiments of Conrad and merits the praise James gave it.

240 ————. *Into the Unknown: The Evolution of Science Fiction from Francis Godwin to H. G. Wells*. Berkeley and Los Angeles: University of California Press, 1970.

Approaches sf "as a strategy of narrative presentation—a rhetorical strategy in Wayne Booth's sense"—and suggests that it "mythically displaces, and interpretatively deforms, areas of historical reality"—i.e., prophesies. Significant because of its formal approach and because of its solid documentation.

241 Plank, Robert. "Names and Roles of Characters in Science Fiction," *Names*, 9 (September 1961), 151–159.

Finds three categories of names in sf: Anglo-Saxon (the heroes and their helpers); foreign (often the villains); and 'out-of-the-world' (guardian characters and aliens who have a superior intelligence and help man). The same pattern holds true for Soviet sf.

242 ————. "The Golem and the Robot," *Literature and Psychology*, 13–15 (1963–1965), 12–27.

Traces the literary evolution of characters created by man. Accompanied by Simon O. Lesser's "Our Feelings About Man-Made Creatures, Imaginary and Real," a commentary on the paper given at the Literature and Psychology section of MLA. Lesser concentrates upon computers instead of the details of the paper itself.

243 Pratt, Fletcher and Lee De Forest. "Introductions," in *Ralph 24C41+: A Romance of the Year 2660*, by Hugo Gernsback. New York: Frederick Fell, 1950.

Praises this 1911 novel which celebrated the scientist-inventor as a hero who "belongs to the state," not himself; filled with descriptions of technological paraphernalia that completed the early, basic formula for the Gernsback magazines. Such periodicals as *Time* and the *New Yorker* have cited it as the first sf novel.

244 Priestley, J. B. "Who Goes There," *New Statesman*, 6 September 1958, pp. 268, 270.

Everywhere he finds dystopias portrayed, resulting in "one of the dreariest trips I have ever made." Rumors in trade that sf is on the way out. It provides him with a point of departure to indict the "military budget" and wish that the "world divided in the wrong way" could unite.

245 Pritchett, V. S. "The Scientific Romances," *The Living Novel*. London: Chatto & Windus, 1946, pp. 116–124.

Concentrates upon Wells, with whose ideas he disagrees. Calls him an "anarchist" who did not adequately reckon with the inner "reserve" of man. Speaks of his "intoxicated response to the front-page situation of his time," but declares that *The Time Machine* will "take its place among the great stories of our language." This chapter was omitted from the second edition.

246 Pulvertaft, Thomas B. "Five Types of Science Fiction," *Spectator*, 11 December 1955, p. 702.

Denies Wells and Verne; Gernsback did start sf. Types range from "modern western *cum* fairy tale" to better stories, in which there is "a feeling of desolation, of emptiness—a strange ruined terrain and freezing wastes of outer space."

247 Reilly, Robert. "The Artistry of Ray Bradbury," *Extrapolation*, 13 (December 1971), 64–74.

Examines Bradbury's themes and styles as illustrated by *The Martian Chronicles, Fahrenheit 451,* and *Something Wicked This Way Comes.* Concludes that "while Bradbury is important, he is also pure delight."

248 Robinson, Guy S. "Science in S.F.: Hypertravel," *Listener*, 17 December 1964, pp. 976–977. (See I, 78.)

249 Rogers, Alva. *A Requiem for Astounding*. Chicago: Advent, 1965.

Includes comments by Harry Bates, Orlin Tremaine, and John W. Campbell. A nostalgic history of what was the foremost sf magazine during the 1930's and, at least, through World War II. Covers that period 1930 to 1960, when it took the new title *Analog*. Excessively detailed reminiscence, yet the book contains information that might have been lost if not preserved in such a memorial volume.

250 Rogers, Ivor. "The Time Plays of J. B. Priestley," *Extrapolation*, 10 (December 1968), 9–16.

Suggests that Priestley, one of the few writers not to live outside the scientific tradition, has also been one of the few to explore "the realm of scientific ideas as opposed to technology," particularly the concepts of time. Main influences upon him have been E. A. Abbott (author of *Flatland*), J. W. Donne, and P. D. Ouspensky. Proceeds to an analysis of the concept of time in various of Priestley's plays, both thematically and structurally.

251 Rottensteiner, Franz. "Kurd Lasswitz: A German Pioneer of Science Fiction," *Riverside Quarterly*, 4 (August 1969), 4–18.

Surveys works of Lasswitz, best known for *Auf zwei planeten* (1897). Gives most attention to his short stories. He accepted technology as a matter of course; his utopias stressed the happiness of society gained through the development of individual rather than mass (class) consciousness. Such external influences as the World Wars have limited his reputation and influence. (Reprinted in Clareson, *SF: The Other Side of Realism*, II, 71.)

252 Russ, Joanna. "Dream Literature and Science Fiction," *Extrapolation*, 11 (December 1969), 6–14.

Cites such works as Lindsay's *Voyage to Arcturus* to typify "dream literature," the "thin and schematic" projections of daydreaming. The resultant literature is stylistically and structurally bad, with "unvisualized scenes, unreal characterization, melodrama." It is "the ineffable and inexpressible that makes daydreaming so exciting; but art must express the inexpressible or cease to exist."

253 Sackett, Samuel J. "A Motif Index for Science Fiction," *Extrapolation*, 1 (May 1960), 38.

Citing the indices by Antti Aarne and Stith Thompson in folklore, he suggests that a motif or type index would be invaluable to the study of sf, partly as a way of avoiding the difficulties of abstract definition of the genre.

254 Sapiro, Leland. "The Faustus Tradition in the Early Science Fiction Story," *Riverside Quarterly*, 1 (August 1964), 3–18; 1 (November 1964), 44–57; 1 (February 1965), 118–125.

Examines fiction in Gernsback's magazines to show the persistence of the myth of the scientist destroyed because he had sought/attained knowledge belonging to God. Some rejection of a mechanistic philosophy also discernible in the stories.

255 ———. "The Mystic Renaissance: A Survey of F. Orlin Tremaine's *Astounding Stories*," *Riverside Quarterly*, 2 (June 1966), 75–88; 2 (November 1966), 156–170; 2 (March 1967), 270–283.

Examines numerous stories to show that an element of mysticism entered in *Astounding's* fiction, particularly through those stories dealing with "thought-variants." They often exhibit the "diffuse banality so characteristic of occult writings." Ties this topic to the sin of intellect developed in the Faustian article. (See II, 254.)

256 Scarborough, Dorothy. "Supernatural Science," in *The Supernatural in English Fiction*. New York and London: G.P. Putnam's Sons, 1917, pp. 251–281.

Although concentrating upon Wells, she does give some attention to his contemporaries. What is most important, she accepts the "scientific romance" as a lineal descendant of the Gothic and thus part of the established literary tradition.

257 Schmerl, Rudolf B., "The Two Future Worlds of Aldous Huxley," *PMLA*, 77 (June 1962), 328–334.

Analysis of *Brave New World* and *Ape and Essence*. BNW shows to advantage because Huxley did "not gain as a propagandist what he lost as a novelist." BNW satirized "the limited visions" of such as Thomas Huxley and strove to rise from "the criteria of morality to the criteria of sanity." Names BNW and *1984* as the "two most widely discussed English fantasies of this century." Suggests fantasy "may be defined as the deliberate presentation of improbabilities through any one of four methods—the use of unverifiable time, place, characters, or devices."

258 ————. "Fantasy as Technique," *Virginia Quarterly Review*, 43 (Autumn 1967), 644–656.

Departing from such sources as Forster and Gerber, he explores the nature of fantasy. It denies "the totality of our knowledge of what our culture regards as real." Yet the fantasists of the past have deliberately tried to lend plausibility to their materials. The "sacrifice of pretenses of actuality distinguishes modern fantasy." It is "the intentional and purposeful contradiction of our experience, the deliberate presentation of improbabilities," and thus it becomes a deliberate literary technique to gain the author's ends. Emphasizes that it merges with satire and allegory. (Reprinted in Clareson, SF: *The Other Side of Realism*, II, 71.)

259 ———. "Who's Afraid of Fantasy?" *Arts in Society*,
6 (Summer–Fall 1969), 177–181.

Paper at the first "Secondary Universe" Conference, University
of Wisconsin-Milwaukee, 1968. Questions the future that science
is providing, and suggests that fantasy, "by presenting a future
in the past tense, can illuminate present processes in ways simply
not available to the writer of realistic fiction." Suggests, too,
that fantasy is "a peculiarly appropriate literary method with which
to attack totalitarianism."

260 Scholes, Robert. "Speaking of Books: For Non-Realistic
Fiction," *New York Times Book Review*, 22 October
1967, p. 2.

"A novelist of the realistic persuasion will resist bitterly my view
that life can and should be presented in fiction through non-
realistic means." Attacks the assumptions of literary realism, based
as they are on "a social psychological typology." Instead, "fiction
must abandon the worn-out type of realism and focus on the
world in different ways." Cites such writers as Barth, Barthelme,
Vonnegut, who have been "victims of vicious and hysterical
criticism." Asks that writers "find fictional forms for a new vision."
Does not explicitly name sf.

261 ———. "Fabulation and Satire," in *The Fabulators*.
New York: Oxford University Press, 1967, pp. 35–55.

Discusses Vonnegut in the context of "Black Humor," in which
both topics receive one of their ablest handlings. "The sensibility
and compassion which characterized the great novels of the
nineteenth century are being modified by the wit and cruelty of
Black Humor." Its writers have "faith in art" but reject "all
ethical absolutes." Focuses upon *Cat's Cradle* and *Mother Night*.
Like his contemporaries, Vonnegut cannot indulge in the
"rhetoric of moral certainty" traditional to satire. Regards Black
Humor as a sign of health and life, not sickness.

262 Schwartz, Sheila. "The World of Science Fiction,"
NYS English Record, 21 (February 1971), 27–40.

"Science fiction reflects the contemporary world with greater
authenticity than other contemporary literature." Gives a detailed
sketch of the history of the genre as well as an enumeration of
its themes, exploring four in detail: (1) "Man on Other Planets,"
(2) "Other Planets on Earth," (3) "Man's Destruction of
Earth," and (4) "Utopia and Anti-Utopia." The article has special
value as an introduction to the field on two counts: (1) the
wealth of references to specific novels, and (2) the references to
sf films, including a final listing of some 50 film titles; to critical
works; and to three recordings. Discusses the genre in the frame
of its use in the classroom.

263 "Science in Science Fiction," *Advancement of Science*,
26 (August 1965), 195–207. (See I, 83.)

264 Searles, A. Langley, ed. *Edison's Conquest of Mars*,
by Garrett P. Serviss. Los Angeles: Carcosa House, 1947.

Thought to be an imaginary title by Serviss until Searles found it
in the sole remaining file (at the LC) of the *New York Evening
Journal*. This is its first publication in book form. Serialized in
1898, it was undoubtedly Serviss's sequel to Wells's *War of the
Worlds*, just serialized in *Cosmopolitan*. Another celebration
of the scientist as a hero of epic proportion, the novel was, Serviss
declared, "the evolution of earth against the evolution of Mars"
(p. 35). Serviss, a newspaperman, once wrote a column on
astronomy and later served as editor of Collier's sixteen-volume
Popular Science Library.

265 Shackleton, C. C. "Give Me Excess of It, That Something
Snaps," *SF Horizons*, 1 (Winter 1964), 58–62.

Delightful criticism-parody of the hero-versus-menacing-alien-
hordes type story. In the 1920's the hordes were "crazy scientists,
bent on establishing a technocracy"; in the 1930's, "giant

anthropoidants"; in the 1940's, "soldiers from a vast galactic empire"; in the 1950's, "pulse-stopping entities that could change shape"; and now, "mindless U.N. members."

266 ———. "How Are They All on Deneb IV?" *SF Horizons*, 2 (Winter 1965), 61–63.

Delightful humor and irony on the changing story lines in sf treatment of flights to alien planets from the "space opera" to the "New Wave."

267 Shanks, Edward. "Other Worlds Than Ours," *New Statesman*, 14 October 1930, pp. 305–306.

Salutes *Amazing Stories*, for a magazine "which prints nothing else" but sf provides a "phenomenon which is deserving of study." Objects somewhat to the typical story-line and finds earth "surrounded by enemies." Without referring to titles, he summarizes some of the plots and predictions. "But on the whole, the scientifictionists [*sic*] take a rather gloomy view of posterity."

268 Sheppard, R. Z. "Future Grok," *Time*, 29 March 1971, pp. 86, 88–89.

Sympathetic appraisal of the current sf scene: concentrates upon Herbert's *Dune* and Heinlein's *Stranger in a Strange Land*, and gives special emphasis to Samuel R. Delany among the younger writers. Also notes the increasing academic attention to sf, suggesting as many as 70 colleges offer courses in the genre.

269 Silverberg, Robert, ed. *The Mirror of Infinity*: *A Critic's Anthology*. New York and London: Harper & Row, 1970.

A provocative collection of eleven stories, each introduced by a different critic; American and British, academic and "professional" points of view are represented. Silverberg's own introduction names many of the issues fundamental in the development of modern sf. (A paperback edition was issued by Canfield Press, 1970.)

270 Simak, Clifford. "Face of Science Fiction," *Minnesota Libraries*, 17 (September 1953), 197–201.

Surveys the nature and potential of sf. Since the sf writer does not have the "ready-made, tailored-to-order background" of the realistic novel to rely on, he must spend time and effort to banish the skepticism of his readers regarding "alien concepts" and "unfamiliar background." This necessity may be the principal reason that sf has not achieved the degree of literary quality that some may demand before regarding it as "literature."

271 Sisario, Peter. "A Study of the Allusions in Bradbury's *Fahrenheit 451*," *English Journal*, 59 (February 1970), 201–205.

Close reading of literary and biblical allusions reveals a deeper theme than a simple dystopian warning. Literary allusions to such writers as Swift, Boswell, and Arnold emphasize the emptiness of the world portrayed; biblical allusions reveal the concept of the natural cycle and express faith in the future. The central metaphor of the novel remains that of the Phoenix.

272 Skeels, Dell R. "Science Fiction as Myth," *The Trend in Engineering at the University of Washington*, 29 (October 1971), 10–15, 31.

Calls sf the "myth of science, of technology, and of the future," saying that it is essentially a mythology of hope. It follows the age-old forms of myth and folklore; stresses two basic patterns: the "centripetal" (the intrusion of a force from the unknown into the known society) or the "centrifugal" (the going forth and, sometimes, return of the hero). Both can be either negative or positive in tone and theme.

273 Slate, Tom. "Edgar Rice Burroughs and the Heroic Epic," *Riverside Quarterly*, 3 (March 1968), 118–123.

Draws a parallel in subject matter and method between ERB's Tarzan and John Carter stories and the traditional epics like

Beowulf and the *Iliad*. Suggests the similarity is precisely why his critics do not like him: the hero is out of fashion. "The heroic spirit, like every other form of spiritual exaltation, makes social control difficult . . . especially in a commercial and industrial society such as our own."

274 Slater, Joseph. "The Fictional Values of *1984*," in *Essays in Literary History*, ed. Rudolph Kirk and C. F. Main. New York: Russell & Russell, 1965, pp. 249–264.

Acknowledges original impact of Orwell's "ugly vision," and examines "certain fictional matters which were at first obscured by fact." Emphasizes its "structural tightness" and praises the "sharply drawn and memorable" minor characters.

275 Smith, Curtis C., "Olaf Stapledon: Saint and Revolutionary," *Extrapolation*, 13 (December 1971), 5–15.

Focusing primarily on *Last and First Men*, Curtis emphasizes Stapledon's role as a mythmaker who would have mankind achieve a "new communal consciousness." His myth would help modern man face the "problems of alienation and powerlessness" facing the individual in the 20th century.

276 Solomon, Eric. "Prophetic War Novels," *Notes & Queries*, 204 (January 1959), 36–37.

Brief commentary on "future war" motif, concentrating upon Louis Tracy's *Final War*. Calls "these visionary books . . . sensational hackwork, similar to modern science fiction." Ascribes *The Battle of Dorking* to a "Mrs. Brown." (See Bergonzi, II, 30.)

277 Solon, Ben. "Lovecraft on the Doorstep," *Haunted: Studies in Gothic Fiction*, 1 (June 1968), 87–88.

Asserts "The Thing on the Doorstep" is one of HPL's finest stories, including characterization, because in it "Lovecraft as he really was [came] face to face with Lovecraft as he wished to be."

278 Spacks, Patricia Meyer. "The Myth-Maker's Dilemma:
Three Novels by C. S. Lewis," *Discourse*, 2 (October
1959), 234–243.

First traces the Christian meaning and then the use of both
Christian and Classical myths in the Ransom trilogy. Finally
suggests the sf framework trivializes the Christian meaning for
the non-Christian reader. [Christopher]

279 Speer, Diane Parkin. "Heinlein's *The Door into Summer*
and *Roderick Random*," *Extrapolation*, 12 (December
1970), 30–34.

Points out "striking similarities" between the novels in terms of
plot and character development.

280 Spinrad, Norman. "*Stand on Zanzibar*: The Novel as
Film," in *SF: The Other Side of Realism*, ed. Thomas D.
Clareson. Bowling Green, Ohio: Bowling Green University
Popular Press, 1971, pp. 181–185.

Argues that Brunner's novel "is not a novel; it is a film in book
form," citing the table of contents and then discussing it in terms
of "Brunner's own technique"; i.e., in terms of some of the
types of segments he includes in *Stand on Zanzibar*.

281 Staggers, Anthony. "Now Read On," *New Statesman*,
21 July 1956, pp. 64–66.

Essentially unfavorable, although he acknowledges a "certain
bizarre popularity . . . displacing the detective story." He finds
three types of stories: (1) interplanetary corps, (2) totalitarian
states, and (3) Noble Savage. Sf sociology and anthropology
are "disappointing." "Morals and religion are uniformly Accepted
20th Century Conventional (probably because the U.S. Postal
office is notoriously old-maidish about what goes through the
mails)." Finds sf as "exciting as a colony of penguins."

282 Stevenson, Lionel. "The Artistic Problem: Science Fiction as Romance," *Extrapolation*, 4 (May 1963), 17–22.

Based upon 1962 MLA Seminar. The "real prominence" of sf began "as a genre about seventy years ago," coinciding with the increased general interest in the physical sciences. Emphasizes, too, that the whole concept of literary realism "was profoundly contrary to the principle that the arts are not concerned with fact and logic but with imagination and feeling." Thus, sf became the mode of the new romantic novelists, and H. G. Wells proved the one to seize upon the "naive tale of adventure for boys," transforming it "into something new and astonishingly subtle." Then suggests the complex criteria by the achievement of which sf can gain "a permanent niche in literature." (Reprinted in Clareson, *SF: The Other Side of Realism*, II, 71.)

283 ————. "Purveyors of Myth and Magic," in *Yesterday and After: The History of the English Novel*. New York: Barnes & Noble, 1967, pp. 111–154.

This volume marks the first time that such writers as Machen, Blackwood, M. R. James, Shiel, and Eddison, for example, have received a full and unbiased treatment in a standard history of the novel. While this chapter has special significance, there is also an excellent chapter on Wells, and treatments of Huxley, Orwell, Golding, T. H. White, Richard Hughes, and Iris Murdoch are included. "By the middle of the twentieth century the two elements of fantasy and science fiction had become . . . thoroughly reconciled. The present chapter has been intended to demonstrate the vitality with which symbolism and the supernatural survived during the decades when realism was nominally in the ascendency."

284 Suvin, Darko. "The SF Novel in 1969," in *Nebula Award Stories 5*, ed. James Blish. New York: Doubleday, 1970, pp. 193–205.

Analysis of novels nominated by members of SFWA for the 1969 award. Gives particular attention to Norman Spinrad's *Bug Jack*

Barron, John Brunner's *Jagged Orbit*, Thomas Disch's *Camp Concentration*, and Ursula LeGuin's *Left Hand of Darkness*. Defines sf as the "literature of cognitive estrangement," employing the concept of estrangement as developed by Victor Shklovsky and "underpinned" by Bertolt Brecht and emphasizing the "scientific rigor" (cognition) with which sf elaborates its material in a "supposedly factual" manner. That is, it is the genre "whose necessary and sufficient conditions are the presence and interaction of estrangement and cognition, and whose main formal device is an imaginative framework alternative to the author's empirical environment." Praises the emergence of a "New Left" in sf, which has to do "with sensibility and world view much more than personal politics."

285 ———. "Significant Themes in Soviet Criticism of Science Fiction to 1965, with a Selected Bibliography," *Extrapolation*, 11 (May 1970), 44–52.

Surveys some of the most important articles which develop the major themes in Soviet criticism of both Soviet and American sf.

286 ———., ed. *Other Worlds, Other Seas: Science-Fiction Stories from Socialist Countries*. New York: Random House, 1970.

The most notable anthology dealing with Eastern European sf, particularly because of Suvin's introduction, in which he sketches the development of modern sf in those nations.

287 Takeo, Okuno. "Japanese SF," *SF Horizons*, 2 (Winter 1965), 51–52.

Notes sf not popular in Japan until recently; however, it "began as mainstream literature." The "first lengthy" work was Abe Kimifusa's *Fourth Interglacial Period*. Mentions also Komatsu Seicho, Hoshi Shinichi, and Mishima Yukio. (The title is available in the U.S. as *Inter Ice Age 4*, by Kobo Abé.)

288 Tenn, William. "The Fiction in Science Fiction," *Science Fiction Adventures*, 2 (March 1954), 66–78.

Perhaps Tenn's major essay. Praises certain stories which "like all good fiction, are essentially stories of human relationships, individually and communally." Wisely emphasizes that all literature is the popular art of its own period. Emphasizes, too, that the author is true to the scientific theories of his own day, whatever may eventually happen to those theories. The special job of sf is "to take the utterly fantastic . . . and make it seem as real as today's tabloid newspaper." Stresses that in all fiction the writer "wanders as far afield as he can, *without jeopardizing the sense of reality.*" Finds sf's roots "locked intricately around the great social issues of our own time."

289 Thale, Jerome. "Orwell's *Modest Proposal,*" *Critical Quarterly*, 4 (Winter 1962), 365–368.

1984 shows "a way of life that obliterates man." Orwell and Kafka "stand out for the sheer terror of the nightmares they created." Orwell saw that the private nightmare is an indulgence and impossibility; so in *1984* the ethical and political come together: an "allegory of the present state of things."

290 Ulanov, Barry. "Science Fiction and Fantasy," in *The Two Worlds of American Art*: *The Private and the Popular.* New York: Macmillan, 1965, pp. 298–308.

Fantasy and sf "cannot be separated from each other on the basis of positive and negative attitudes toward the future or the present." Since the "devotee" of sf is likely to be of "a categorical mind, feeding on a kind of fiction in which category is all," there are two results: (1) a "remarkably toneless" language and (2) inadequate portrayal of "the interior life of the characters." At present no writer equals "the dimension of Hawthorne or James," although he does praise Bradbury, Sheckley, Pohl, and Matheson. Fantasy and sf "do not often produce novels of quality"; suggests the genre's chief function is that of story-telling.

291 Vonnegut, Kurt, Jr. "Science Fiction," in *Page 2*: *The Best of 'Speaking of Books' from the New York Times Book Review*, ed. Francis Brown. New York: Holt, Rinehart, and Winston, 1970, pp. 117–120.

Denounces sf as a "file-drawer" from which he "would like out, particularly since so many serious critics regularly mistake the drawer for a tall white fixture in a comfort station." Flays widely at those responsible for the verdict, and, incidentally, says his career began with *Player Piano*.

292 Weinkauf, Mary S. "Edenic Motifs in Utopian Fiction," *Extrapolation*, 11 (December 1969), 15–22.

Utopian fiction moves toward the mythic level in that it makes specific, wide usage of many traditional motifs and symbols that recall the Edenic scene.

293 West, Anthony. "The Dark World of H. G. Wells," *Harpers*, 214 (May 1957), 68–73.

One of the earliest and most brilliant reassessments of Wells, coming to grips with the intellectual dilemmas facing Wells throughout his life. He "dealt with the ideological basis of pessimism" in his early works. These were the twin ideas to which a mechanistic view of the universe is hostile: (1) "The conception of evolutionary progress depends upon a picture of the universe in which mind is increasingly valuable"; and (2) as a result there is, increasingly, orderliness. His early works "describe the collapse of human dreams in the face of the realities of human nature." Once he attained some success and movement in society, he took to the idea that "the minority of men of good will everywhere, in all lands," might be able to "take hold of the meaningless proliferation of industrialism and give it a coherent direction." This led to the assumption "that human nature is plastic" and can be directed by an act of will. The conflicts among these ideas lay behind any apparent optimism and caused much of his despair, apparent in his works of all periods.

294 ———. "Men and Ideas (XII): H. G. Wells," *Encounter*, 41 (February 1967), 52–59.

Revised, including a new opening based on a biographical incident, this remains essentially a re-write of the earlier article. Both should be read, however, for examples and phrasing. (See II, 293.)

295 West, Robert H. "Science Fiction and Its Ideas," *Georgia Review*, 15 (Fall 1961), 276–280. (See I, 92.)

296 Wilkins, A. N. "Robert Paltock and the Bishop of Chester," *Notes & Queries*, n.s. 5 (October 1958), 438–440.

Suggests Paltock knew Bishop John Wilkin's *Mathematical Magick* (1648) when he wrote *The Life and Adventures of Peter Wilkins, A Cornish Man* (1751), in that the Bishop argues that man may fly, and Paltock describes a race of men (Glumms) who can fly.

297 Williams, Pat. "Ulysses in Space," *Books and Bookmen*, 12 (July 1967), 17–18.

The appeal of sf lies in that it expands the seeming limitations of the world. Answers three chief criticisms of the genre: (1) the lack of characterization; (2) the "impoverished" writing and imagination; and (3) the pointlessness of "going outside one's ordinary society to write about us humans." Suggests that "western learning has caged us inside a society which confuses culture with the people who live in it." To answer the first two, he develops a labored analogy with the *Odyssey*—perhaps because of his audience—to show the mythic level of both Homer and sf.

298 Williams, W. T. "Science in S. F.: Alien Biology," *Listener*, 24 December 1964, pp. 1003–1004. (See I, 93.)

299 Williamson, Jack. "H. G. Wells, Critic of Progress,"
Riverside Quarterly, 3 (August 1967), 6–31; 3 (March
1968), 96–117; 3 (August 1968), 187–208; 3 (March
1969), 272–293; 4 (August 1969), 24–33.

Wells's criticism of progress underlies the unity of his art as well
as the conflicts within his mind. He defines progress as successful
adaptive change to meet the conditions of survival; he explores
the limits set upon the human future both by the nature of the
cosmos and the nature of man. Eventually he foresees as the
essential change the replacement of the traditional by "a new
scientific class of technicians and engineers." At this point he
becomes the prophet whom later critics have condemned. The early
romances remain of paramount importance to his art and
thought. (This will be published by Mirage Press.)

300 Wilson, Colin. "The Vision of Science," in *The Strength
to Dream: Literature and the Imagination.* London:
Gollancz, 1962, pp. 94–117.

Relates sf to the mainstream of literary tradition, seeing it as the
expression of "the scientific imagination." It expresses a faith
in truth and knowledge, a "feeling that there is a fundamental
rightness about nature," and a sense that "the main evil of the
world is human stupidity. . . ." Contrasts it with primitive myth,
which saw the world as an "alien and dangerous place." Most
individual attention is given to Taine and Lovecraft; some to
vanVogt, Blish, and Aldiss. Sets sf in opposition to the *cul-de-sac*
of the "Beckett school" and, by implication, to realism.

301 Wilson, Robert H. "Some Recurrent Symbols in Science
Fiction," *Extrapolation*, 2 (December 1960), 2–4.

Traces occurrence of the robot figure from medieval times.
Appeal of many of these stories is not their prediction of scientific
or social developments, "but images of what we already know
about the human condition."

302 Winandy, Andre. "The Twilight Zone: Imagination and Reality in Jules Verne's *Strange Voyages,*" *Yale French Studies,* 43 (1969), 97–110.

In Verne's stories the journey becomes symbolic of "adventure, discovery, escape, liberation of the imagination." The motif here called "the mark of the other"—exemplified by Arnie Saknussemm's runic signature—permits a "link between the past, present, and future" while moving the narrative into "the nowhereland of timelessness." Emphasizes that the scientific possibility of the journeys "can always be charted"; also Verne used a "graphic language" which created a sense of immediacy and rendered experience "beautiful, familiar though distant," thus helping him to hold his imagination at "the intersection of myth and reality."

303 Wollheim, Donald A. *The Universe Makers: Science Fiction Today.* New York: Harper & Row, 1971.

This is a highly personal memoir of "a life for science fiction," in a world that sf "conjectured in most of its aspects." Establishes Verne and Wells as the two traditions and breaks sf into four divisions: "Imaginary Voyages, Future Predictions, Remarkable Inventions, and Social Satire." Insists that the essential view held by sf is optimistic.

304 Yershov, Peter. *Science Fiction and Utopian Fantasy in Soviet Literature.* New York: Research Program on the U.S.S.R., Mimeographed Series No. 62, 1954.

A 66–page pamphlet. Definitely a political bias, as he sketches the history of sf and utopian fantasy in terms of examples, concentrating upon "First Russian Experiments" (to 1917); "the Soviet Regime" (1919–1929); and "Fantasy in the Service of Communism" (1929–1951). An additional chapter notices "Zigzags" in the criticism of the field. Concentrates upon those works "annoying to the Bolsheviks" and, of course, finds Zamyatin as a model, for Yershov sees the Russian people "being subjected to a totalitarian state in the way" Zamyatin predicted. A wealth of detail and titles for the first half of this century.

305 Zamyatin, Yevgeny. "H. G. Wells," in *A Soviet Heretic*: *Essays by Yevgeny Zamyatin*, ed. Mirra Ginsburg. Chicago and London: University of Chicago Press, 1971, pp. 259–290.

Considers the range of Wells's work, with attention to the "scientific romances," which he calls Wells's "urban fairy tales." Acknowledges the power of Wells, but concentrates upon his gadgets and predictions.

306 Zaniello, Thomas. "Outopia in Jorges Luis Borges's Fiction," *Extrapolation*, 9 (December 1967), 3–17.

Draws upon Lewis Mumford's description of an archetypal utopian city as well as ancient mythology to establish the context for Borges's studies of the "labyrinth." Asserts that "the special mirror of Borges's art . . . inverts our world." Completes article with "A Selected Bibliography: Articles (in English) About Borges."

III. SF: Book Reviews

1 Adams, J. Donald. "Speaking of Books," *New York Times Book Review*, 12 July 1953, p. 2.

Extended comment on Bretnor's book of essays. Notices that the genre is discussed as though Verne and Wells had never written.

2 Adams, Phoebe. "Potpourri," *Atlantic*, 192 (January 1964), 120.

Finds Pierre Boulle's *Planet of the Apes* "respectably descended" from Swift and Verne. He draws "ethical and political inferences" but remains "clever and never dramatic" because he has "refrained from following any line."

3 Adams, Robert M. "H. G. Wells Reconsidered," *Scientific American*, 217 (1967), 124–129.

Ostensibly a review of Richard H. Costa's *H. G. Wells*, this soon dismisses the book as incompetent and evaluates the permanence of the "scientific romances." [Mullen]

4 Allen, Dick. "Pop Epics," *Poetry*, 117 (November 1970), 115–117.

Holding Your Eight Hands: An Anthology of Science Fiction Verse, edited by Edward Lucie-Smith, contains "carefully crafted selections" which rouse the "same unexpected wonder" that occurs in stories by Borges or Isaac Singer.

5 Amis, Kingsley. "Adventures on a Distant Star,"
New York Times Book Review, 24 November 1963, p. 60.

David Lindsay's *Voyage to Arcturus* "is not science fiction, which
is a realistic genre. It is in intention, perhaps, a religious allegory,"
but fails of strong "underpinning" because it is not based on a
"great public myth" like Christianity. Finds in it an "abundance
of cheapjack novelties."

6 ———. "A Cosmic Despair," *New York Times Book
Review*, 22 October 1967, p. 6.

Ostensibly reviews Mark Hillegas's *Future as Nightmare*, but
becomes Amis's own reflections on Wells. The perfect societies are
"straightforwardly totalitarian," while the early romances
range from "vivid horror" to "cosmic despair." As a result of his
personal reactions "Mr. Hillegas's vigorous defense [of Wells]
leaves me cold," although he did not realize the indebtedness
of later writers to Wells. Nevertheless, their importance rests
finally in their "autonomy."

7 Andreyev, Kirill. "Ray Bradbury," *Soviet Literature Monthly*,
no. 5 (1968), pp. 176–180.

Calls Bradbury's *Dandelion Wine* the work of a "genuine
humanist" and praises him as one of the world's finest sf writers.

8 "Apes in Heaven," *Times Literary Supplement*, 6 February
1964, p. 101.

As a "quaint old-fashioned piece of pre-science fiction" Pierre
Boulle's *Monkey Planet* [British title] can be "readily appre-
ciated." In his satire he does not give any "impression of an unduly
agonized social conscience," but the novel is "an agreeable
diversion for an allegorist."

9 Bacon, Leonard. "The Imaginative Power of C. S. Lewis,
Saturday Review of Literature, 8 April 1944, p. 9.

An enthusiastic and allusive review of *Perelandra*. [Christopher]

10 Baker, Robert H. "Bored with the Good Earth," *Saturday Review*, 8 August 1952, pp. 18–20.

An informational review of three non-fiction titles: Hans Haber, *Man in Space*; Patrick Moore, *Guide to the Moon* (which represents "current thinking of many astronauts"); Kenneth Heuer, *The End of the World: A Scientific Inquiry*.

11 Balliett, Whitney. "Books," *New Yorker*, 2 April 1960, pp. 159–160.

Devoted almost entirely to a plot summary of Walter Miller's *Canticle for Leibowitz*, it concludes, "But irony, after all, is only a kind of high-toned mockery. It entertains, but it changes nothing."

12 "Beneath the Surface," *Times Literary Supplement*, 9 May 1958, p. 258.

Praises Brian Aldiss's *Non-Stop*: "The first two-thirds is excellent, a moving allegory of the human condition that deserves to be read as literature in its own right. The writing is good, the development fascinating." But the last part "reminds us we are reading" sf because the plot must be resolved and explanations "are piled on top of us."

13 Berkvist, Robert. "Science Fiction for Boys," *New York Times Book Review*, 9 June 1963, p. 38.

One of the occasional catalogues of titles approved for the juvenile audience, this time including Heinlein's *Podkayne of Mars*, Clarke's *Dolphin Island*, Norton's *Key Out of Time*, and Piper's *Junkyard Planet*.

14 Boucher, Anthony. "Criminals at Large," *New York Times Book Review*, 8 November 1964, p. 68.

Uses the column to celebrate Conan Doyle's Professor Challenger when *The Poison Belt* is re-issued. Had Doyle written a "few more stories," Challenger would be to sf what Sherlock Holmes is to the detective story. Had Doyle written no historical novels or Sherlock Holmes, he would still be known as "skilled purveyor of entertaining fiction" because of Challenger.

15 ———. "In Step with Science," *New York Times Book Review*, 27 February 1966, p. 18.

Applauds Bruce Franklin's *Future Perfect*, which studies the "aspirations and attitudes toward science of 19th century America through its science fiction." It gives an "admirably clear perspective on speculative fiction and its cultural and social functions."

16 Brophy, Brigid. "Rare Books," *New Statesman*, 14 June 1963, pp. 904–905.

Primarily a plot recapitulation of three re-issues: Visiak's *Medusa*, Shiel's *Purple Cloud*, and Lindsay's *Voyage to Arcturus*. Dismisses *Medusa*, but finds Shiel has "more psychological interest" and a "period charm." *Voyage to Arcturus* has "a displeasing smell of repression, of morbid hygiene . . . a genuine curio, but aesthetically of the same order as an embryo pickled in a bottle."

17 Brutenhuis, Peter. "A Battle Between the Sexes Was the Answer," *New York Times Book Review*, 27 October 1963, p. 4.

Finds Anthony Burgess's *Wanting Seed* an ambitious "counter-Utopian novel," which is "comprehensively comic and gruesomely detailed." Yet his themes are not "translated into human terms," perhaps because the difficulty of creating an unfamiliar world leaves little energy for characterization. Since he does not seem committed, "we cannot, in the end, take his theme seriously."

18 Brynes, Asher. "Adventure on the Moon," *New Republic*, 23 October 1961, pp. 25–26.

Primarily a plot summary of Clarke's *Fall of Moondust*, which he judges to be sf of "the *applied* problem, closely resembling the type of technological or engineering fiction written about sunken submarines. . . ."

19 Burgess, Anthony. "H. G. Wells," *New York Times Book Review*, 3 August 1969, pp. 1, 18.

Lovat Dickson's *H. G. Wells: His Turbulent Life and Times* is praised because of its "exhibition of the demonic in Wells" and because it treats his affair with Rebecca West. Wells's art was "a half-made gift sprung from an overweening libido," but his sf remains "better than anything written since because it enshrines not only startling novelties but intense, and exactly observed, humanity."

20 Carey, Graham. "Real World of Science Fiction: [Reply]," *Commonweal*, 26 June 1953, p. 300.

Suggests Seymour Krim examine works of C. S. Lewis. (See III, 55.)

21 Clareson, Thomas D. "Two Contrasting Studies of Science Fiction: A Review," *English Literature in Transition*, 11 (1968), 226–229.

Sam Moskowitz's *Explorers of The Infinite* provides information necessary to the study of the genre, while I. F. Clarke's *Voices Prophesying War*, which analyzes the "future war" motif, provides a model for further studies.

22 ———. "Miriam Strauss Weiss, *A Lively Corpse: Religion in Utopia* and Lois and Stephen Rose, *The Shattered Ring: Science Fiction and the Quest for Meaning*," *Christian Scholar's Review*, 1 (Winter 1971), 177–179.

Miss Weiss, while detailed in her treatment of classic utopian titles, seems satisfied with description rather than analysis and gives no attention to the contemporary scene. The Roses set out on a personal quest that has little relation to the meaning of sf and is erroneous in much of its factual material.

23 ———. "*More Issues at Hand: Critical Studies in Contemporary Science Fiction,*" *Journal of Popular Culture,* 5 (Summer 1971), 247–249.

Praises James Blish's second collection of critical essays because Blish argues for high literary standards and sees sf as part of a continuing tradition. The essays cover various aspects of the field during the 1960's.

24 Coffey, Warren. "*Slaughterhouse-Five,*" *Commonweal,* 6 June 1969, pp. 347–348.

Vonnegut has been "a writer's writer, serious, technically accomplished, uninterested in accommodating himself to the book trade or the great thundering herd." He is "an inventive, skillful author working in a bad line, humor, at a bad time." Much recapitulation of plot.

25 Cosman, Max. "Post World War III," *Commonweal,* 5 May 1961, pp. 157–158.

Despite devices echoing Wells, Huxley, and Orwell, L. P. Hartley's *Facial Justice* "has a flair of its own" in its attack upon the new egalitarianism. It is "a work of intellectual fancy and play, yet serious enough to know the danger of 'mistaking the appearance for the reality.' It is worth reading."

26 Crispin, Edmund. "Makrokosmos," *New Statesman,* 18 June 1955, p. 854.

Mentions a number of current titles, insisting that the essence of sf must be a sense of the wondrous rather than "the sober-paced, dismally predictable accounts" of space-launchings or of "post-atomic totalitarianism." Judges Clarke's *Earthlight* to be "solid, *reliable*" because it "depends for its wondrousness on

serious scientific fact." Christopher's *Year of the Comet* "is of
fine quality even if lightweight," but he objects to its political
and economic backdrop, though calling them original.

27 Dennis, Nigel. "Lovers vs. Bombers," *New York Times
Book Review*, 20 August 1961, p. 4.

J. B. Priestley's *Saturn over the Water* "has one great virtue: one
can read it and even enjoy it without, as it were, paying the
slightest attention to it. And that is really all one asks of a
romantic adventure story." Objects that Priestley divides all
people into Lovers (Uranus) or Bombers (Saturn) in his desire
to warn of threats facing society.

28 DuBois, William. "Books of the Times," *New York Times*,
27 August 1953, p. 23.

Clarke's *Childhood's End* contains many of the devices of sf, but
he has "mixed them with a masterly hand." Recapitulates plot:
"*homo sapiens* fights back to the end with resourcefulness
and wit."

29 Edelstein, J. M. "The Future Without Humanity,"
New Republic, 9 October 1961, pp. 24–25.

Primarily a plot summary of Hugh Sykes Davies's *Papers of
Andrew Melmoth*, which he finds "terrifying." Commends
Davies's "extraordinary style and skill as a novelist" and finds his
"meaning" to be that "man no longer can make a choice." A
brief comparison to Alan Sillitoe's book of poetry, *The Rats*.

30 Erisman, Robert O. "Trolls and Witches of a Coexistent
Cosmos," *New York Times Book Review*, 27 August
1961, p. 27.

Poul Anderson's *Three Hearts and Three Lions* is an "imaginative
yarn told with skill and polish." Yet if sf is to have a wider
audience, it must make up its mind, for, as here, it contains "a
mixture of qualities that make it uncertain whether the story
is intended for intellectuals, adult readers of mysteries or
teenagers seeking fictional adventure."

31 "Fantastica," *Times Literary Supplement*, 5 July 1963, p. 497.

Extended praise for Lindsay's *Voyage to Arcturus*, whose "impact . . . is tonic and terrible . . . its aim sublimity." A "sympathetic reading" produces a "sense of the remarkable profundity and coherence of the vision." Finds in *The Purple Cloud* something "coarse and self-indulgent in Shiel's imagination," while *Medusa* depends upon a "disquieting atmosphere."

32 "Fiction," *Library Journal*, 1 February 1961, p. 596.

Konstantin Tsiolkovsky's *Beyond the Planet Earth*, concerned with a manned flight to outer space and the moon, is "a fascinating work, much in the tradition of Jules Verne and H. G. Wells." Contains a commentary about Soviet Rocket achievement in the 20th century.

33 "Fiction," *Library Journal*, 15 March 1961, p. 1160.

Leo Szilard chose "satire to express his views of politics and science" in *The Voice of the Dolphin*, which contains "clever stories, but with limited appeal. Only for large libraries."

34 "Fiction," *Library Journal*, 1 January 1964, pp. 134–135.

David Lindsay's *Voyage to Arcturus*, now first published in the U. S., "is full of symbolism and hidden meanings which make the reading difficult. Recommended for thoughtful readers and larger collections."

35 "Fiction," *Library Journal*, 1 May 1966, p. 2357.

Says of J. G. Ballard's *Crystal World*, "This strange and remarkable creation is not for the mystery shelves but is for the sf buff and metaphysicist." Of sf: occasionally it "concentrates upon the metaphysical and psychological rather than technological aspects of outer space."

36 Fraser, G. S. "New Novels," *New Statesman*, 28 September
    1957, p. 390.

> Superficial commentary on Fred Hoyle's *Black Cloud* and John
> Wyndham's *Midwich Cuckoos*, concentrating upon Hoyle's "really
> thrilling book." Both "divert and excite" and are "rattling
> good stories," but the characters are two-dimensional because
> neither novel is introspective.

37 Fremont-Smith, Eliot. "Books of the Times," *New York
    Times*, 13 January 1967, p. 212.

> Criticizes I. F. Clarke's *Voices Prophesying War* because it does
> not relate the literature of disaster to the literature of Utopia and
> "doesn't even touch the implications of happy-ending" sf.
> Nevertheless, "stimulating and amusing," the book should spur
> further interest in this "curious, prevading, perhaps prophetic"
> literature."

38 Gorer, Geoffrey. "There Is a Happy Land," *Encounter*,
    1 (July 1962), 83–86.

> Huxley's *Island* is "only technically a novel; it is a Utopia."
> Analyzes it "as a social anthropologist" might analyze the report
> of a traveller.

39 Green, Martin. "Russian Science Fiction," *Commonweal*,
    26 March 1965, pp. 27–28.

> Anthology of Russian sf edited by Robert Magidorf reveals a
> Soviet view of the future both optimistic and narrow, with sf as
> simple pedagogy to instill the right kind of interest in science and
> technology. Fantasy predominates over sf, and there is much
> "heavy-footed, old fashioned bric-a-brac." Selection may not be
> fully representative of Soviet sf.

40 Hatch, Robert. "Lucky Jim and the Martians," *Nation*,
    19 March 1960, pp. 257–258.

> Amis's *New Maps of Hell* provides an "enticing introduction
> to a literature officially considered sub-literature and unavailable

to cultivated minds." Stresses the role of sf as a medium for social criticism. Feels Amis is an advocate rather than critic of the genre.

41 Hayakawa, S. I. "From Science-fiction to Fiction-science," *Etc*, 8 (1951), 280–293.

Brief sketch of sf as background to review of L. Ron Hubbard's *Dianetics*, put forth as a new revelation of truth rather than as fiction. Has no regard for theory: "There is no wheat." [Plank]

42 Hillegas, Mark. "Other Worlds to Conjure," *Saturday Review*, 26 March 1966, pp. 33–34.

Praises Franklin's *Future Perfect* as part of the increasingly serious critical appraisal of sf; regrets no scholar like Franklin is now writing about the contemporary scene.

43 ———. "Satiric Fantasy," *Nation*, 22 January 1968, pp. 120–121.

Speaks highly of story collection *The Dragon* by Zamyatin, the "master at alloying fantasy with realism." Katayev's *Holy Well* most interesting for its dream sequence of a visit to America.

44 Holmes, H. H. "Science and Fantasy," *New York Herald Tribune Book Review*, 20 September 1959, p. 15.

Regularly-featured column. Concentrates upon Aldiss's American debut in novel *Starship* and story collection *No Time Like Tomorrow*. "More than anyone else young Aldiss resembles the young Ray Bradbury of a dozen years ago—a cock-eyed poet and prophet in love with humanity and with words, who happens to cast his poetic vaticinations in the nominal form of science fiction. As with Bradbury, the closer his attempts come to strict s.f. the less successful they are; but his more absolute imaginings can be wonderful stimulants."

45 ―――. "Science and Fantasy," *New York Herald Tribune Book Review*, 4 December 1960, p. 60.

Praises Judith Merril's "enlightened and enlightening remarks" on the state of sf in her *5th Annual*. Finds Greye La Spina's *Invaders from the Dark* satisfactory, but Poul Anderson's *High Crusade* is "a wholly captivating light novel, as outrageous and as delightful as *The Mouse That Roared*."

46 Hopkins, D. F. "Impacts of Literary Science," *Chemistry and Industry*, 16 March 1963, pp. 440–442.

Reviews P. A. Barker's *Atoms and the Cell*, and praises Ballard's *Drowned World*, which "succeeds by credibility," not by debasing science or introducing a "pseudo-masquerade of scientific ideas." Calls the period of Verne and Wells an "isolated event" and asserts that ties between it and modern sf are rarely "discernible."

47 "I Sing the Body Electric," *New York Times Book Review*, 28 December 1969, p. 16.

Two-pargraph notice of "these fictional odds and ends by Ray Bradbury." He does maintain an "enthusiasm" for both the natural and supernatural which "sends a tingle of excitement through even the flimsiest conceit."

48 "In the Realm of the Spacemen," *New York Times Book Review*, 13 August 1950, p. 19.

Basil Davenport finds de Camp's *Castle of Iron* to be "pure extravaganza and pure delight." Villiers Gerson thinks "fairy tale" most correctly describes Beyer's *Minions of the Moon*. And Edward Dahlberg finds personal mysticism in Blackwood's *Tales of the Uncanny and Supernatural* and gives plot summaries.

49 "In the Realm of the Spacemen," *New York Times Book Review*, 24 September 1950, p. 33.

Villiers Gerson merely names some of the stories in Bleiler and Dikty's *Best Science Fiction*, 1950 while Fletcher Pratt believes

Bond's *Lancelot Briggs, Spaceman* shows how close sf and fantasy are. Pratt also believes that Theodore Sturgeon spoils *The Dreaming Jewels* with a "welter of corn, telepathy, violence, and the hackneyed properties of sentimental fiction."

50 "Interplanetary Frolics," *Times Literary Supplement*, 4 October 1957, p. 598.

Praises Hoyle's *Black Cloud* for its "lively logic" and command of "scientific reference." Commends *Fallen Star*, in which Blish reveals his "terse, graphic and often wryly humorous way of telling a story," but Wyndham's *Midwich Cuckoos* "lacks the force of his previous ventures."

51 Josselson, Diana. "Shorter Reviews," *Kenyon Review*, 25 (Summer 1963), 559–560.

Primarily sketches the plot of Burgess's *Clockwork Orange*, briefly comparing it to Golding's *Inheritors* and suggesting it also be compared to sf. Finds last chapter disappointing; "in retrospect," the whole book is "false . . . put together with mild ingenuity but to no purpose."

52 Kennebeck, Edwin. "The Future Church," *Commonweal*, 4 March 1960, pp. 632–634.

Lengthy sketch of plot of Miller's *Canticle for Leibowitz*, called a novel about "the role of the Church as the preserver of wisdom and spiritual life in dark ages." Finds it an "admirable contrast" to the film, *On the Beach*, which "cheapens the serious problems with which it pretends to deal." Miller's problem is the "two-dimensional limitations" of his characters; he does not have "the penetration of a Graham Greene." Yet it is "imaginative, amusing, and diverting."

53 Kilpatrick, Clayton E. "Round-up of Westerns, Mysteries, Horror, and Science Fiction," *Library Journal*, 1 February 1958, pp. 356–360.

Calls these forms "off-shoots of fiction" but insists "some of the best writing" is being done in them. Lists and comments upon the plots of some current sf.

54 Klein, Marcus. "A Slouch Toward Bethlehem," *Nation*, 19 November 1960, pp. 398–402.

Ostensibly reviews Berriault's *The Descent*, Fitzgibbon's *When the Kissing Had to Stop*, Miller's *Canticle for Leibowitz*, Roshwald's *Level 7*, and Shute's *On the Beach*. Becomes an attack upon the apocalyptic novel in general, which maintains "so pure a rage of testifying," and has both "obvious sincerity" and an "astonishing sameness of novelistic inspiration." Each author presses home his own solution. *When the Kissing Had to Stop* is the best of these five, "and independent of them [is] a very good novel, the most thinking of them, the most engaged, the most severe and the least liberal."

55 Krim, Seymour. "The Real World of Science Fiction," *Commonweal*, 12 January 1953, pp. 252–254.

Reviews Bretnor's *Modern Science Fiction*, but has its significance in pointing out that the "mainstream" of literary tradition draws from literature, philosophy, and art, having little or "nothing to do with science." Thus, "our finest writers can enlarge the significance of their imaginative journeys by adapting some of the symbols already crudely posed by science-fiction writers."

56 Lardner, Rex. "Fiction in Brief: *The Martian Chronicles*," *New York Times Book Review*, 7 May 1950, p. 21.

A one-paragraph commentary which finds Bradbury's novel "suspenseful and, at times, funny." Reports that the earliest "reception" by the Martians "is unfriendly," but they soon die of chickenpox.

57 Leiber, Fritz. "Way-Out Science," *National Review*,
9 April 1963, pp. 289–291.

Praises both Clarke's *Profiles of the Future* and Sir Bernard
Lovell's *Exploration of Outer Space* for coming to grips with the
immensity of the universe. Clarke provides a "splendid
introduction" to materials used during the past half century by
sf writers.

58 ———. "Utopia for Poets and Witches," *Riverside
Quarterly*, 4 (August 1970), 194–205.

Thinks highly of Robert Graves's *Seven Days in New Crete*.
Names conventions by which fantasists can explore the past
—simple time travel, alternate worlds, parallel worlds—
and emphasizes that the "past explored may be that of reality
or of myth or of folklore" so that the potentiality is greater
than the devices themselves suggest.

59 "Let Imagination Soar," *Newsweek*, 30 May 1955, p. 84.

Reviews Davenport's *Inquiry into Science Fiction*. "Summing
up: Spacemen have dignity."

60 Levin, Martin. "Incubator of a New Civilization," *New
York Times Book Review*, 27 March 1960, pp. 42–43.

Miller's *Canticle for Leibowitz* is at its best in its "early medieval"
part but "bogs down" in its Neo-Renaissance. Miller is guilty
of a "heavy-handed approach to allegory" and indulges in "far too
explicit moralizing"; yet the novel comes "close enough to the
mark" to make one nostalgic for *R.U.R.* and *Brave New World*.

61 ———. "Reader's Report," *New York Times Book Review*,
7 March 1965, p. 38.

Christopher Hodder Williams's *Main Experiment* combines the
"exotic kernel of science fiction with so much *Hound of
Baskervilles* atmosphere" to produce "as wild a mixture of spook
and science story as I've come across in many a day."

62 ———. "Do Human Beings Matter?" *New York Times Book Review*, 25 April 1965, p. 41.

Vonnegut's *God Bless You, Mr. Rosewater* requires the services of "a social historian rather than a book reviewer." If the novel as a literary form projects "a view of life by means of character, this is not a novel." His ethics are a "parfait."

63 ———. "Reader's Report," *New York Times Book Review*, 15 May 1966, p. 41.

In "science fantasy" the villain has become "old Mother Nature herself," as in Ballard's *Crystal World*, a "haunting shocker." Ballard is "one of the most elegant of the dark fantasists."

64 Ley, Willy. "Space Travel: Science Fiction and Science Fact," *Publishers' Weekly*, 24 October 1953, pp. 1742–1748.

Essentially an extended review of both sf (11 titles) and science non-fiction (7 titles) available for the juvenile audience. Basic point is that an sf story, "especially one for young readers, has to pass its science test first. It is not a question of whether the reader is taught a little or a lot, the point is that whatever he is taught must be correct." Reinforces this by suggesting that "Science Doesn't Mix Well With Whimsy" in criticizing two novels for their lack of accurate science.

65 "Little Hmān, What Hnau?" *Time*, 11 October 1943, pp. 100, 102, 104.

Basically summarizes plot of Lewis's *Out of the Silent Planet*, filling it with Malacandrian terms.

66 Maddocks, Melvin. "The Novel as Science-Non-Fiction," *Life*, 30 May 1969, p. 15.

Mixed reaction to *Andromeda Strain*. Suggests Crichton is to Verne as Truman Capote is to Conan Doyle. Recounts the plot and emphasizes lack of characterization; it can be interpreted as another "man vs blob," but some readers will see it as a warning because some of the "horror" of sf "doesn't rest in hopped-up dangers of the future but in what man must become to survive." Crichton is "too cool, too scientific" to moralize.

67 "Making Up a Mind," *Times Literary Supplement,* 21 July 1966, p. 629.

Welcomes British publication of Daniel Keyes's *Flowers for Algernon* because it is "that kind of science fiction which uses a persuasive hypothesis to explore emotional and moral issues." It "can stand on the shelf" alongside Wyndham's titles and Miller's *Canticle for Leibowitz,* "which use the mode of science fiction to ask real questions about human beings."

68 Mascall, E. L. *"Out of the Silent Planet," Theology,* 38 (April 1939), 303–304.

A perceptive brief review points out the reversal of Wellsian assumptions about aliens in Lewis's novel and praises in particular the translation of scientific humanism into one-and-two-syllable words. [Christopher]

69 "Mixed Fiction," *Time,* 22 February 1960, p. 110.

Miller's *Canticle for Leibowitz* "belongs to the growing literature of the A-cum-H jitters." Calls it "chillingly effective" in communicating a "post-human lunar landscape of disaster." Yet remains uncertain whether Miller believes that "better bomb shelters or more Roman Catholics are the answer."

70 Morgan, Edwin. "Unconcerned," *New Statesman,* 15 April 1966, p. 545.

Ballard's *Crystal World* excels in "atmosphere, action, visualization." In addition, as "a human adventure in a suddenly alien and frightening environment, the book is convincing and powerful," but its metaphorical level comes off less well.

71 Morgan, W. John. "New Novels," *New Statesman*,
5 November 1960, p. 708.

Brief praise of Hugh Sykes Davies' *Papers of Andrew Melmoth*.
"The story-telling is all the more effective for being rather
indirect. We seldom meet Andrew head on, but his tormented
personality comes through."

72 "Mystery—Detective—Suspense," *Library Journal*,
1 November 1964, p. 4390.

Lovecraft's *At the Mountains of Madness and Other Stories*
provides "a poetic and hypnotic combination of imaginative horror
and realistic science fiction."

73 Naipail, V. S. "New Novels," *New Statesman*,
21 May 1960, pp. 764–765.

L. P. Hartley's *Facial Justice* "can best be read as a pure fantasy;
it is as accomplished as we expect. Mr. Hartley's gift for the
macabre is well known; his novel abounds in chilling surprises."

74 "Never Too Old to Dream," *Time*, 30 May 1949, p. 87.

Ostensibly a review of Weinbaum's *Martian Odyssey*, it becomes
a sketch of the sf field at the time. Mentions small, specialist
publishers, fandom and fanzines. Verne and Wells, Leinster called
"Deans" of the field, while Heinlein and vanVogt are "best."
Weinbaum's "dream-beasts come startlingly close to what the
human race has been running across, for a good many years, in its
childish nightmares."

75 "New Novels," *Spectator*, 17 September 1954, p. 350.

Sturgeon's *More Than Human* recalls Bradbury; it falls between
the schools of sf and poetic fantasy.

76 Newman, James R. "An Examination of the History and Present State of Science Fiction," *Scientific American*, 203 (July 1960), 179–180.

Reviews Amis's *New Maps of Hell*. Suggests the "mainstream" and sf have common ground: "dissent, revulsion, indignation, even bewilderment over the less lovely aspects of society." Insists that sf "does not exist in isolation, however queer it may seem." Amis has convinced him it has value, and he hopes that it prospers.

77 "Nightmares and Realities," *Times Literary Supplement*, 13 August 1951, p. 545.

In *Day of the Triffids*, Wyndham proves "rather too fertile in imagination" because of his two premises: the widespread blindness and the carnivorous plants. "In addition the viewpoint is that of a Londoner." However, the "language is excellent," and the scene of disaster in London "has all the qualities of a vividly-realized nightmare."

78 "Novels of the Week: *Out of the Silent Planet*," *Times Literary Supplement*, 1 October 1938, p. 625.

Brief review compares Lewis to Wells, finding Wells the better in "dramatic sharpening, running characterization, other-worldly exposition and vivid incident." Does like opening and spaceflight section of Lewis's novel. [Christopher]

79 Poore, Charles. "Books of the Times," *New York Times*, 29 March 1962, p. 31.

Utopists "like to lecture their contemporaries. . . . No doubt sinful mankind is dreadfully in need of this sort of thing." Aldous Huxley is the Dean of those who cry "Havelock Ellis and let slip the dogs of Evelyn Waugh." Reviews *Island*, and feels turned loose in a "mass of notes and resource material for a novel not written yet."

80 "Potpourri," *Atlantic*, 192 (November 1953), 112.

Clarke's *Childhood's End* raises sf beyond the pulps to the "far-distant world of the novel of ideas." It is "highly stimulating . . . wildly fantastic but far from frivolous" because of the questions it asks.

81 Pratt, Fletcher. "What's The World Coming To?" *Saturday Review of Literature*, 2 April 1938, pp. 3–4.

Seemingly the first of his columns featured here. He uses Wells's *When the Sleeper Wakes* as his cornerstone to any picture of the "future adumbrated in imaginative literature." Summarizes plot motifs.

82 ————. "Science Fiction and Fantasy—1949," *Saturday Review of Literature*, 24 December 1949, pp. 7–9.

Commentary on year's titles. Praises Orwell's *1984*, but finds Stapledon's *Worlds of Wonder* "wordy and complicated." Suggests sf will replace detective story as the most popular form of escape fiction. Emphasizes that any theme may be dealt with.

83 ————. "Beyond Stars, Atoms, and Hell," *Saturday Review of Literature*, 17 June 1950, pp. 32–33.

Praises Anthony West's *Vintage*. Finds in Bradbury's *Martian Chronicles* the "implied statement that the destruction of the planet need not involve the downfall of the human spirit."

84 ————. "Sci Fi & Fantasy—1950," *Saturday Review*, 30 December 1950, pp. 16–17.

Praises Judith Merril's *Shadow on the Hearth* and Frank Norris's *Nutro 29*. Surprised that Norris "should have played the game so well without knowing the rules." Asserts that method of sf "consists in working out the implications of a single concept." This explains why short story and anthology are most frequent forms.

85 ———. "Time, Space, and Literature," *Saturday Review*, 25 July 1951, pp. 16–17.

Repeats idea of short story as form and single concept as method. Mentions Willy Ley's *Rockets, Missiles and Space Travel*: "If the fiction bores you, read the facts and marvel."

86 ———. "Fiction Flights in Space and Time," *Saturday Review*, 23 February 1952, pp. 20–21.

Survey of titles has been reduced to a chart called "Guide to Science Fantasy Fiction."

87 ———. "Of Time and Space," *Saturday Review*, 2 August 1952, p. 34.

Of Clarke's *Sands of Mars*: "This is what sci fi can do when a real writer who is a real scientist gets hold of it."

88 ———. "Of Time and Space," *Saturday Review*, 18 October 1952, p. 43.

Announces Bradford Day's *Index*: "indispensable."

89 ———. "Trail of the Paper Comet," *Saturday Review*, 7 March 1953, pp. 26–27.

Publishers are trying to appeal beyond the core of enthusiasts. It has been "a poor year for fantasy."

90 ———. "Of Time and Space," *Saturday Review*, 29 August 1953, p. 40.

Chart of titles only.

91 ———. "Of Time and Space," *Saturday Review*, 12 September 1953, p. 50.

Only three titles in the chart.

92 ———. "The Season's Science Fiction," *Saturday Review*,
7 August 1954, pp. 14–15.

In "a rather poor season" for sf and fantasy, he mentions novels
by Asimov, Nearing, Shafer, Sturgeon, and Tucker.

93 ———. "Science Fiction's Second Wind," *Saturday Review*,
27 November 1954, p. 14.

Surveys titles. Suggests that, like the detective story, sf has
conventions with "case-hardened" rules. It must "be in the future
or in space, preferably both. The surroundings include
mechanical wonders, lovingly described. Let the action be rapid
and emotional material be held to a minimum."

94 Prescott, Orville. "Books of the Times," *New York Times*,
4 August 1961, p. 19.

Heinlein's *Stranger in a Strange Land* is "dull, a non-stop orgy
. . . combined with a lot of preposterous chatter."

95 Prescott, Peter S. "Looking at Books: You're Putting Me on,
I Hope," *Look*, 10 June 1969, p. 12.

Crichton's *Andromeda Strain* "lacks the literary tone" of the best
of Verne and Wells and gains a "spurious air of legitimacy
because [he] seems to know a lot about government security
procedures." Yet the story is "frighteningly relevant." Merle's
Day of the Dolphin uses "science fiction gimmicks" to carry
satire and social criticism, while Gilbert's *Ratman's Notebooks*
is, succinctly, "spellbinding."

96 "Pretty Gentlemen and Betafied Lady," *Times Literary
Supplement*, 20 May 1960, p. 317.

Hartley's *Facial Justice* is "a kind of religious science-fiction,
part fantasy about the future and part satirical fable about
the standardization of men and women." Because he does not
"entirely succeed" in fusing together "the various elements
of satirical fable and religious fantasy . . . and perhaps because of

its ambiguities and obscurities, he has written a sincere, brave, and unfashionable work of the imagination whose implications deserve as much thought as he himself has evidently given them."

97 "Questing Characters," *Times Literary Supplement*, 25 November 1960, p. 753.

Praises Davies' *Papers of Andrew Melmoth* for "the high quality of its style" and for the "distinction" with which its themes have been "meditated and assessed." He is equally successful in his "judicious psychological portrayal of people."

98 Richardson, Maurice. "After the Apocalypse," *New Statesman*, 30 October 1954, pp. 554, 556.

Cursory account of the plots of Sturgeon's *More Than Human*, Kuttner's *Mutant*, Castle's *Satellite E One*, Crowcroft's *Fallen Sky*, Dexter's *World in Eclipse*, and Pangborn's *West of the Sun*. Suggests sf is a phenomenon "more sociological, really, than literary"; believes that because of its interest in telepathy and in the "clinical-psychological," much of it is "merely fantasy" and wells up from "deep unconscious levels."

99 ———. "New Novels," *New Statesman*, 9 April 1960, p. 533.

Calls Miller's *Canticle for Leibowitz* "a fascinating allegorical fantasy, a piece of satirical science fiction." Its "post-apocalyptic scenery" is "well done" and its "level of theological disputation . . . high."

100 "Rifts in the Moonscape," *Time*, 5 August 1957, pp. 78–79.

Reviews Evans's *Jules Verne: Master of Science Fiction*. Although Verne's novels were filled "with inaccuracies," his characters remain "strictly human, strictly Victorian." Dislikes Judith Merril's anthology, calling its characters "deader than the planets they visit."

101 Rowland, Stanley J. "With Moral Passion," *Christian Century*, 25 May 1960, pp. 640–641.

Miller's *Canticle for Leibowitz* explores "the possible consequences of man's mastery of nature through technology." Its "operating pressure" is neither plot nor character, however, but "moral indignation in a broad and somewhat journalistic sense." Finds the heart of its "artistic integrity" in its "uncompromising Christian morality."

102 Samuels, Charles Thomas. "Age of Vonnegut," *New Republic*, 12 June 1971, pp. 30–32.

Completely hostile analysis of Vonnegut's novels occasioned by the Delacorte edition of them. He "borrows the debased formulas of science fiction and comic books as a travesty of our present condition." His "one-dimensional grotesques" imitate people, while "random structure facilitates digression." He is "uninventive to the point of repetition"; his books are "arrogant" in that they are aimed for an audience already well familiar with his ideas so that his books "demand no exertion" from that audience. Samuels is disconcerted that critics and adults like Vonnegut, for this is to have "faith in any nostrum that bears the certifications of novelty and youth."

103 Schickel, Richard. "Black Comedy with Purifying Laughter," *Harpers*, 232 (May 1966), 102–106.

Reviews Vonnegut's *Player Piano* and *Mother Night*. "Over the years Vonnegut has advanced from diagnostician to exorcist, finding in intensified comic art the magic analgesic for the temporary relief of existential pain." His maturity—"Purifying laughter"— separates him from the black comedians. Mentions sf as "a distinctly *declasse* popular genre which no important literary person takes seriously."

104 Schott, Webster. *"The Andromeda Strain,"* New York *Times Book Review,* 8 June 1969, pp. 4–5.

Calls Crichton's novel a "reading windfall—compelling, memorable, superbly executed." It is a "fictional entree to the operations-research logic, the statistical totalitarianism of our military-scientific-space establishment," and it anticipates the "future, when the novel will organize and synthesize the findings of technology and science."

105 "Science Fiction Presents a Strange Picture of Science," *Science Newsletter,* 10 May 1958, p. 296.

One-paragraph notice of Hirsch's study of the sociology of sf. (See Hirsh, I, 35.)

106 Scott, J. D. "New Books," *New Statesman,* 15 September 1951, p. 290.

Essentially unfavorable toward Wyndham's *Day of the Triffids* because he introduces both widespread blindness and ambulant, canivorous plants: this is "surely going too far, even for the space monthlies." Asserts that this type of story has not been effective since Wells and 1914 because science and technology— and apparently their horrors—are so familiar to modern society. "Wells's success in this genre has never been repeated and can now never be approached."

107 Southern, Terry. "After the Bomb Came the Ice," *New York Times Book Review,* 2 June 1963, p. 20.

Vonnegut's *Cat's Cradle* is an "irreverent and often highly entertaining fantasy" which is far more meaningful than the "tripe" most people "consider serious" literature.

108 "Space Ahoy," *Time,* 14 August 1950, pp. 87–88.

Supplements comments on Nelson Bond's *Lancelot Biggs: Spaceman* with remarks about such matters as Buck Rogers and the comics. Bond's novel is "chiefly notable as a publisher's trailblazer," the sixth title released by Doubleday. American readers "can brace themselves for more long rides into space."

109 Spencer, Theodore. "Symbols of a Good and Bad England," *New York Times Book Review*, 7 July 1946, p. 10.

Reviews Lewis's *That Hideous Strength*. Emphasizes that placing fantasy (particularly involving Merlin) in a realistic, earthly setting makes the fantasy seem silly—unlike the imaginative suspension of disbelief Lewis gave to the first two volumes of the trilogy. "The titular director [of N.I.C.E.] is a patent caricature of H. G. Wells." [Christopher]

110 Sturgeon, Theodore. "Science Fiction: A Function for Fable," *National Review*, 23 September 1961, pp. 201–202.

Uses new titles as a point of departure. Calls the best of sf "a species of literature of strength and scope . . . which affords a proving ground for ethical and sociological concepts new and old, along with rattling good, or provocative, or brilliant, or even beautiful *story*." Introduces the term *speculative fiction* into his discussion. Judges Clifford Simak to be "one of the very best of modern sf writers [and] the least lionized."

111 ———. "Men, Monsters, Moondust," *National Review*, 16 December 1961, pp. 421–422.

"Good sf is good fiction." Praises Heinlein's *Stranger in a Strange Land*: "the reader who can control his outrage sufficiently to read it all the way through will be left wondering whether he has not after all been given a glimpse of love, of worship, of honor and devotion more basic and more pure than anything Earth has seen since the days of Apostolic Christianity."

112 ———. "Of Time and Tithes," *National Review*, 24 April 1962, p. 298.

Cites Fritz Leiber's assertion that sf aims to "awaken, in a story, a world on the very edge of impossibility, and then, in the midst

of the story, on the verge between the written and the unwritten,
to study and search with all the passion of a scientist scrutinizing
his experiment, or an analyst his patient's thought-stream, or a
Holmes a Moriarity, or a lover his beloved."

113 ———. "Literati vs. Cognoscenti," *National Review*,
23 October 1962, pp. 231–232.

Praises *The Hugo Winners*, edited by Asimov, but attacks
Spectrum, edited by Amis and Conquest.

114 ———. "The Science Fictionist," *National Review*,
20 November 1962, pp. 403–404.

Criticizes Clarke's *Tales of Ten Worlds* when he writes of
"Things" or sentimentally of "People," but admires his finest.
Repeats the "Ninety percent of science fiction is crud" remark,
referred to by Pohl as Sturgeon's law. That is his *"Revelation"*;
his law is that *"Nothing is absolutely always so."*

115 ———. "A Viewpoint, a Dewpoint," *National Review*,
12 February 1963, pp. 119–120.

Devoted entirely to Russell Kirk's *Surly Sullen Bell*; despite
certain philosophical objections, calls it the best of its kind since
Candide.

116 ———. "Jackets and Footnotes," *National Review*,
26 March 1963, pp. 244–245.

Diatribe against dust jacket blurbs, taking off from Heinlein's
Podkayne of Mars. Clifford Simak "has never written a bad book."
Praises William Tenn's "Time Waits for Winthrop."

117 ———. "Science and Song," *National Review*, 16 July
1963, pp. 25–26.

Devoted entirely to Harry Martinson's poem, *Aniara*; its
"crowning achievement is the communication at last of galactic
immensity."

118 ———. "One Prize, One Pleasure," *National Review*,
24 March 1964, pp. 246–247.

Praises both Pangborn's *Davy*, citing Heinlein's comparison of it
to *Huck Finn*, and Leiber's *Wanderer* as "entertainment in the
grand manner."

119 ———. "Chromium Quaint—and an Oddment!"
National Review, 11 August 1964, pp. 693–694.

Robert Magidorf's *Russian Science Fiction* suggests that "these
writers handle technology with such awe." The Soviets seem to be
"producing *science*-fiction and not science-*fiction*." Praises
Farmer's *Inside Outside*.

120 ———. "Anyone for . . . ?" *National Review*, 1 December
1964, pp. 1074–1075.

Comments upon Heinlein's *Farnham's Freehold*, Leiber's *Pail
of Air*, and Anderson's *Trader to the Stars*.

121 ———. "Science Fiction and Index," *National Review*,
9 March 1965, pp. 200–201.

Praises Walter Sullivan's *We Are Not Alone* for the soundness
of its speculations concerning life on other worlds. Commends
W. P. Cole for his index to 200 anthologies, listing 2700 stories.
(See Cole, VIII, 9.)

122 ———. "The Next Great Name Is Smith," *National
Review*, 1 June 1965, pp. 471–472.

Lavishes praise upon Cordwainer Smith in a review of his
Planet Buyer. Will not be surprised if future literary historians
call Smith "another Tolkien."

123 ———. "It Takes All Kinds," *National Review*,
21 September 1965, pp. 835–836.

Additional praise of Smith in a review of his *Space Lords*.

124 ———. "Fine Fat Packages," *National Review*,
25 January 1966, pp. 76–77.

Perfunctory notice of Nolan's *Pseudo-People*; *Three by Heinlein*; *Analog 3*; and *Spectrum 4*.

125 ———. "Beginning with the Nineteenth Century,"
National Review, 5 April 1966, pp. 320–322.

Finds Franklin's *Future Perfect* "all the perfect anthology should be": entertaining and instructive.

126 ———. "A Brace, Three Singles, and a Ten Strike,"
National Review, 17 May 1966, pp. 478–480.

With its "thesis-like introduction," Sam Moskowitz's *Modern Masterpieces of Science Fiction* contains 23 stories that are "masterpieces in some respect" and exemplify "Sam's carefully defined and hard-held 'sense-of-wonder.' " His *Seekers of Tomorrow*, containing biographical sketches, suggests that Moskowitz's "vitality lies in his positiveness."

127 ———. "Of Storytelling: How and What," *National Review*, 12 July 1966, pp. 689–690.

Salutes Ellison's *Paingod* as the work of a young writer who will become "a major prose stylist." Praises Pangborn for his ability to tell an old story "beautifully" in *A Princess and Three Suitors*.

128 ———. "From Terra to TANSTAAFL," *National Review*, 13 December 1966, pp. 1278–1281.

Favorable review of Biggle, Heinlein, Hoyle, and Spinrad.

129 ———. "Anthologies: The Old and the New," *National Review*, 30 May 1967, pp. 594–596.

Moskowitz has produced a "truly extraordinary book" in *Masterpieces of Science Fiction*, "quite the most complete, the most fascinating, and one of the most generous historical arrays of (any) *genre* fiction I have ever seen."

130 ———. "Titanic Tome from the Tic-Toc Man," *National Review*, 7 May 1968, pp. 456–458.

Focuses exclusively on Ellison's *Dangerous Visions*, tracing the development of the book from its original concept to its completed form.

131 ———. "Merril-y We Wave Along," *National Review*, 18 November 1969, pp. 1174–1175.

Focuses exclusively on Judith Merril's new anthologies and a reprint of three of her novels. Becomes a discussion of the so-called "New Wave," calling Merril its "chief exponent," and saying that her "capitalized SF has come to mean Speculative Fiction."

132 ———. "I List in Numbers," *National Review*, 10 March 1970, pp. 266–267.

New anthologies serve as a point of departure for an analysis of John W. Campbell's influence on the genre. Suggests that the field is "yeasting as never before, judging by the quality and quantity of anthologies and the diversity of their contents."

133 ———. "The Odd Coupling of Hugo and Edgar," *National Review*, 14 July 1970, pp. 743–744.

Becomes a discussion of the similarities of sf and detective fiction.

134 ———. "Best of the Best," *National Review*, 3 November 1970, pp. 1170–1171.

Focuses exclusively on *Science Fiction Hall of Fame*, volume 1, edited by Robert Silverberg. This anthology contains stories chosen by the Science Fiction Writers of America from the "era ending December 31, 1964," the year before the first Nebula Awards.

135 ———. "Momento Mori—Et Seq.," *National Review*, 12 January 1971, pp. 39–40.

Focuses upon Ursula LeGuin's novels, *A Wizard of Earthsea* and *City of Illusions*.

136 "Sums and Scrubbers," *Times Literary Supplement*,
14 April 1966, p. 332.

On the basis of Ballard's *Crystal World*, asserts that he has
"established himself as one of the most sensitive and enigmatic
novelists of the present day." Compares the novel to elements
in Conrad, Graham Greene, and Poe.

137 "The Monkey's Pa," *Time*, 8 November 1963,
pp. 101–102.

Pierre Boulle's *Planet of the Apes* "clings prehensilely to this one
turnabout joke, but rings nearly as many satiric changes on it as
Swift did on the horsey Houyhnhnms." Concludes that Boulle's
meaning is based on the idea that "human dignity is both
precarious and precious; too often it is based on pride in
achievements that can be matched by clever mimics of what has
been done before."

138 "Theological Thriller," *Time*, 10 June 1946, pp. 52–54.

Of *That Hideous Strength*: "As in many moral tales, Good is
less sharply drawn than Evil; some readers may think Dr. Ransom's
mysterious sources of power more druidical than Christian. . . .
The devil abroad in his 20th Century world is the ultra-rational
scientist-technocrat." [Christopher]

139 Trevor, William. "New Novels," *The Listener*,
18 February 1965, p. 273.

Aldiss's *Earthworks* achieves a "certain Orwellian chilliness"
despite the introduction of undeveloped characters. Judges him
superior to most sf writers: "neat and to the point."

140 Walbridge, Earle F. "New Books Appraised: Fiction,"
Library Journal, 1 May 1960, p. 774.

Late review of *Martian Chronicles*. Bradbury "has the most striking
imagination of the newer generation" of sf writers, as well as
"the most original and controlled style (though his taste is a bit
uncertain)." Some of these tales are "quite dazzling."

141 Walsh, Chad. "Can Man Save Himself?" *New York Times Book Review,* 1 April 1962, p. 4.

Calls Huxley's *Island* a "philosophic romance," containing his "final word about the human condition and the possibility of a good society."

142 Weales, Gerald. "Reader to Rider," *Commonweal,* 2 June 1961, pp. 253–255.

Reviews Morton H. Cohen's biography of Rider Haggard. Gives much attention to Haggard's story-line, "on which he hangs a number of separate scenes, and the myth-quest kind of tale serves this purpose well." Finds in him a mixture of adventure and admonishment as well as a kind of melancholy tone.

143 Yaffe, James. "Modern Trend Toward Meaningful Martians," *Saturday Review,* 23 April 1960, pp. 22–23.

In *New Maps of Hell,* Amis "lines himself up with forces that are gradually destroying science fiction as a genuine and enjoyable form." In recent years sf has become "snobbish." It is to sociology what the detective story is to psychology. This has been the ruin of both forms, for "as soon as they pretend to the stature of literature, they oblige us to judge them by the standards of literature." Implores sf to be "the pleasant intellectual game it was intended to be."

144 ———. "The Well-Trod Way to Holocaust," *Saturday Review,* 4 June 1960, p. 21.

Despite sympathy for Miller's themes, he does not think *Canticle for Leibowitz* can stand up under judgment as a novel. Miller falls back on "style" to conceal his "defects," which include poor characterization, "banal" ideas, and "feeble" drama.

145 ———. "Of Fission and Fish," *Saturday Review,* 20 April 1961, pp. 14, 16.

"Rarely does one find a work of fiction which is at once so stimulating and so exasperating, so hardheadedly perceptive and so sophomorically muddled" as Leo Szilard's *Voice of the Dolphin and Other Stories*. It is "satisfying as a work of art," particularly for its tongue-in-cheek satire and straightforward comment" in picturing great movements of men, not individuals. Yet the book is not thought through "carefully and rationally."

146 Young, B. A. "Space Time," *Punch*, 1 June 1966, p. 820.

Perfunctory plot summaries of six new sf titles, including Ballard's *Crystal World*. "Mr. Ballard seems to be turning his back on SF and moving on to a pleasing poetic fantasy."

IV. SF: The Visual Arts

1 Agel, Jerome, ed. *The Making of Kubrick's 2001*. New York: New American Library, Signet Film Series, 1970.

The most important book on a single sf film. Compiles documents, particularly interviews and reviews, tracing the diverse reactions to *2001* as well as an account of its planning and production. Includes an elaborate photo insert.

2 Aldiss, Brian. "SF Art," in *The Saturday Book*, ed. John Hadfield. New York: Macmillan, 1964. 24: 170–183.

Surveys the different styles of cover illustrations used by sf magazines. Calls the 1930's the "horror phase" of sf art, with scenes "of destruction or potential destruction." In the 1940's *Astounding* developed "atmosphere and dimension," while later Ted Carnell and Brian Lewis, with *New Worlds* and *Science Fantasy*, moved the closest to the use of abstractions. Judges sf covers "abominable . . . at their best merely curious or charming," largely because their artists have held "firmly to representation at a rather literal level."

3 Alpert, Hollis. "Day They Did It," *Saturday Review*, 10 February 1962, p. 35.

Review of British film, *The Day the Earth Caught Fire*, which provides an "apt symbol of the wanton destructiveness known as 'testing.'" The film is a "model of expert moviemaking, continually and excruciatingly suspenseful."

4 ————. "Fantastic Voyage," *Saturday Review*, 20 April
1968, p. 48.

Wonders if "effort justified" in production of *2001: A Space
Odyssey*. Kubrick, fascinated by space hardware, has discovered
"new possibilities for the screen image"; however, some may wish
for "speedier space travel." Hal the most "human" character.

5 Amory, Cleveland. "Review/*Star Trek*," *TV Guide*,
25 March 1967, p. 1.

Reviews "Shore Leave," panning it as silly, but suggests that
the show is colorful enough to amuse children. [Berman]

6 Anderson, Howard A., Linwood G. Dunn, and Joseph
Westheimer. "Out-of-this-world Special Effects for
Star Trek," *American Cinematographer*, 48 (October
1967), 714–717.

Detailed discussion, with illustrations, of the many different
special effects used by the program. [Berman]

7 Asimov, Isaac. "Mr. Spock Is Dreamy," *TV Guide*,
29 April 1967, pp. 9–11.

Humorously explains that Spock's sex appeal results from a change
in attitude toward science: intelligence is at last "in." On the
other hand, maybe it's all in the ears. [Berman]

8 Baxter, John. *Science Fiction in the Cinema*. New York:
A. S. Barnes, 1970.

A history of the sf film from 1895 to 1968. "Particularly good
is a treatment of the genre from 1900 to 1940 with an emphasis on
Metropolis, and *Things to Come*." Attempts to deal with the
aesthetics of the film genre, pointing out that "most sf films are
really 'anti-science fiction,' based on a crude Hollywood anti-
intellectualism or, as in Europe, a simplistic brand of anti-technol-
ogy." [Al Jackson, in *Luna*]

9 Beja, Morris. "*2001*: Odyssey to Byzantium," *Extrapolation*, 10 (May 1969), 67–68.

"When Dave Bowman goes on his odyssey to outer (and inner) space, he is on precisely the same sort of journey that Yeats is making when he sails to Byzantium." (Reprinted in Clareson, *SF: The Other Side of Realism*, II, 71.)

10 Boone, Andrew R. "Hollywood Planets Wage Space War," *Popular Science Monthly*, 165 (November 1954), 168–169.

Discusses models and special effects used to produce Raymond F. Jones's *This Island Earth*.

11 Brody, Alan. "*2001* and the Paradox of the Fortunate Fall," *Hartford Studies in Literature*, 1 (1969), 7–19.

Lead article in the Symposium on the film, which is "in the tradition of American literary romance." It combines the motifs of the fall ("The Dawn of Man") and the cyclic journey as part of the theme of self-realization.

12 Cantril, Hadley. *The Invasion from Mars*. Princeton: Princeton University Press, 1952.

Subtitled "A Study in the Psychology of Panic," this presents the whole of Howard Koch's script of the 30 October 1938 Mercury Theatre Production of *The War of the Worlds*. It must serve as a model for this type of analysis. The five sections consider the nature and extent of the panic, "how the stimulus was experienced," the immediate reactions to it, the historical setting, and individual cases.

13 Clarens, Carlos. *An Illustrated History of the Horror Film*. New York: Capricorn Books, 1968.

Profusely illustrated, this book provides a widely-ranging survey of the horror film and contains many bits of information that might otherwise have been lost. Although sf films are referred to throughout the text, of special interest is the chapter, "Keep Watching the Sky."

14 Clareson, Thomas D. "John A. Mitchell's *Drowsy*: A Most Unusual Country," *Extrapolation*, 12 (May 1971), 99–105.

A folio of six moonscapes from Mitchell's 1917 novel. The artist was Angus Peter Macdonnel, the well-known contributor to such periodicals as *Scribners* and *Harpers*.

15 Crowther, Bosley. "Outer Space Comes of Age," *Atlantic*, 189 (March 1952), 91–92.

A discussion of Hollywood's "current rush toward outer space," in which various sf films are named. Concludes that *Destination Moon* alone deserves "to be taken at least semi-seriously."

16 Dempelwolff, Richard F. "Backstage Magic for a Trip to Saturn," *Popular Mechanics*, 127 (April 1967), 106–109.

On technical background of *2001* at Borehamwood studios near London. Describes some problems met (centrifuge) and some model sizes used (30 x 30 lunar landscape atop a three-story scaffold).

17 ———. "How They Made *2001*," *Science Digest*, 63 (May 1968), 34–39.

Another treatment of the technical problems encountered, largely repetitious of the earlier article. (See IV, 16.)

18 Doyno, Victor A. "*2001²*," *Hartford Studies in Literature*, 1 (1969), 131–132.

Explores the structure of the film in terms of such visual motifs as eyes, bars, and spears to show their relationships to "the dominant concerns of consciousness and ritualized progression."

19 Fenichel, Robert R. "Comment," *Hartford Studies in Literature*, 1 (1969), 133–135.

Final entry in *2001* Symposium; a series of brief objections to points in principal articles.

20 Fuller, Richard. "Fuller's Earth," *Colloquy*, 4 (May 1971), 37–45.

Well illustrated highly personal discussion of sf films. Refers to many titles, but climaxes with a consideration of *2001: A Space Odyssey*.

21 "Gadgets from Hollywood," *Business Week*, 21 February 1953, p. 27.

Brief discussion of Oscar Dallons and his brothers who do Special effects for sf films and TV.

22 Goodstone, Tony, ed. *The Pulps: 50 Years of American Pop Culture*. New York: Chelsea House, 1970.

Fantasy and sf receive attention in a single chapter, "Extension of the Infinite." A few covers from sf pulps are included in an excellent folio.

23 Grant, Allan. "When a Camera Gets Under the Skin," *Popular Photography*, 59 (October 1966), 118–119.

The author, a "photojournalist," gives a brief account of the sets and special effects used in photographing the film, *Fantastic Voyage*, based on the Asimov novel in which the submarine and its crew are miniaturized to enter the blood stream. Allan found his own photography (stills) "a remarkable voyage of discovery . . . [an] exciting trip . . . and creatively . . . rewarding."

24 Grigorescu, Dan. "Forecasts, Not Prophecies," *Romanian Review*, 22 (1968), 57–58.

Incidental mention of sf in a discussion of the fine arts.

25 Gunn, James. "An Author Watches His Brain Child Die on Television," *TV Guide*, 13 February 1971, pp. 7–12.

Gunn's commentary after watching the failure of the series based on his novel, *The Immortal*. TV buys a " 'property' because it is different and then turn[s] it into a product that looks and sounds and feels and smells like everything else." Only one person concerned with pilot film worked with series.

26 Hamburger, Philip. "Television: Now I Lay Me Down to Sleep," *New Yorker*, 22 December 1951, pp. 57–59.

His 4-year-old son has rejected usual TV fare for *Captain Video*. Parodies plot-line.

27 Hauser, Frank. "Science Fiction Films," in *International Film Annual*, ed. William Whitebait. New York: Doubleday, 1958, pp. 87–90.

Suggests the post-World War II films reflect the same concerns that bother such writers as Bradbury. Two patterns: "When the aliens are seen as enemies, scientists, ministers, and humanitarians are dangerous fools. When the aliens are beneficent, soldiers, politicians, and hard-boiled realists are the villains." Praises *The Thing From Another World* and *The War of the Worlds*. As for the many monster films, "They are but little bugaboos dressed up in atomic hats." Feels that the rush of titles is over and that "whatever their defects of viewpoint and intellectual grasp, science fiction films usually took more trouble to entertain and give at least technical value for money than the nondescript comedies and flatulent epics which have succeeded them."

28 Hoch, David G. "Mythic Patterns in *2001: A Space Odyssey*," *Journal of Popular Culture*, 4 (Spring 1971), 961–965.

Based upon Joseph Campbell's analysis of myth in *The Hero with a Thousand Faces*, this emphasizes the transformation of the apes into man and of Bowman into "a higher form of life."

Much attention is given to the "atonement with the father"; that is, the final sequence climaxing with Bowman's encounter with the "father" monolith. The film follows "the pattern of the monomyth with mankind as its hero."

29 Hodgens, Richard M. "A Brief, Tragical History of the Science Fiction Film," *Film Quarterly*, 13 (Winter 1959), 30–39.

During the 1950's sf films have distorted their sources, while their premises have been impossible and inconsistently developed. They have relied on monsters and have tied them to such problems as atomic energy to reinforce their hysteria. Underscores the antiscientific basis of these films. Comprehensive. (Reprinted in Clareson, *SF: The Other Side of Realism*, II, 71.)

30 Holland, Norman N. "*2001*: A Psychosocial Explanation," *Hartford Studies in Literature*, 1 (1969), 20–25.

"A remarkable documentation of the psychosocial issues of 1968," the film structures itself around a basic pattern: "a life support system, a struggle for it, a failure of communication, the intervention of the Slab, and victory, leading to a new evolutionary phase."

31 "Hollywood Builds Flying Saucers," *Popular Science Monthly*, 161 (November 1952), 132, 134.

Briefly explains how images of flying saucers were produced for George Pal's *War of the Worlds*.

32 "Hollywood Goes to Mars," *Science Digest*, 30 October 1951, pp. 69–71.

Calls sf "a vast body of literature beloved by millions of readers." Otherwise a superficial survey of current films.

33 "Interplanetary Cop," *Time*, 11 August 1952, pp. 46–47.

Brief notice of *Buzz Corey, Space Patrol* on ABC: no sex, no nightmares, an overabundance of interplanetary sound effects.

34 Kivu, Dinu. "Hybrid Genres?" *Romanian Review*,
22 (1968), 59–60.

A brief survey of the "totally different" uses Romanian drama
and film make of "the data and principles" of sf. Ion Popescu-
Gopo, film; Horia Lovinescu, Horia Arama, and A. Mirodan,
drama.

35 McConnell, Frank. "Rough Beast Slouching: A Note on
Horror Movies," *Kenyon Review*, 32 (1970), 109–120.

An astute analysis of the "distinctively American" tradition of
the horror film, suggesting that *Dracula* (1931) and *Frankenstein*
(1931) established the limits and potentials of the form. He
finds them both to be "translations . . . of English romanticism
into a profoundly Americanized mental landscape . . . in the sense
that D. H. Lawrence described the compulsion of classic American
writers to translate and revalue the inherited burden of
European culture." Cites James, Hawthorne, and Whitman.
Despite this, the "principal ingredient of their nightmarishness
is precisely the bland theatricality, the decadent ease, with which
they establish themselves as bad dreams." In contrast, in the
post-World War II sf films, "the insect and vegetable monsters
are only more resolutely insensate, more unredeemable material
inversions of the myth of imperial intelligence." These films
make a romantic search for "landscape appropriate to the
expansive energies of the mind." They deal with the "horror of
incarnate history . . . of the uncontrollable atomic future in
which man . . . finds himself displaced from total control by 'alien'
worlds in the process of borning."

36 Malone, Nancy. "Star Alien," *Read*, 15 March 1968, pp. 6–9.

An interview with Nimoy on Spock's appeal to young people.
Nimoy suggests its cause is Spock's sophistication and ethical
behavior combined with his self-control. He has received letters
from college students who say their English classes have studied
Spock as an example of modern folk hero—cool and rational
instead of big and strong. [Berman]

37 "Monster of the Month: *Outer Limits*," *Newsweek*,
27 January, 1964, p. 55.

Louis Stefano has taken the ABC *Outer Limits* to the top 20
programs. He declares that if there is a "message," it is a
"strong preachment against violence, bigotry, and prejudice.
They come from outer space and we don't ask them to do the
things we do here."

38 Morgenstern, Joseph. "Kubrick's Cosmos," *Newsweek*,
15 April 1968, p. 87.

Essentially unfavorable review of *2001*, stressing lack of plot.
Doesn't like ending with its "cute little embryo."

39 Morsberger, Robert E. "Shakespeare and Science Fiction,"
Shakespeare Quarterly, 12 (Spring 1961), 161.

Notes that much of the plot of *Forbidden Planet* came from *The
Tempest*. Despite the "pseudo-Freudian horror at climax,"
consciously or unconsciously "the main situation is almost identical
with Shakespeare's old play," which he calls the sf or at least
fantasy fiction of its time. As with modern critics, so Jonson
complained "of wonders" and of gracing "the stage with
monsters" like Caliban.

40 Plank, Robert. "Sons and Fathers, A.D. 2001," *Hartford
Studies in Literature*, 1 (1969), 26–33.

2001 follows "a pattern well established in fiction about imagined
beings." The humanoids—those involved with the Slab—are
"unapproachable but on the whole benign," while the android
(Hal) leans "toward malevolence and rebellion." Thus the
humanoids become father figures; the android, the figure of an
"artificial" son.

41 ———. "1001 Interpretations of *2001*," *Extrapolation*, 11 (December 1969), 23–24.

Replies to Morris Beja, emphasizing the need for ambiguity in the finest art and suggesting several ways of approaching an interpretation of *2001*. (Reprinted in Clareson, *SF: The Other Side of Realism*, II, 71.)

42 Raddatz, Leslie. "*Star Trek* Wins the Ricky Schwartz Award," *TV Guide*, 18 November 1967, pp. 25–28.

Article reports the intensity of fan involvement in the *Star Trek* series. Quotes Nimoy and Shatner on their attitudes toward the series and the fans. Examples cited include the Smithsonian request for a print of one episode and a fan's letter containing a 21–page description of the Vulcan solar system. [Berman]

43 "Rape of the Future," *Esquire*, 65 (May 1966), 112–116.

Many pictures, little copy. Review of both Saul David's film *Fantastic Voyage* and Kubrick's *2001*. Emphasizes the hardware and special effects.

44 Rogers, Ivor. "Extrapolative Cinema," *Arts in Society*, 6 (Summer–Fall 1969), 287–291.

Notes inadequacy of sf films and criticism of them. Undertakes survey of sub-genres of the extrapolative film: political (*Seven Days in May* to *Dr. Strangelove*); social (*Man in the White Suit*); "[the]authentic extrapolative exploration of time" (*Last Year in Marienbad*); and that type which uses an sf framework for for philosophical comment upon man (*The Lord of the Flies*). Ends with a discussion of *2001*.

45 Rogers, Robert. "The Psychology of the 'Double' in *2001*," *Hartford Studies in Literature*, 1 (1969), 34–36.

The film which seems to celebrate technology omits "the most wonderful thing about man—his mind." With the possible exception of Hal, the characters are "mindless automatons."

46 Rosenfeld, Albert. "A Searching Moon Sets Off a Weird Quest," *Life*, 5 April 1968, pp. 34–35.

The film *2001* "dazzles the eyes and gnaws the mind." Praises accuracy of technology, which was used as a "realistic" point of departure "into realms more metaphysical than physical." The deliberate ambiguity lifts *2001* "out of the literal realm of science fiction."

47 Sanz, Jose. *SF Symposium / FC Simposio*. Rio de Janeiro, Brazil: Instituto Nacional do Cinema, 1970.

Contains the major speeches given at the Science Fiction Film Symposium held in Rio in 1969, including those by vanVogt, Brunner, Aldiss, Clarke, and Poul Anderson. While most of the speakers discussed the sf film, the general topics ranged widely and are valuable for the different views expressed. Sanz did an extensive introduction. The text is in both Portugese and English. [Wollheim]

48 Sargeant, Winthrop. "Through the Interstellar Looking Glass," *Life*, 21 May 1951, pp. 127–130.

The sf "fad is made for Hollywood." Emphasizes fandom in fun-filled cliches. In 11 June issue (p. 8) occur the replies: John W. Campbell on dianetics and Richard Shaver on Deros, both protesting Sargeant's remarks.

49 Schwartz, Sheila. "The World of Science Fiction," *NYS English Record*, 21 (February 1971), 27–40. (See II, 262.)

50 Scobie, Steven. "Concerning Horses; Concerning Apes," *Riverside Quarterly*, 4 (March 1971), 258–262.

Uses *Gulliver's Travels* as the model against which to analyze and evaluate the satire in *Planet of the Apes* and *Beneath the Planet of the Apes*. Finds their satire to be "simplistic, even . . . whimsical," but asserts that the films' "manipulation of [the]

audience's identification with the hero is . . . even more subtle
than Swift's manipulations of attitudes to Gulliver." Emphasizes
that the hero's pride remains constant throughout the films and
is a major fact in the final catastrophe.

51 Seelye, John. "Arrgh! The Collected Works of *Buck Rogers
In The 25th Century*," *New Republic*, 21 January 1970,
pp. 24–26.

A sympathetic study of the Buck Rogers comic strip as a metaphor
anticipating NASA and President Kennedy's "New Frontier."
Citing Ben Fussell, he suggests that Buck Rogers is a projection of
America's permeating myth of the old frontier; traces the
metamorphoses that occurred in the strip. Indians became
Mongolian hordes, Martian cat-men, Martian Tigermen, and
finally the Monkey Men of Planet X. Dr. Huer "began as a
parody of Einstein" but lost that identity to become merely an
eccentric who supplied machines for Buck to use. Rogers is "a
mythic hero lighting out from poor old earth for howling
adventures amongst the Indians of outer space . . ." Concludes by
warning that sf "is fun," but fiction must not be confused with
fact. He is concerned about correct priorities.

52 Shatnoff, Judith. "A Gorilla to Remember," *Film Quarterly*,
22 (Autumn 1968), 56–62.

Frames the article with a discussion of Darwin. Pans *Planet of
the Apes* as something akin to "the Victorian battle between
apes and angels," making use of all Hollywood's stereotypes and
an "entire textbook of Hollywood-simple pronouncements." In
contrast, praises the "spectacular universe of *2001*." Criticizes
story-line, but it is "a beautiful film ultra-modern in its admiration
for the material wonders it displays." (King Kong is the "ape to
remember"; he was "the true child of Darwin in Hollywood's
cartoon of life.")

53 Shayon, Robert Lewis. "TV and Radio: The Interplanetary Mr. Spock," *Saturday Review*, 17 June 1967, p. 46.

Discusses *Star Trek's* potential contribution "to rational public thought" about what the future may bring, including the possibility of having to adjust to non-human intelligences. [Berman]

54 Shuldiner, Herbert. "How They Filmed *2001: A Space Odyssey*," *Popular Science Monthly*, 192 (June 1968), 62–67, 184–186.

Concerned with the gadgetry and special effects of the film; nothing new.

55 Sontag, Susan. "The Imagination of Disaster," *Commentary*, 40 (October 1965), 42–48.

Defends sf film as expression of fantasy which "allows most people to cope with [the] twin specters of . . . unremitting banality and inconceivable terror" characteristic of our time. Judges the art of the sf film to be higher than the art of sf fiction; moreover, the film can give something the fiction can never give—"sensuous elaboration." The core of the film lies in "the imagery of destruction" which reflects and satisfies the "powerful anxieties" that modern historical reality and concern for the individual psyche have brought about. They mirror "an intersection between a naively and largely debased commercial art product and the most profound dilemmas of the contemporary situation." Calls sf films "one of the most accomplished of the popular art forms." (Reprinted in Sontag, *Beyond Interpretation*. New York: Farrar Straus, 1966.)

56 "*Space Patrol* Conquers Kids," *Life*, 1 September 1952, p. 33.

Space Patrol replaces Hopalong Cassidy. Text minimal and cliche-ridden.

57 Spinrad, Norman. "*Stand on Zanzibar*: The Novel as Film," in *The Other Side of Realism*, ed. Thomas D. Clareson. Bowling Green, Ohio: Bowling Green University Popular Press, 1971, pp. 181–185. (See II, 280.)

58 Stacy, Paul. "Cinematic Thought," *Hartford Studies in Literature*, 1 (1969), 124–130.

Emphasizes the differences inherent in literature and cinema because "literature, being linguistic, is certain to be conceptual and discursive," while film "favors action, violence, surface qualities."

59 Van Horne, Harriet. "Space Rocket Kick," *Theatre Arts*, 35 (December 1951), 40–41.

Says writers of sf take "scientific license," primarily in that they employ gadgets "the present day technologists haven't got around to yet." Discusses the TV science fiction programs, concentrating upon *Captain Video* and *Tom Corbett*. Praises Willy Ley's part in the latter program and speaks of its "imagination" and "idealistic" thinking, calling it "carefully researched, well written."

60 Walton, Harry. "How TV Tricks Take You Space Traveling," *Popular Science Monthly*, 161 (September 1952), 106–108.

Describes how characters act against a black backdrop while a second camera zooms close to anything from a photograph to a bowl of breakfast cereal in order to "create" the proper alien environment. Reference to *Tom Corbett* series.

61 Whiteside, Thomas O. "Onward and Upward with the Arts: No Lobster Men from Neptune," *New Yorker*, 1 March 1952, pp. 32–34.

Of sf on TV, with memories of Buck Rogers, breakfast foods, Superman, and Cocomalt. Met with Allan Ducovny, "man in charge" of *Tom Corbett*. Concludes this program has "believability within the limits of pulp possibility."

62 Whitfield, Stephen E. *The Making of Star Trek*.
New York: Ballantine, 1968.

A chatty, informative, heavily illustrated history of the genesis
and operation of the television show which ran on the NBC
network for three years. Gene Roddenberry, producer of the show,
gave Whitfield access to the complete files. Correspondence,
diagrams, photographs, and partial contents of the program's
guidebook for script writers comprise more than half of the book,
connected by running narrative commentary on Roddenberry's
problems with selling the concept, obtaining special effects, and
compromising enough with network officials to get the considerable
financial support he needed. Although the narrative voice is full
of hero-worship, the book is valuable for the large amount of
information, much of it in undigested form, which it contains in
easily available format. [Samuelson]

63 Wright, James W. "TV's *Star Trek*: How to Mix Science
Fact with Fiction," *Popular Science Monthly*,
161 (December 1967), 72–74.

Concerned with gadgetry and special effects; suggests that all
are based on accepted scientific theories or refinements of such
devices as today's lasers.

V. SF: Futurology, Utopia, and Dystopia

1 Alden, Robert C. "Sociology Taught by Fiction," *Social Studies*, 47 (January 1956), 30.

The "ideas of sociology can be pointed out in literature." He names a number of utopian novels, essentially to illustrate that "science fiction is an excellent medium for the development of different types of cultures."

2 Allen, Dick. *Science Fiction: The Future*. New York: Harcourt, Brace, Jovanovich, 1971.

An anthology designed for use as a text in a variety of courses explores "concepts of the future as seen by SF writers," but includes materials outside the genre in order to establish "First Perspectives" and to anchor the concern for the future as widely as possible. The main body of the book concerns "Alternative Futures" and ends with "Theories."

3 Armytage, W. H. G. "Extrapolators and Exegetes of Evolution," *Extrapolation*, 7 (December 1965), 2–17.

An early discussion of the impact of Darwin's theory on British fiction, serving as background for part of chapter 4 of *Yesterdays Tomorrows*. (See V, 6.)

4 ———. "Superman and the System," *Riverside Quarterly*, 2 (March 1967), 232–241; 3 (August 1967), 44–51.

Discussion of the "Nietzschean Gospel," focusing upon German disciples, Wells, Shaw, and Lawrence; incorporated into chapter 7 of *Yesterdays Tomorrows*. (See V, 6.)

5 ———. "The Disenchanted Mechanophobes in Twentieth Century England," *Extrapolation*, 9 (May 1968), 33–60.

This is the early version of chapter 8 of *Yesterday's Tomorrows*. (See V, 6.)

6 ———. *Yesterdays Tomorrows*: *A Historical Survey of Future Societies*. London: Routledge & Kegan Paul; Toronto: University of Toronto Press, 1968.

The most comprehensive study of the mythic use of the future from Graeco-Roman times to the present. Since "Christianity has been demythologized . . . and exhausted until it is merely a philosophy of existence," contemporary forays into the future represent "a valid modern mythology." Not confined to sf, it explores the whole of the modern temper, but the concern throughout makes the study valuable to futurologists, emphasizing as it does the forecasting of the future.

7 Asimov, Isaac. "Life in 1990," *Science Digest*, 58 (August 1965), 63–70.

To predict, Asimov "must take a condition that *will certainly* exist in the future and try to analyze the possible consequences. And to decide on a condition that is certain for the future, it is best to look at the conditions that prevail today." Examples include air and water pollution and a society more gadget-centered and scientific.

8 Atkins, John. *Tomorrow Revealed*. New York: Roy Publishers, 1956.

A most amusing effort to write the history of the future (1960–3750), based upon a dozen or so of the major sf works of the period, primarily Wells, Orwell, and vanVogt, concluding with Robert Graves. Some illustrations, with a time chart reminiscent of Stapledon. [Wollheim]

9 Bloomfield, Paul. *Imaginary Worlds; or, The Evolution of Utopia.* London: Hamish Hamilton, 1932.

A literary history of utopias from "heaven" and Plato to Huxley's *Brave New World.* Individual chapters on Wells, Shaw (*Back to Methusaleh*), Haldane (*The Last Judgment*), Theodore Hertzka (*Freeland*), and Huxley.

10 Burgess, Anthony. "Utopias and Dystopias," in *The Novel Now: A Guide to Contemporary Fiction.* New York: W. W. Norton, 1967, pp. 38–47.

All too brief, the chapter concentrates upon Wells, Huxley, and Orwell. Bright spot is the more detailed discussion of L. P. Hartley's *Facial Justice.*

11 Churchill, R. C. *A Short History of the Future.* London: Werner Laurie, 1955.

Similar to the Atkins title, *Short History* bases its history of the future (1930–6601) on a wider range of well-known sf materials such as Robert Graves, Nevil Shute, James Wellard, George Orwell, and Kurt Vonnegut. Contains time charts and a valuable index. Less amusing than Atkins but more substantial. (See Atkins, V, 8.) [Wollheim]

12 Clarke, I. F. "The First Forecast of the Future," *Futures,* 1 (June 1969), 325–330.

First of the series, "The Pattern of Prediction 1763–1973." Focuses upon *The Reign of George VI* (1763) as the "first major forecast of its kind," introducing a form of fiction which has become "a dominant device" for commenting upon the state of society and possible patterns of development. Its author foresaw a static world changed by "political and military moves within the European monarchical system."

13 Elliott, Robert C. "Saturnalis, Satire, and Utopia," *Yale Review*, 55 (June 1966), 535–536.

Utopia as a secularization of the myth of the Golden Age, a myth incarnated in the festival of Saturnalia. Two modes, Utopia and satire, joined in the work of such as Thomas More. "Utopia necessarily entails a negative appraisal of present conditions."

14 Frye, Northrop. "Varieties of Literary Utopia," *Daedulus*, 94 (Spring 1965), 323–347.

Issue was dedicated to studies of Utopia. Concepts of social contract and of Utopia expressed "only in myth." In it "behavior of society is described *ritually*," partly because "behavior of society is presented as rationally motivated" as a result of such conventions as the Socratic Dialogue and the guide. Three patterns: pastoral (Arcadian), cyclical return; classical (More) "derived form" from the city state; modern, "from a uniform pattern of civilization spread over the whole globe."

15 Gerber, Richard. *Utopian Fantasy: A Study of English Utopian Fiction Since the End of the Nineteenth Century.* London: Routledge & Kegan Paul, 1955.

Concerned with the wider range and popular force of recent utopian fiction. Not concerned with the "practical details of social planning and only superficially with special literary devices." Origin of the modern movement lies in a "quasi-religious belief in the miraculous growth of unlimited evolutionary progress." "An adequate literary genre" has developed, enabling writers "to attain the closest possible connection with present-day reality and the reader's mind." Does not discuss works beyond Huxley's although an appendix lists utopian titles from 1901–1950.

16 Glicksberg, Charles I. "Anti-Utopianism in Modern Literature," *Southwest Review*, 37 (Summer 1952), 221–228.

Although the romantic impulse in literature is kept alive by the utopian dream, concern here is with the emphasis upon "futurism," because it is intrinsically totalitarian and because it breaks so completely with the past. The anti-utopian swing of modern literature results from the failure of the Soviet experiment. Orwell and Huxley only writers given detailed attention.

17 Granin, Daniel. "A Journey into the Future," *Soviet Literature*, no. 5, (1968), pp. 151–158.

Focuses upon man's growing concern for the future, with some review of past accomplishments, but more attention to the potentiality the future has for the 20th century. In looking forward, one should bring "out the best in 20th century man" in a world ever more entwined because of "the appearance of universal problems and efforts."

18 Grunwald, Henry Anatole. "From Eden to the Nightmare," *Horizon*, 5 (March 1963), 73–79.

A popular account of the utopian literary tradition, emphasizing the usual writers from More and Campanella to Huxley and Orwell. Acknowledges indebtedness to Amis for a brief account of the negative utopias in sf, which foresee a "technologically supported totalitarianism."

19 Hillegas, Mark. "Dystopian Science Fiction: New Index to the Human Situation," *New Mexico Quarterly*, 31 (Autumn 1961), 238–249.

Suggests sf has long reflected the belief that "by extending man's power to the performance of all things possible," science "will inevitably improve the human condition." This optimism has been countered by the dystopian phenomenon which asserts that science and technology "may well enslave, dehumanize, and even destroy man." Since it is a popular literature, it should "produce sufficient mass awareness to help avert some of its own predictions."

20 "Inspirational Value of Science Fiction," *Science Digest*, 53 (March 1963), 34.

In "What's on Your Mind" department. Refers to Arthur C. Clarke's Kalinga prize speech. Notes that sf "assumes the future will be profoundly different from the past" but does not "attempt to predict the future in detail." (See Clarke, I, 13.)

21 Kenkel, William F. "Marriage and the Family in Modern Science Fiction," *Journal of Marriage and the Family*, 31 (February 1969), 6–14. (See I, 41.)

22 Knox, George. "Apocalypse and Sour Utopias," *Western Humanities Review*, 16 (1962), 11–22.

Through a discussion of "mainstream" writers only, focusing upon the late 19th century in greatest detail, Knox traces the failure of the utopian vision. Emphasis upon the concern of many of these writers over the loss of religious ideals and their replacement by a "secularized eschatology." There has grown the "fear that the powers we have deified and sold our souls to have already transcended" our control.

23 Leeper, Geoffrey. "The Happy Utopias of Aldous Huxley and H. G. Wells," *Meanjin Quarterly*, 24 (1965), 120–124.

Brave New World, a satire of Wells's *Men Like Gods*, and an attack upon "happy" utopias. Huxley's contemporaries thought *BNW* "a reactionary tract." But his last, *Island*, was itself a "happy" utopia, exhibiting a "hatred of metropolitan life, a sentiment for the country." It fell flat because the "fashion is still the defeated style of Orwell's *1984*." Discursive.

24 Livingston, Dennis. "Science Fiction and Futurology: Some Observations at a Science Fiction Convention," *The Futurist*, 2 (June 1968), 47–48.

A brief account of the "natural links" between the sf and futurist communities and the benefits of more communication between the two. "Science fiction can give the futurist an emotional feel for the human significance of various alternate futures, and thereby influence the desirability accorded by policy makers to working for the achievement of one such future rather than another."

25 ———. "Science Fiction as a Source of Forecast Material," *Futures*, 1 (March 1969), 232–238.

"As the only branch of literature that has taken within its scope an exploration of the varied possible futures open to mankind," sf would seem to be "a logical source of material for those concerned with the future. They may use it to stimulate their thoughts, to corroborate forecasts they have worked out, and to generally provide multiple simulations of the futures occupying their research." Science fiction predictions are categorized into five types and evaluated for their utility to futurology.

26 ———. "The Study of Science Fiction as a Forecasting Methodology," in *Challenges from the Future: Proceedings of the International Future Research Conference*, ed. Japan Society of Futurology. 4 vols. Tokyo: Kodansha, 1970. 1: 71–79.

Science fiction has two aspects to its role as data source for futurology. It is itself an agent that affects society, and it is a literary form that uses as a major theme predictions of future technology and of the social consequences of future science and technology.

27 ———. "Science Fiction Models of Future World Order Systems," *International Organization*, 25 (Spring 1971), 254–270.

An analysis of eight works of sf, including Brunner's *Stand on Zanzibar*, Orwell's *1984*, and Pohl and Kornbluth's *Space Merchants*, according to the societal models they present and the nature and status of international factors implied in these models. The ways in which the societies described institutionalize their international relations fall into several patterns, as do the linkages between domestic and international politics. "Serious sf is seen as speaking to the same issues being raised in non-fiction, social science and literature."

28 Lokke, Virgil L. "The American Utopian Anti-Novel," in *Frontiers of American Culture*, ed. Ray Browne *et al.* Lafayette, Ind.: Purdue University Studies, 1968, pp. 123–149.

Surveys the wave of novels following Bellamy, with some attention to their literary values. The utopian writers saw the novel "as the means by which to persuade society of the need for change." They operated on "a particular theory of mass communication"— the mass, elite, and intermediaries—which saw women possessing "instinctively a capacity" to respond to "spiritualized" love in fiction, thereby becoming the ones to "educate quickly and painlessly."

29 Maddison, Michael. "The Case Against Tomorrow," *Political Quarterly*, 36 (April–June 1965), 214–227.

Praises Heinlein as best, and says sf needs "no fierce apologetics or defense." The "technocratic visionaries have been dethroned"; sf now has "a clear-cut humanistic and radical alignment." Emphasis upon American dystopian sf. "Science fiction has presented a formidable case against tomorrow—a case that the sociologist and political scientist can ill afford to ignore." Not pessimistic: "a desire to demonstrate the total inadequacy of last century optimism, and, more important, an affirmation of man's responsibility for the present—and the future."

30 Morton, A. L. *The English Utopia*. London: Lawrence and Wishart, 1952.

Surveys *English* Utopias from More to William Morris, with a single chapter devoted to "Yesterday and Tomorrow," covering such writers as Wells, Chesterton, Huxley, Orwell, and Herbert Read. Utopia is no longer a perfect, static state but portrays "a society moving toward ever new goals."

31 Muller, Herbert J. "A Note on Utopia," *The Children of Frankenstein*: *A Primer of Modern Technology and Human Values*. Bloomington and London: Indiana University Press, 1970. (See I, 58.)

32 Negley, Glenn R. and J. Max Patrick. *The Quest for Utopia*: *An Anthology of Imaginary Societies*. New York: Henry Schumann, 1952.

Excerpts from 28 Utopias, none later than 1919. Chapter 2 discusses "Modern Utopias: 1850–1950" and includes checklist of titles. (Reprinted by Doubleday, Anchor (A 326), 1962.)

33 Parrington, Vernon Lewis, Jr. *American Dreams*: *A Study of American Utopias*. Providence, R. I.: Brown University Press, 1947.

A significant, pioneer work which remains the fullest statement on the utopian tradition in American literature. A few titles such as *Symzonia* are omitted, but it is particularly comprehensive for the period at the end of the 19th century and contains a checklist of titles from 1659 to 1946. Of special interest to sf is the chapter, "Mars and Utopia." Relates the literary expression to actual experiments taking place.

34 Patrick, J. Max. "Inside Utopia," *Extrapolation*, 8 (December 1966), 20–24.

Reprint of the essay first published as a pamphlet some ten years earlier in connection with an exhibit in the Paul Klapper Library of Queens College, with a postscript updating it. The definition and sketch of the history of Utopia.

35 Plank, Robert. "The Geography of Utopia: Psychological Facts Shaping the 'Ideal' Location," *Extrapolation*, 6 (May 1965), 39–49.

The utopian writer "must present his settings as not co-existent with the reader's setting." He must "displace" the reader in time and space. Various settings have been tried, most often the island.

36 Rojas, Billy, ed. *Future Studies*. Amherst, Mass.: University of Massachusetts Press, 1970.

Three numbers have been issued. The first is a 108 page bibliography, not annotated, concerned "with aspects of future history"; many of the titles are from sf, and all of them establish an elaborate context for the study of sf. The second number describes courses offered in future studies; the third provides a directory of individuals and organizations in the field.

37 ———. "Futuristics at Massachusetts," *Extrapolation*, 12 (December 1970), 60.

Describes the Program for the Study of the Future in Education begun at the University of Massachusetts in 1969. Although it is still in its formative stages, he suggests several of the projects already underway or planned for the present year.

38 "Utopias You Wouldn't Like," *Harpers*, 210 (April 1955), 87–88.

"Mr. Harper," in "After Hours" department, suggests sf has turned against science. At time of Wells and Gernsback, the stories were essentially utopian, and the writers "advance guards of a materialist's millenium." Focuses upon third issue of Ballentine's *Star Science Fiction*, in which nine of ten stories are anti-scientific. "Obviously each of these is not adventure fiction, but social satire, edged with bitterness against the science-minded society of today, let alone tomorrow."

39 Walsh, Chad. "Attitudes Toward Science in the Modern 'Inverted Utopia,' " *Extrapolation*, 2 (May 1961), 23–26.

Paper presented at "Literature and Science" group of MLA, 1960. A persistent theme is that "social stability can be achieved only if men become something less than fully human." Science provides the tools to gain this end. Writers see science not as good or evil in itself, but as "a powerful tool in the hands of society," as well as a force that will make us forget "our role as a part of nature."

40 ———. *From Utopia to Nightmare*. New York and
Evanston: Harper and Row, 1962.

Walsh documents not only the passing of Utopia but also of
humanism before the diverse forces of the 20th century.
"Theoretically, the loss of utopian hopes could mean that man is
abandoning his humanistic delusions and returning to
Christian realism. But it can equally well mean that a mood of
total pessimism, as unreasoned as the earlier utopian hopes,
is engulfing our minds and our spirits." He makes much
comparison between the utopian and dystopian dreams, on the
one hand, and the Old Testament prophets on the other. One of
the most important recent studies; if it has a limitation, it is
that he relies heavily upon traditional examples and ignores such
contemporaries as Bradbury.

41 Webb, Honor A. "Science Fiction Writers: Prophets of
the Future," *Library Journal*, 15 (December 1955),
pp. 2884–2885.

Cites Campbell's remark that sf should be "technical—
philosophical," dealing with "the hopes and dreams and fears
(for some dreams are nightmares) of a technically based society."
Mentions Asimov and Gerald Heard. But concludes that "our
present imagination cannot envision a new technology that of
itself, with no social implications, can interest us."

42 Weinkauf, Mary. "The God Figure in Dystopian Fiction,"
Riverside Quarterly, 4 (March 1971), 266–271.

"The dystopian dictators are dramatically conceived caricatures of
the Judeo-Christian God traditionally accepted in the British,
American, and Russian societies of the novels' audiences." The
article analyzes the characteristics of such figures in Orwell,
Huxley, Zamyatin, Hartley, C. I. Moore, Burgess, and Evelyn
Waugh.

43 Weiss, Miriam Strauss. *A Lively Corpse: Religion in Utopia.*
New York: A. S. Barnes; London: Thomas Yoseloff,
1969.

A detailed commentary upon the various aspects of religion in
the classical Utopia from More to Wells. Skinner's *Walden Two*
is the latest title mentioned. Descriptive rather than analytical.

44 Woodcock, George. "Utopias in Negative," *Sewanee
Review*, 64 (1956), 81–97.

Sketches history of Utopia, emphasizing end of the 19th century
through Huxley and Orwell. Before World War I the dystopias,
such as they were, attacked collectivist ideas. World War I
precipitated attacks upon "industrial regimentation" and the
"closer regulation of daily living." Stresses the importance of
Zamyatin's *We*, emphasizing how much Orwell and Huxley seem
to have followed it.

VI. SF: Classroom and Library

1 Arnold, John E. "SF on the Drawing Board," *Science*, 34 (September 1953), 39–43.

Condensed from *Astounding*. Outlines Arcturus IV project as MIT, in which students create, design for, and supply an imagined fourth planet of Arcturus.

2 Asimov, Isaac. "Sword of Achilles," *Bulletin of Atomic Scientists*, 19 (November 1963), 17–18.

Names self as sf writer, one of whose books has sold 400,000 copies. "A number of these have been bought by libraries, where perhaps dozens of people have read each copy." An adult art, sf is interested in the world that will develop as a result "of changes in science and technology." English teachers not interested in science or sf, but it should be made "freely available in school libraries."

3 ————. "SF: Clue to Creativity," *Library Journal*, 15 February 1964, pp. 914–917.

"Today's sf fans may be tomorrow's creative scientists." If sf is freely available and if students are not browbeaten out of reading it, it may help develop new scientists.

4 Banks, William H., Jr. "Classroom Ideas: Homework Assignments," *Science Teacher*, 29 (February 1962), 36, 39.

Made writing assignment meaningful to a ninth grade general science class by allowing them to write sf stories on the topic, "How Inertia Can Be Overcome." Includes sample themes.

5 Barron, R. Neil. "Anatomy of Wonder: A Bibliographic Guide to Science Fiction," *Choice*, 6 (January 1970), 1537–1545.

Aimed at libraries, this is the most comprehensive evaluation yet published of available resource materials. After an essay devoted primarily to hardback volumes of criticism and history, it concerns itself with "Indices and Bibliographies," "Other Reference Aids," "Major Collections," "Suppliers," and "Fanzines." Particularly valuable in these last categories.

6 Bowers, Dorothy W. "Science Fiction for College Libraries," *Choice*, 6 (June 1969), 478–483.

Stresses need for sf in college libraries; calls it "one of the kinds of books that sell, that people really read." Names Bradbury, Clarke, Heinlein.

7 Brague, Paul E. "Escapism Plus," *Library Journal*, 15 April 1968, p. 1603.

In the department, "Magazines." General commentary about sf. Lists as the best magazines *Analog*, *Galaxy*, and *Magazine of Fantasy and Science Fiction*.

8 Bulman, Learned T. "Using Science Fiction as Bait," *Library Journal*, 15 December 1955, pp. 2885–2886.

In "Junior Libraries" section. Advocates sf for school libraries. Praises Heinlein's *Red Planet*. Calls the genre "a good drawing card" and a "painless means of encouraging the use of" the science section of a library. Genre has kept some youngsters "with us" until "they have found, or we have discovered for them, more important and more lasting reading interests."

9 Cochell, Shirley. "Martians in the Classroom," *Senior Scholastic*, 6 March 1963, pp. 9T–10T.

Describes the sf classroom project she carried out: "earthmen colonizing a distant planet," with students working out all details of the world and of the landing.

10 Cooper, Jean E. "Original Science Fiction Useful in Teaching the Geologic Time Table," *American Biology Teacher*, 16 (October 1954), 17–19.

Allowed her students to write "fiction stories about prehistoric animals"; man could be present only as an observer unless he actually lived at the time. Declares the assignment successful; includes two sample themes.

11 Dodd, Alan L. "Science Fiction in the Elementary School," *Science Teacher*, 25 (December 1958), 463.

Favors student reading of sf to see how much of its science is verifiable: "intelligently interpret it in terms of scientific truths."

12 Donovan, R. M. "Bug Eyed Monsters," *Ontario Library Review*, 36 (February 1952), 28–30.

Encourages interest in sf because it records impressions of possible effects of science upon humanity "in an easily digestible form." Seems to use J. O. Bailey as source for his historical sketch of genre. Lists 25 titles.

13 Dovey, Irma. "Sister, Board That Space Ship," *Elementary English*, 31 (October 1954), 345–346.

Encourages teachers to gain knowledge of sf in order to help students interested in the field. "It is our job to help them distinguish space opera from space facts."

14 Field, Ruth R. "Browsing without the Bem's," *Alabama Librarian*, 8 (January 1957), 5–8.

A bibliography of recommended sf made up of 34 titles ranging from Mary Shelley, R. L. Stevenson, and Conan Doyle through John Campbell, Frederik Pohl, and Clifford Simak to Huxley, Orwell, James Hilton, and J. B. Priestley. Includes some anthologies. Davenport only critic named. Only Wells and Arthur C. Clarke have more than one title. Third of the Maxwell AFB papers. (See Giffin, I, 27; Lambert, II, 180.)

15 Fox, Dorothea M. "Weird Tales in the Library," *Library Journal*, 1 August 1941, pp. 652–653.

Notes new interest in fantasy as escapism, but discusses non-fiction, such titles as Seabrook's *Witchcraft*. No sf by name.

16 Gallant, Joseph. "A Proposal for the Reading of 'Scientific Fiction,' " *High Points*, 33 (April 1951), 20–27. (See II, 123.)

17 Grimsley, Juliet. "*The Martian Chronicles*: A Provocative Study," *English Journal*, 59 (December 1970), 1239–1242.

Used Bradbury's novel in a ninth grade class and here catalogues elements of his "vitriolic, satirical philosophy" expressed in "descriptively lovely prose."

18 Gross, Elizabeth H. "Science Fiction as a Factor in Science Education," *Science Education*, 43 (February 1959), 28–31.

Finds the role of sf "difficult to interpret" and therefore remains inconclusive. But it may well play a "significant role" in the motivation of "practicing and would-be" scientists.

19 Gulbin, Suzanne. "Parallels and Contrasts in *Lord of the Flies* and *Animal Farm*," *English Journal*, 55 (January 1966), 86–88.

A listing of somewhat superficial similarities between the novels. Used them in a freshman high school class during study "of social criticism in novel form."

20 Hall, H. W. "SF: The Other Side of the Coin," *Library Journal*, 15 June 1970, pp. 2240–2241.

In department, "Magazines," notices favorably sf critical magazines shown at ALA Convention in Detroit in 1970: *Luna, Extrapolation, Riverside Quarterly, SF Review,* and *SFWA Bulletin*, "the trade magazine."

21 Hanlon, Mercedes. "Needed: Science Stories for Young Readers," *School Science and Mathematics*, 58 (December 1958), 677–689.

Provides principles for such stories, complete with a "variation of root words permissible" chart. Mentions as a topic "Aboard a Space Ship," but no other sf as such.

22 Hillegas, Mark. "The Course in Science Fiction: A Hope Deferred," *Extrapolation*, 9 (December 1967), 18–21.

Based on personal experience. Accuses English Departments of an intellectual conservatism making courses devoted to sf difficult to achieve. Among the reasons for this is an anti-scientific stance taken by the discipline as a whole.

23 Hurley, Richard J. "A Librarian Looks at Science Fiction," *Publishers' Weekly*, 18 July 1953, p. 179.

In "Books on Trial" department. Objects to sf because of a "lack of standards" and because of "extraneous sex angles especially in jacket and cover illustrations." Yet it is "here to stay." Notes that 36 titles were accepted, 11 rejected.

24 ———. "Letter to the Editor," *Publishers' Weekly*, 29 August 1953, p. 747.

Notes that 27 of the 36 titles approved were juveniles; 10 of the 11 rejected, adult. He is concerned with this possible bad influence upon youngsters. Moreover, sf is "open to charges of materialism." (See VI, 23.)

25 Jenkinson, Karl. "Science Fiction in High Schools," *Wilson Library Bulletin*, 25 (October 1951), 158–159.

Repeats many of the expected remarks about sf: that it must be probable; that its origin causes its disrepute; that the best sf is "different" because of its social criticism. Lists 13 titles for school libraries.

26 Knight, Damon. "Science Fiction Basics," *Library Journal*, 1 June 1966, pp. 2777–2779.

Three brief lists of books: (1) a collection of sf titles all libraries should have; (2) supplementary list including contemporary writers; (3) critical materials.

27 Lederer, Richard. "Shaping the Dystopian Nightmare," *English Journal*, 56 (November 1967), 1132–1135.

As an assignment, he had students write a sketch of a dystopia, and read several of E. B. White's humorous pieces, such as "The Decline of Sport," as examples. Quotes from several papers. In an extended note, the final page and a half traces the rise of the word dystopia.

28 Levin, A. and A. Velikovich, "Science Fiction and the Schoolchild," *Soviet Review*, 11 (Fall 1970), 250–257.

Reports results of a questionnaire circulated by the sf fan clubs at Moscow University and in Baku, giving most attention here to those returned by seventh to tenth graders, average age 15. The actual state of science fiction is incomparably richer and more diverse than any "universal" formulations about it, and the interests of its readers are just as "diverse." One out of five schoolchildren prefers it to other genres. Calls for books that describe the history and "distinctive characteristics" of sf.

29 Livingston, Dennis. "'Science Fiction Is Valuable Means to Psychically Prepare for the Future," *Trend*, 7 (Spring 1971), 15, 26.

Much more than mere adventure fiction, sf is being used "as a way to look at future societal and technological alternatives." It is therefore valuable not only as a part of an English curriculum but also in the natural and social sciences.

30 ———. "Science Fiction in the Teaching of Futurology," in *Proceedings of the First General Assembly of the World Future Society*, ed. Edward Cornish, forthcoming.

Explains how teachers of courses about the future may use sf as a source of predictions of the possible outcomes of present trends; as a source of speculations on issues directly relevant to the futures field; and as a source of imaginative experiences that can be used to simulate possible futures.

31 ———. "Science Fiction as an Educational Tool," in *Learning 21*, ed. Alvin Toffler. New York: Random House, forthcoming.

Analyzes sf as a literature that explores problems of forecasting, postulates alternative societies, and describes technology-related public policy issues, and thus may be used to enhance both cognitive and affective modes of education.

32 McCauley, Virginia C. "'Out of This World': A Bibliography of Space Literature for Boys and Girls," *Elementary English*, 36 (February 1959), 98–101.

Almost no commentary; listing divided equally between "Space Information" and "Space Fantasy." Heinlein and Andre Norton have most titles, eight each.

33 McCreight, Cathryn. "Hardware," *Colloquy*, 4 (May 1971), 46–47.

Recommends a variety of books, both fiction and criticism of sf.

34 McCusker, Lauretta G. "Creative Teaching Through Fiction," *Education*, 77 (January 1957), 276–280.

On teaching history through novels; science also may use "historical science fiction that interprets the life of primitive man such as the anthropological stories of cave men." Notices "new" sf by such authors as Heinlein and Asimov, which makes reader "think regarding problems social and scientific."

35 Madsen, Alan L. "That Starlit Corridor," *English Journal*, 53 (September 1964), 405–412.

Suggests that English teachers have failed to concern themselves with science, personally or academically. Then describes a project that he undertook with his ninth grade class.

36 Marshak, Alexander. "How Kids Get Interested in Science," *Library Journal*, 15 April 1958, pp. 13–15.

In "Children's and Young People's Libraries." Finds sf "false psychologically and inept scientifically"; therefore, it is not the best influence, for it does not lead to the "deeper purpose of science—unravelling step by step the patterns of reality." Because we know the patterns of the "major phenomena," there is a need for synthesis, integration, simplification of ideas.

37 Marshall, David F. "The Great Curriculum in the Sky," *Colloquy*, 4 (May 1971), 32–33.

"Religious educators ignore sf at a loss to their calling and perhaps to the church's future." Finds in it three notable themes: "the search for order in the universe even in the face of catastrophe, the quest for self-understanding and a rapprochment with injustice, and the pursuit of wholeness which balances man's scientific thinking with religious emotion. . . ." Ends by sketching a possible class that might be conducted by the church.

38 Mooney, Ernest W., Jr. "An Untapped Dimension in
   Fiction," *Virginia Journal of Education*, 47 (December
   1953), 20–21.

   Advocates the use of sf in the classroom. Feels that he cannot
   "deprive" his students of the sf titles that he knows are "good
   reading, as well as good writing."

39 Moore, Robert E. "Science Fiction in a Junior College
   Reading Program," *Journal of Reading*, 9 (April 1966),
   329–332.

   Suggests sf for "The Student Who Doesn't Like to Read,"
   particularly if he is "truly technical-minded." Gives data, based
   on the Flesch formula, regarding ease-of-reading in the genre.
   Calls Clarke and Heinlein the "best contemporary counterparts"
   of Verne.

40 Murray, Tony and Roger Mansfield, eds. *Fantasy, Fiction
   and Fact.* Glasgow: Blackie & Sons, 1965.

   Intended as a text, with lists of suggested reading in sf and
   sociology, this anthology includes short stories and excerpts from
   novels. Ranges from Huxley and Wyndham to Michael Young
   and Alan Sillitoe. Each story is followed by a commentary by the
   editors and discussion questions for class use. [Wollheim]

41 Panshin, Alexei. "Books in the Field: Science Fiction,"
   Wilson Library Bulletin, 44 (February 1970), 616–620.

   Lists 35 "best" contemporary titles; names Delany and Zelazny
   as the "current paragons"; and suggests that current writers
   realize that "the science of which they write is only a metaphor."
   Does not deal with criticism, but does mention several library
   collections.

42 ———. "A Basic Science Fiction Collection," *Library Journal*, 15 June 1970, pp. 2223–2227.

Presents a collection "representative of creative fantasy of the last century" chosen by a committee of eight members of SFWA. Speaks of fantasy as a "minor tradition" in European literature, and suggests that its isolation in the American specialist magazines has prevented U.S. recognition. (Reprinted in *Colloquy*; see VI, 44.)

43 ———. "Science Fiction Bibliography and Criticism," *American Libraries*, 1 (October 1970), 884–885.

Intended as an introduction to the field, article notices the growing academic interest in sf. Emphasizes sf as an "expanding form"; lists a bibliography of 17 titles.

44 ———. "A Basic Science Fiction Collection," *Colloquy*, 4 (May 1971), 13–25.

Reprint of the article in 15 June 1970 *Library Journal*. (See VI, 42.)

45 Porges, I. "Mathematics Motivated Through Science Fiction," *School Science and Mathematics*, 56 (January 1956), 1–4.

Highly general and inconclusive, seeking ways sf can be of aid to the teacher in presenting ideas.

46 Russ, Joanna. "Communique from the Front: Teaching and the State of the Art," *Colloquy*, 4 (May 1971), 28–31.

Discusses a class she taught at Cornell in 1969. Asimov's "Nightfall" is named as the favorite story; Clarke's *Childhood's End* as the favorite novel. Praises Samuel R. Delany's *Einstein Intersection* at length. Speculates about the future of sf, stressing that its "intellectual content" is greater than other fiction in addition to its having the sense of wonder. Ends with the list of books she used, and those she would now add.

47 Schwartz, Sheila. "The World of Science Fiction," *NYS English Record*, 21 (February 1971), 27–40. (See II, 262.)

48 "Science Fiction for Young Adults: A Selected Book List," *Top of the News*, 18 (December 1961), 44–46.

Merely lists 30 books, annotated as to contents and plot line, without any critical evaluation.

49 Scoggins, Margaret C. "The Outlook Tower: Science Fiction Roundup," *Horn Book*, 31 (June 1955), 220–222.

Synopses of 12 plots.

50 Scott, Alan. "Science Fiction Best Seller," *Instructor*, 77 (March 1968), 59.

Reports on both a school book sale in which fifth grade ten-year-olds bought 400 copies of sf in 3 days and a writing project with fourth graders in which groups no larger than 5 each wrote a chapter of a novel.

51 Sewell, Margaret and Martha Irwin. "Satellite Stimulates Science Fiction Stories," *Florida Libraries*, 8 (December 1957), 11.

Calls sf a "respectable form of literature," although only a few titles merit a place in libraries. Repeats usual points in rationalizing why librarians should be "thoroughly informed" about the genre.

52 Simpson, D. J. "Analogists," *Assistant Librarian*, 53 (December 1960), 233–237.

Intended to acquaint librarians with the genre, article sketches the types of sf story but gives way to Simpson's conviction that sf has helped its readers to want to "numerate" (a word coined by a Ministry of Education report); that is, it has made them want to "understand the scientific approach to the study of phenomena and to think quantitatively," characteristics essential in the modern world.

53 Sister Mary Bennet. "Science Fact or Fiction: Which—
and Why?" *Catholic Library World*, 25 (March 1954),
179–181.

Report of an "experiment to verify a hunch" that high school
students, especially those headed for college, prefer reading science
fact to sf. Students from a senior physics course and a junior
chemistry course were given 10 pairs of books to read. Results
verify the popularity of science fact; implication is that the
better students prefer science fact.

54 Smith, Charles C. "Science Fiction: Asset or Liability?"
Science Teacher, 5 (October 1953), pp. 233–235.

Resents having sf coupled with comics and dismissed; teacher
must "have vision" to see that if books are wisely selected, sf
can be used "for motivating and teaching."

55 Solomon, Stanley. "Science Fiction for the Space Age,"
Scholastic Teacher, 21 (January 1966), 20–21.

Would promote the use of sf in the classroom. The real world
so full for students that "ordinary fiction" cannot attract them.
Finds sf "as much concerned" with the present as the future.

56 Stockton, H. G. "Science Fiction Today," *Assistant Librarian*,
47 (August 1954), 124–126.

A general article which sketches the history of sf since 1926 and
cites various judgments of it. Most important, Stockton rejects
Heinlein's assertion that its scientific content must be "valid."
Instead, sf should also be judged "by those qualities of exposition,
motivation, syntax, 'readability,' and so on, by which we normally
judge creative writing."

57 Weaver, Edward K. and Elfred Black, "The Relationship
of Science Fiction Reading to Reasoning Abilities,"
Science Education, 49 (April 1965), 293-296.

Based on Black's M.A. thesis for Atlanta University (1959).
Problem: to discover how sf reading affected "the ability of a

selected group of secondary school pupils to reason and use scientific knowledge to solve problems." Results did not show that reading sf measurably influenced "the structure of reasoning abilities as measured by the STEP science test." Instead, as opposed to the scientific method, sf reading fosters "creative, inductive, imaginative, and holistic or organismic" behavior so that its readers may develop "two thinking behavior patterns," one for sf reading and one for the "formal science classroom." Calls for more tests.

58 Wells, Lester G. *Fictional Accounts of Trips to the Moon.* Syracuse, N. Y.: Syracuse University Press, 1962.

A pamphlet giving brief descriptions, with illustrations, of books in the Syracuse library holdings. Gives summaries of the stories, including Lucian, Joseph Atterley's *Voyage to the Moon* (1827), Poe, Verne, and Wells.

59 Williams, Paul. "Science Fiction Magazines," *Library Journal*, 15 December 1962, pp. 17–19.

In "Children's and Young People's Libraries." The fourteen-year-old author discusses sf generally, citing Martha Foley's use of sf stories in her short story annual. Names 9 magazines in the field, 3 of them British.

60 Williamson, Jack. "Science Fiction Comes to College," *Extrapolation*, 12 (May 1971), 67–78.

A brief discussion of the increased academic interest in the field, followed by an annotated listing of some 70 courses offered at the college and university levels during the academic year 1970–1971.

61 ————. "Science Fiction: Emerging from Its Exile in Limbo," *Publishers' Weekly*, 5 July 1971, pp. 17–20.

Excellent survey of the new academic interest in sf, stressing new courses, critical materials, and library collections as well as the increased interest of trade publishers. Sets this discussion in the context of the development of the genre over the past century; emphasizes the "conflicting ideas that still motivate much science fiction . . . the optimistic faith that applied human reason can create a better world [and the] pessimistic implication that even the most perfect world is not forever." Believes that "with very few taboos, science fiction can deal with nearly every social and moral and technical problem that the human race must meet, from nearly any point of view."

62 Woolever, John D. "Science Fiction for Science Students," *Science Education*, 35 (December 1951), 284–286.

Believes sf can be used in classroom after the teacher determines if "the story has anything worthwhile of scientific value, whether it be facts, applications, phenomena, or philosophy." If regular sf writers do not fill the need, "our scientists and science teachers" should perhaps "write the types of stories we need"—stories meant to "inspire and entertain" the younger readers.

VII. SF: Publishing

1 Ashmead, Lawrence P. "Specialized Needs at Doubleday:
   Mystery-Suspense and Science Fiction," *Writer*,
   82 (May 1969), 23–24.

   General suggestions to writers submitting Mss. to Doubleday:
   of science fiction—"The range is from pure fantasy through the
   classic space opera to the introspective psychological novel."
   Emphasizes the concept of the single assumption and the problems
   faced by the writer who must create a completely unknown
   world for his readers.

2 Asimov, Isaac. "Other Worlds to Conquer," *Writer*,
   64 (1951), 148–151.

   Accepts as the "best" definition that which calls sf "that branch
   of literature which is concerned with the impact of scientific
   advance upon human beings." Stresses that the genre deals
   "first and foremost with human beings" who are "subjected to
   an alien environment." Also emphasizes that "the jargon of the s-f
   story is science," though this does not mean the writer must
   have technical training or a college degree. Closes with six general
   suggestions to the writer, of which only "Don't contradict a
   known scientific fact" is unique to sf.

3 ———. "S-F Market Still Healthy," *Writer*, 69 (August 1956), 218.

Letter to the editor, answering Richard A. Lupoff's article in the May issue. Speaks of the " 'boom' of 1950-53" being over, but points out that new sf magazines are being planned (See Lupoff, VII, 18.)

4 ———. "Imagination in Orbit," *Writer*, 74 (March 1961), 16–18, 37.

Suggests sf to new writer. It concerns itself with "the impact of scientific and technological advance upon human beings." Asserts that "the jargon of the sf story is science." Lists seven rules of thumb.

5 ———. "Imagination in Orbit," in *The Writer's Handbook*, ed. A. S. Burack. Boston: The Writer, Inc., 1966, pp. 309–315.

Reprint of article from *Writer*, March, 1961. (See VII, 3.)

6 "Avoid 'Typhoid Mary,' Editors Warned," *Publishers' Weekly*, 6 September 1952, p. 915.

Alfred Bester, Theodore Sturgeon, and Martin Greenberg (Gnome Press) were the speakers at the Editors' Lunch Club on 20 August. Bester warned book publishers that they "face the same dilemma" sf magazines did twenty years earlier and that they are mistaken if they think that all the public wants is "erotic stimulation" reflected in suggestive stories and cover art work which he termed the "Typhoid Mary" variety. To keep ahead of science, Sturgeon suggested, sf writers must "turn to philosophy and psychology." Greenberg asked how a book publisher can compete with the sf magazines which pay up to $1200 for a 70,000 word story while all he can advance is $500. Notes that sf book sales have increased from an average of 1500 copies to 4000 copies a title. But booksellers "are afraid of science fiction," ordering very small quantities.

7 Campbell, John W., Jr. "Science Fact: *Science Fiction,*" *Writer,* 77 (August 1964), 26–27.

Gives requirements for *Analog* stories. Only taboo: "no point in offending any one or any group without purpose. . . . Sex as genetics is another matter." Asks for nonfiction pieces. The genre explores "just beyond the borders of current science." Novels to be no more than 120,000 words; stories, no more than 18,000. Payment 3 or 4 cents a word, with readers' opinion finally deciding higher rate. Likes concept of hero; asks if current writers are "afraid to write of men bigger and better than themselves."

8 ———. "Science Fiction We Can Buy," *Writer,* 81 (September 1968), 27–28.

Advises persons submitting Mss. to *Analog.* Although he cannot "tell you" the difference between sf and fantasy or what sf is, those persons "who don't know the difference between science fiction and fantasy" waste everyone's time and effort by submitting to *Analog,* whose readers "want nothing but science fiction." As a major criterion for the stories, he asks for a genuine hero with a real purpose, a hero with whom readers can pleasurably identify; and he reminds would-be-authors that "Sex in suburbia—or elsewhere—is *not* the only motivating force in a real yarn."

9 Christopher, John. "Not What-If But How-He," *Writer,* 81 (November 1968), 15–17.

All stories should show the "reaction to the environment of the characters concerned." Divides sf into two traditions: "The Old English" (Wells, Wyndham) and the "Far Out (New American)," in which the writers are "dwarfed by the gadgets" and by the "details of a background completely unknown" (Cordwainer Smith and Zelazny). Uses his *Little People* for discussion of how he/one plans a novel. An author must keep control of his material, but how profound his questions and answers are finally determines the merit of the work.

10 Darrach, Brad. "Back to the Gore of Yore," *Time*,
    5 July 1971, pp. 70–71.

> Describes the success Bantam has had in reprinting 61 of the 181
> *Doc Savage* titles. Ten and a half million copies in print have
> realized "about $4.5 million in sales." Sketchy on Lester Dent,
> the author, and essentially satirical in tone toward "The Man
> of Bronze," who is a "funhouse mirror of the America that loved
> him and apparently still does—a big square joe with the body
> of Charles Atlas, the brain of Thomas Edison, and the implacable
> innocence of Mickey Mouse." Yet he admits that "as stories
> most of them are bloody good."

11 Eshbach, Floyd, ed. *Of Worlds Beyond: The Science of
    Science Fiction Writing*. Chicago: Advent, 1964.

> First published in 1947, this is a symposium intended for would-be
> writers of sf. Campbell, de Camp, Heinlein, "Doc" Smith,
> John Taine, vanVogt, and Williamson discuss the ingredients
> and methods they feel are essential to the genre. It remains of
> historical interest because it represents the view held after the War
> on the eve of the first widespread interest in the genre.

12 Estrade, Jackie. "The Science Fiction Market," *Writer's
    Digest*, 49 (April 1969), 48–52.

> Concentrates upon the views of Campbell and Pohl. Closes with
> Harry Harrison's list of the seven most common faults in works by
> beginning writers.

13 Harrison, Harry. "Science Fiction: Short Story and Novel,"
    Writer, 83 (May 1970), 16–18.

> While sf "is *not* about science," its writer must be a "fan" of
> science. He must be "humanistic" and "must feel man is
> perfectible." Stresses that sf is "idea-oriented" and that its reader
> enters a "wholly new and logical world."

14 Kauffman, Stanley. "1953: Year of the Blast Off,"
   Publishers' Weekly, 19 December 1953, pp. 2393–2396.

   Surveys publication of sf, especially in paperback, since World
   War II. Cites Donald Wollheim's *Book of Science Fiction* as
   one of the first notable paperbacks. Up to 1950 the outstanding
   sales were of A. Merritt's novels, of which *Burn, Witch, Burn*
   sold half a million copies. "About 1950" the tide changed in
   favor of sf because of such factors as the Doubleday and Simon &
   Schuster programs, the appearance of such a writer as Ray
   Bradbury, and the selection of Max Ehrlich's *Big Eye* by a book
   club. "By keeping in balance the growing importance of s-f"
   the paperback publishers "can do a great deal to keep it growing
   and to help gifted writers build a body of books which need
   ask concessions from no one."

15 Kuttner, Henry. "Selling the Fantasy Story," *Writer's
   Digest*, 18 (March 1938), 29–33.

   Emphasizes need for characterization; whether on Mars or in the
   fourth dimension, the characters will have "problems, desires,
   motives similar to present-day ones." He has found "desire for lost
   treasure" and "sex perversion—sadism (dangerous stuff; handle
   with care)" the most useful motivation. Insists "eeriness" is
   essential and may be achieved through "atmosphere, characterization, menace, situation, or a combination."

16 ———. "Selling Science Fiction," *Writer's Digest*,
   19 (October 1939), 34–38.

   Suggests sf "today" follows Wellsian formulas, but emphasizes
   than an adventure story set on another planet is not adequate.
   Some stories "are chiefly psychological in treatment and
   development"; thus, characterization is always important, as is
   novelty and logic. Takes examples from his own and other recent
   stories. Lists 9 magazines as the core of the market.

17 Leinster, Murray. "Writing Science Fiction Today," *Writer*, 81 (May 1968), 16–18.

Discursive. Once sf was only "fantastic places and incredible events," but even then sf not "worse than the standard stuff edited and composed for an educated public." Ninety percent of Poe inferior; *Frankenstein* one of the worst-written tales ever put into print." Very small percentage of "all printed matter" is a permanent contribution to literature. Suggests that Sputnik "changed" all sf. Calls it as "distinct a genre as satire or comedy or farce."

18 Lupoff, Richard A. "From Our Rostrum: What's Left of the Science Fiction Market," *Writer*, 69 (May 1956), 165–167.

"Boom" of early 1950's led 31 magazines, "the great majority . . . heavy with *avant garde* social science fiction." Decline followed because of over-expansion of the field, poor quality of sf. Quotes Howard Browne: sf "was no longer fun to read . . . fiction of the future no longer concerns itself with *heroes*, but *victims*." Lists fourteen magazines still publishing. (See Asimov, VII, 3.)

19 McComas, J. Francis. "The Spaceman's Little Nova," *New York Times Book Review*, 20 November 1955, p. 53.

Suggests "boomlet" in sf over. Part of trouble was that publishers knew nothing of sf or its writers, but the chief problem in sf publishing has been "its silly preoccupation with the anthology." Eighty-three anthologies between 1949 and 1954. But there does remain "a splendid group of younger writers" who promise to sustain "a faint and steady glow" with their fiction.

20 Malec, Alexander B. "Science Fiction Characters," *Writer*, 82 (August 1969), 19–21.

Asserts that "a good chunk of sf smells" and "reader involvement is almost nil." Exhorts the young writer to "write till the real you emerges. . . . Write. For one of you" will create "the *Moby Dick*" of sf. Makes fun of characterization in the older stories, insisting that now "we" characterize.

21 "Media Information," *Publishers' Weekly*, 21 February 1953, p. 961.

Announces that Hugo Gernsback has launched *Science Fiction +* on the 27th anniversary of the first sf magazine. Sam Moskowitz is to be managing editor; gives table of contents.

22 Meek, Captain S.P. "The Pseudo-Scientific Story," *Writer's Digest*, 11 (May 1931), 37-39.

Describes the ingredients in the formula for the "pseudo-scientific yarn," the most popular of which is "the inter-planetary yarn," Advises, "once on a new planet, let your imagination run wild." Aliens need not resemble humans, while a girl and hordes of monsters should usually be "found," thus giving "the thread of romance." Names the lost-race story and the super-scientific detective as other established formulas. But the author "who wants to keep both feet on the ground will have the earth invaded by monsters from space." A caption identifies Meek as the author of 18 "Pseudo-Scientific Stories" published in "Various National Magazines."

23 "Overtaking the Future," *Newsweek*, 8 October 1962, p. 104.

Special issue: "The Space Age." Seems rewrite of earlier articles. Estimates U.S. science fiction audience at 500,000 and blames recent decline on "state of puerile space novels." Nothing on sf as literature, though anyone "wanting to look more than 10 years ahead" must have acquaintance with sf.

24 Purdom, Tom. "The Medium and the Marketplace," *Colloquy*, 4 (May 1971), 34-36.

Suggests that a new reader start with the anthologies; sketches the various forms of publication of sf, emphasizing the magazines. Ends by insisting upon the diversity within sf.

25 "Science Fiction Rockets into the Big Time in Entertainment," *Business Week*, 20 October 1951, pp. 82–84.

Brief discussion of films and TV. Refers to sf "pulps . . . limping along since 1920, but it has not been until recently that circulation showed any real gain." Quotes H. L. Gold's assertion of 100,000 to 125,000 for *Galaxy*. Traces increase in interest to Hiroshima.

26 Williamson, Jack. "As I Knew Hugo," *Extrapolation*, 11 (May 1970), 53–55.

A brief account of Williamson's experience as a writer for Gernsback's magazines. Suggests Gernsback saw the fictional elements as a sugar-coating for an instructional process. Gernsback belonged among the optimistic disciples of the culture of science.

27 ———. "Science Fiction: Emerging from Its Exile in Limbo," *Publishers' Weekly*, 5 July 1971, pp. 17–20. (See VI, 61.)

VIII. SF: Specialist Bibliographies, Checklists, and Indices

1 Andrews, Carolyn and Thomas D. Clareson. "Aldous Huxley: A Bibliography," *Extrapolation*, 6 (December 1964), 2–21.

Eighty-eight entries supplement the 1961 bibliography by Claire John Eschelbach and Joyce Lee Shober. (See VIII, 16.)

2 Bleiler, Everett P., ed. *The Checklist of Fantastic Literature: A Bibliography of Fantasy, Weird, and Science Fiction Books Published in the English Language*. Chicago: Shasta, 1948.

Lists 5000 titles, British and American, from medieval period to 1947. Main listing by author is indexed by title. An "annotated list of critical and historical reference works," some 65 titles, focuses upon the Gothic and 19th century.

3 Cameron, Alastair. *Fantasy Classification System*. St. Vital, Manitoba: Canadian Science Fiction Assn., 1952.

Attempts to classify (on Dewey Decimal System) the subjects of fantasy and sf stories. The *System* is actually a detailed description and definition of the genre of fantastic literature. [Lerner]

189

4 Clareson, Thomas D. "An Annotated Checklist of American
Science Fiction: 1880–1915," *Extrapolation*,
1 (December 1959), 2–20.

Lists some 150 titles, mostly novels, identifying them by
motif. A brief note, "Major Trends in American Science Fiction:
1880–1915," introduces the "Checklist."

5 ———. "An Annotated Bibliography of Critical Materials
Dealing with Science Fiction," *Extrapolation*, 11 (May
1970), 56–83; 12 (December 1970), 35–59;
12 (May 1971), 109–145.

The original form of this volume, with a listing by authors only.
The May 1970 installment included some coverage of
Continental materials.

6 Clareson, Thomas D. and Edward S. Lauterbach. "A
Checklist of Articles Dealing with Science Fiction,"
Extrapolation, 1 (May 1960), 29–34.

An annotated listing of some 40 articles dealing with sf.

7 Clarke, I. F. *The Tale of the Future: From the Beginning
to the Present Time*. London: The Library Association, 1961.

Main listing is chronological, with annotations, from 1644 to
1960. Also short title and author listings. Of some 1200 titles only
13 date before 1871. Clarke divides the "Tale of the Future"
into three basic types: Utopia (dystopia), primarily philosophical
in its aim; political, "taken up with immediate problems in the
area of national or international affairs"; and scientific romance,
"for the most part stories of adventure and wonder according
to the pattern that Wells was the first to trace successfully." (A
second, expanded edition is being prepared for publication.)

8 Cockcroft, T. G. L. *Index to Weird Fiction Magazines.*
Lower Hutt, New Zealand: T. G. L. Cockcroft, 1962–1964.
2 vols. Vol. 1: "Index by Title," 1962; Vol. 2,
"Index by Author," 1964.

Bulk of these mimeographed pamphlets is given over to 279
issues of *Weird Tales* from 1923 to 1954, although 7 other
magazines associated with H. P. Lovecraft and his circle are also
included. [Lerner]

9 Cole, Walter P. *A Checklist of Science Fiction Anthologies.*
Brooklyn, N. Y.: W. R. Cole, 1964.

Lists and indexes 227 English-language sf anthologies published
between 1927 and 1963. The books contain over 2600 stories.
[Lerner]

10 Crawford, Joseph H., Jr., ed. *333: A Bibliography of the
Science-Fantasy Novel.* Providence, R. I.: Grandon, 1953.

Provides plot resumés of 333 British and American novels,
primarily from the 1930's and 1940's, although a few are older
and rarer. Identifies them by motif.

11 Day, Bradford M. *The Complete Checklist of Science-
Fiction Magazines.* Woodhaven, N. Y.: Science-Fiction &
Fantasy Publishers, 1961.

A listing of periodicals that published "science-fiction, fantasy,
fantastic adventure, and weird tales," covering the period 1892 to
1960. It is international in scope, but information on non-English
titles is often spotty. Listings are arranged alphabetically under
original title of magazine. [Lerner]

12 ———. *The Supplemental Checklist of Fantastic Literature.*
New York and Denver: Science Fiction & Fantasy
Publishers, 1963.

This lists some 3000 titles not included in Bleiler's *Checklist.* Its
arrangement is similar to Bleiler's, although no appendix or
bibliography of critical materials is given.

13 ———. *The Checklist of Fantastic Literature in Paper-bound Books*. New York and Denver: Science-Fiction and Fantasy Publishers, 1965.

This lists English-language (British, American, Canadian, Australian) "paper-backed books with a sufficient tinge of the supernatural or super-scientific as to warrant placement in the science-fantasy field." It is arranged alphabetically by author and indexed by title.

14 Day, Donald B. *Index to the Science-Fiction Magazines 1926–1950*. Cambridge, Mass.: MIT Science Fiction Society, 1961.

Provides an index to all isues of 58 specialist magazines. Main listing is by author; second by title. Concerns itself only with English-language titles; nothing is included from European magazines. (See Strauss, VIII, 36.)

15 Emmons, Winfred S., Jr. "A Bibliography of H. P. Lovecraft," *Extrapolation*, 3 (December 1961), 2–25.

Not annotated. Covers Lovecraft's fiction, essays, and poetry, as well as critical materials about his work, most of these from "little" or specialist magazines.

16 Eschelbach, Claire John and Joyce Lee Shober. *Aldous Huxley: A Bibliography 1916–1959*. Berkeley and Los Angeles: University of California Press, 1961.

Presents all of Huxley's writings during the period, including reviews and newspaper contributions, as well as an excellent listing of works about him. Contains both name and title indices. (See Andrews, VIII, 1.)

17 Franson, Donald. *A History of the Hugo, Nebula, and International Fantasy Awards*. Dearborn Heights, Mich.: Sciencefiction Sales, 1969.

Following a brief history of conventions and each award, lists the winners and nominees in all categories, both professional and "fan," from 1951 through 1969.

18 Gernsback, Hugo. *Evolution of Modern Science Fiction.*
Chicago: World Science Fiction Convention, 1952.

Mimeographed pamphlet distributed at the World Science Fiction
Convention. In the introduction Gernsback accepts the role of
the "father of science fiction." Valuable for its bibliography
of stories published in such magazines as *Modern Electric, Science
and Invention,* and *Radio News* between 1911 and 1925.

19 Hall, H. W. *Science Fiction Book Review Index*: *Pilot
Issue* (*1969*). Bryan, Tex.: H. W. Hall, 1970.

First of a series of annual indices that will index the reviews in
the "professional sf magazines, library journals, and some of the
more widely circulated fanzines." Will draw from at least 16
journals. Arranged both by author and by title.

20 ———. *Science Fiction Book Review Index*: *1970.* Bryan,
Tex.: H. W. Hall, 1971.

Contains the listing of reviews for 1970.

21 Heins, Henry Hardy, ed. *A Golden Anniversary Bibliography of Edgar Rice Burroughs.* West Kingston, R. I.:
Donald M. Grant, 1964 (rev. ed.).

Valuable for such items as the chronological listing of stories in
McClurg and the reprinting of a variety of short articles, such
as Burroughs's "Tarzan Theme" from *Writer's Digest* (June
1932). But reprints everything, from a selection of illustrations
and dust jackets to advertisements for the books. Names "Carter of
the Red Planet" (1912) as the first story published, and calls
the Mars series the "golden age of scientific romance."

22 Hillegas, Mark. "A Bibliography of Secondary Materials
on Jules Verne," *Extrapolation,* 2 (December 1960), 5–16.

Lists 69 books and articles, most in English, although a few
European titles are included.

23 ———. "An Annotated Bibliography of Jules Verne's *Voyages Extraordinaires*," *Extrapolation*, 3 (May 1962), 32–47.

Listing by date of publication, sketches plots of 64 books by Verne, giving both the French and English titles.

24 ———. "Science Fiction as Satire: A Selected Bibliography," *Satire Newsletter*, 1 (Fall 1963), 20–22.

Defines sf as a "species of Utopian fantasy which describes an imaginary, non-existent world"; it differs from the classic Utopia in its dependence upon "action (character and plot)" instead of upon the blueprint of an ideal world. Lists 20 novels, 30 stories from sf magazines.

25 ———. "The Clarkson Collection of Science Fiction at Harvard," *Extrapolation*, 5 (December 1963), 2–14.

Description of one of the largest library collections: 2000 books and every issue of over 100 magazines. (Professor Hillegas may well have been the last person to examine the collection. Because of its supposed fragility, no one may now have access to it, and funds do not exist for microfilming.)

26 Lewis, Arthur O., Jr. "The Anti-Utopian Novel: Preliminary Notes and Checklist," *Extrapolation*, 2 (May 1961), 27–32.

Brief definition of term, suggesting three categories: anti-totalitarian, anti-technological, and satiric (or combinations). Followed by annotations to 34 titles, mostly from 1950's, but a few as early as Kipling and Chesterton.

27 Manson, Margaret, ed. *Item Forty-Three. Brian W. Aldiss: A Bibliography 1954–1962*. Birmingham: The Dryden Press, n.d.

Annotated by Aldiss himself, the bibliography lists his fiction first by title and then place of publication. 122 stories in 9 years.

Also included are the anthologies he edited, and perhaps most important, a listing of his critical articles, many of which appeared in *The Bookseller*. Unfortunately only 500 copies of this book were printed.

28 Negley, Glenn R. *The Duke University Utopia Collection.* Durham, N. C.: Friends of Duke University Library, 1965.

A listing of some 1200 titles, with some annotation as to content. The collection has given "some particular attention to utopian works in Spanish or South American literature." Main listing is by author, giving full bibliographical data; a chronological listing by authors' names only follows. The works date from 1495 to present. In 1967 a *Supplement* was issued.

29 Owings, Mark and Jack L. Chalker. *The Index to the Science-Fantasy Publishers*: *A Bibliography of the Science Fiction and Fantasy Specialty Houses.* Baltimore: The Anthem Series, 1966.

Includes all publishers "whose output was limited exclusively" to sf or fantasy, "who published at least one hardbound book." Publishers listed alphabetically, each described, with an annotated, chronological listing of their publications.

30 Post, Jeremiah B. "Toward an Atlas of Fantasy," Special Libraries Association: Geography and Map Division, *Bulletin*, no. 75 (March 1969), pp. 11–13.

Discusses the problems of collecting and making an atlas of maps of imaginary lands.

31 ————. "The Bibliophile and the Spaceship," *The Private Library*. 2nd Ser. 3 (Autumn 1970), 120–125.

Discusses problems of collecting sf, with emphasis upon Arkham House and Advent titles.

32 Roemer, Kenneth M. "American Utopian Literature (1888–1900): An Annotated Bibliography," *American Literary Realism*, 4 (Summer 1971), 227–255.

A selective bibliography, it nevertheless triples the number of American Utopias described in any previous bibliography. Stresses the range and diversity of these concepts, though noting they all blended "realism and idealism." The notorious lack of literary quality arose from the authors being, by and large, amateurs who were more interested in conveying ideas than telling a story. Lists titles by the year published; includes some secondary materials; and omits all foreign titles.

33 Scholl, Ralph. "Science Fiction: A Selected Check-List," *Bulletin of Bibliography*, 22 (January–April 1958), 114–115.

Listing of critical articles on sf, called "exhaustive between September 29, 1928, and May 12, 1956." Defines sf as "that imaginative fiction which is the result of extrapolations that take into account the so-called natural laws." No listing of fiction.

34 Sieman, Frederick. *Science Fiction Story Index 1950–1968*. Chicago: American Library Association, 1971.

Lists stories by author and title, keying them to the anthologies in which the stories appear. Of some value, but unfortunately information is fragmented, incomplete, and tends to duplicate work already done by specialist bibliographies (some of which may not be generally available).

35 Stone, Graham. *Australian Science Fiction Index 1925–1967*. Canberra: Australian Science Fiction Association, 1968.

Revision of an earlier *Index* issued in 1964. Lists sf magazines and books published in Australia, excluding many British editions of American magazines. Listing is by author and by title.

36 Strauss, Erwin S. *The MIT Science Fiction Society's Index to the S-F Magazines 1951–1965.* Cambridge, Mass.: MIT Science Fiction Society, 1966.

Indexes all issues of 100 sf magazines from January 1951 through December 1965. Brings Day's earlier *Index* up to date, since annual supplements are issued. Three listings: alphabetically and chronologically by magazine; by title; and by author. Does not include stories in any foreign language. (See Day, VIII, 14.)

37 Sweetzer, Wesley D. "Arthur Machen: A Bibliography of Writings about Him," *English Literature in Transition*, 11 (1968), 1–33.

The most complete listing, yet assembled of critical appraisals and bibliographical materials with annotations. Particularly valuable for the contemporary reviews of Machen's works.

38 Teitler, Stuart A. "A Projected Bibliography: 'By the World Forgot,' " *Extrapolation*, 12 (May 1971), 106–108.

Describes Teitler's efforts to annotate a bibliography of all "lost race" novels of the 19th and 20th centuries. Calls the motif "an example of off-trial fantasy which borders on science fiction" and notes Rider Haggard's influence upon its evolution.

39 Tuck, Donald H. *A Handbook of Science Fiction and Fantasy.* Hobart, Tasmania: Donald H. Tuck, 1959 (2nd ed.).

A dictionary covering sf and fantasy authors, editors, artists, books, magazines, films, societies. Gives brief biographical information for authors; otherwise the entries are concerned with bibliographical data.

40 Viggiano, Michael and David Franson. *Science Fiction Title Changes.* The National Fantasy Fan Federation, 1965.

An alphabetical listing of English-language sf stories appearing under two or more titles. No bibliographical data given; no listing by author. [Lerner]

41 West, Richard C. "An Annotated Bibliography of Tolkien Criticism," *Extrapolation*, 10 (December 1968), 17–49.

Contains the critical entries of the volume, same title, later published by Kent State University Press.

42 ———. *Tolkien Criticism: An Annotated Bibliography.* Kent, Ohio: Kent State University Press, 1970.

By far the most complete bibliography of Tolkien materials yet published: 36 titles by Tolkien, 198 critical items, and extensive reviews of 9 titles.

IX. SF: The Contemporary Scene

1 Aldiss, Brian. *The Shape of Further Things: Speculations on Change.* Garden City, N. Y.: Doubleday, 1971.

Autobiographical in nature, this gives invaluable insight into Aldiss's concerns and, therefore, his themes. It is laced with discussions of sf, ranging from theory to a report of a fan convention. For example, "Science fiction is a particular form of fantasy; although, with regard to form and expression, it generally clings to a somewhat faded realism, in content it comes remarkably close to dream, combining as it does both ancient and modern myth-ingredients."

2 "Arthur C. Clarke: he's so far out, he's in," *Forbes,* 15 April 1967, p. 75.

In section called "Faces Behind the Figures." Brief biographical sketch, including a few of Clarke's predictions.

3 Ash, Lee. "WLB Biography—Ray Bradbury," *Wilson Library Bulletin,* 39 (November 1964), 268, 280.

Little biographical material; primarily quotes from newspapers and magazines concerning each of Bradbury's books.

4 Ballard, J. G. "J. G. Ballard," *Books and Bookmen,* 15 (July 1970), 6.

Denies the influence of any "literary" writer on his own works. Reads "what I term 'invisible literature'": finds his own major interests in the "bizarre verbal collages taken from fashion magazines, weapons, technology, stock market reports and so on." In contrast, for him, most British and American novelists "have nothing of interest to say whatever." He finds Asimov superior to Elizabeth Bowen and believes that sf is "the true literature of the 20th century."

5 Bernstein, Jeremy. "Out of the Ego Chamber," *New Yorker*, 9 August 1969, pp. 40–46, 51–65.

One of the "Profile" series, a warmly sympathetic sketch of Arthur C. Clarke, occasioned by the success of *2001: A Space Odyssey*. Praises Clarke equally for his fiction and his predictions. His style is a "singular amalgam of scientific erudition, speculative imagination, and a profound poetic feeling for the strange and only partly understood objects—stars, moons, planets, asteroids—that populate our universe." Yet the "really distinguishing feature" of his style is "the sense of sadness and loneliness that man must feel over living so brief a time in such a vast universe of which he can have so limited a glimpse."

6 Bradbury, Ray. "Literature in the Space Age," *California Librarian*, 21 (July 1960), 159–164.

Discursive, highly personalized explanation of why he writes sf, giving detailed attention to how and why he wrote "The Nursery." Most important for his explicit rejection of realism as *"reportage* of the worst sort." He also laments the impossibility of using realistic detail to effect characterization.

7 ———. "An Impatient Gulliver Above Our Heads," *Life*, 24 November 1967, pp. 31–37.

Reports on his *Life* assignment to Houston after Saturn V, when for the first time he saw an astronaut and a "spaceship." They were beyond his imagination, but he quotes extensively from several stories.

8 Brunner, John. "One Sense of Wonder, Slightly Tarnished,"
   Books and Bookmen, 12 (July 1967), 19–20.

Brunner recalls the sf he read twenty years ago and decides that
he no longer reacts with the same enthusiasm he once felt,
largely, perhaps, because the "power to wreck the world and
exterminate mankind is no longer the prerogative of tentacled
aliens—the weapons stand ready at airstrips and missile bases."
Yet while the stories and themes have changed, a youngster
such as he was twenty years ago would find the same sense of
wonder in reading such current writers as Cordwainer Smith,
Delany, Ballard, Dick, and Disch, to name but a few.

9 Burroughs, William. "The Hallucinatory Operators Are
   Real," *SF* Horizons, 2 (1965), 3–11.

In a discursive interview, Burroughs names certain sf writers he
likes, particularly C. S. Lewis.

10 deCamp, L. Sprague. *Science Fiction Handbook*. New
    York: Hermitage House, 1953. (See II, 95.)

11 Derleth, August. "H. P. Lovecraft, Outsider," *River*,
    1 (1937), 88–90, 95.

Brief account of HPL's life and work, together with a poem of
lamentation, "Elegy in Providence in the Spring . . . ," and a note
that work is underway on a multi-volume collected edition of
Lovecraft's work. [Mullen]

12 ———. *Some Notes on H. P. Lovecraft*. Sauk Center,
    Wis.: Arkham House, 1959.

A 42-page pamphlet in which Derleth dismisses a number of
myths about Lovecraft's life and works, and discusses both his
unfinished manuscripts and his working habits. The diary notations
of his cousin R. H. Barlow involving a visit by HPL to Barlow's
home in 1934 are reproduced, and finally four letters from
Lovecraft to Derleth are included.

13 Etchison, Dennis. "Presenting! The Amazing! Acker-
monster!" *Cavalier*, 17 (June 1967), 56–57.

A sketch of one of the most colorful individuals in "fandom,"
Forrest Ackerman, emphasizing his collection of properties from
sf films and his magazine, *Famous Monsters of Filmland*. "He
is the necessary monomaniac . . . a man who has given his life to
what he loves. . . ."

14 "Evolution and Ideation," *New Yorker*, 16 September
1967, p. 38.

In "Talk of the Town," an essentially sympathetic report of the
twenty-fifth annual World Science Fiction Convention held in New
York over the Labor Day weekend, 1967. Beginning with
mention of the "debate" between the Old and New Waves, it soon
focuses upon sketches of Gerry de la Ree (as a collector), Robert
Silverberg (then president of SFWA), Fred Pohl (as a long-time
editor), and Harlan Ellison (as "chief prophet of the New
Wave"). Quotes Silverberg: "The era of bug-eyed monsters,
clear-eyed scientists, and plot lines that lean heavily on scientific
hardware is over. The field is evolving, and some of the fans
don't like the evolution."

15 Gibbs, Angelica. "Onward and Upward with the Arts:
Inertium, Neutronium, Chromalogy, P-P-P-Proot!"
New Yorker, 13 February 1943, p. 36 ff. (See II, 126.)

16 Hudson, Derek. "A Study of Algernon Blackwood," in
Essays and Studies for 1961, ed. Derek Hudson.
London: John Murray, 1961. 14:102–114.

Biographical sketch of Blackwood, giving attention to the
sequence of his books. Important for the quotations from his
letters to the Macmillan firm. Considers *The Centaur* (1911) his
most effective work. Quotes Blackwood: "My interest in psychic
matters has always been the interest in questions of extended
or expanded consciousness."

17 Huxley, Julian. "My Brother Aldous," *Humanist*,
25 (January–February 1965), 25.

Brave New World was "extremely opportune satire on the then
current belief that science and technology alone would solve
all our problems." *Island* attempted to demonstrate "the
benevolent possibilities of science and social organization."
Regards Aldous Huxley as "perhaps the greatest humanist of our
age, certainly the one with the most comprehensively illuminating
vision."

18 Kent, George. "Mister Imagination: Jules Verne," *Saturday
Review*, 5 June 1954, pp. 9–10.

Biographical sketch, calling Verne "father of science fiction" and
stressing that he was taken seriously because of "his precise,
indisputable detail."

19 Kontaratos, A. N. "The Amazing 1865 Moon Shot of
Jules Verne," *Look*, 27 May 1969, pp. 74–78.

Illustrations and excerpts from Verne's novels are used to show
"some amazing resemblances" between them and "the reality of
today's headlines." No analysis.

20 LeFranc, Bolivar. "Brian Aldiss," *Books and Bookmen*,
15 July 1970, pp. 18,20.

Interview begins with the background of *The Hand-Reared Boy*,
his best seller, but turns to sf. Asimov and Heinlein tried
"objectively to create a possible future" in their fiction during
the 1940's. Now the sf writer must "more straightforwardly
evaluate the present." Hopes to do "my own sort of philosophical
novel that will have its roots in science fiction."

21 Lovecraft, H. P. *Autobiography: Some Notes on a Nonentity,
with annotations by August Derleth*. Sauk City, Wis.:
Arkham House, 1963.

Thirteen pages of text, in which Derleth has supplemented
Lovecraft's passages with his own parenthetical comments. The

resultant text is divided almost equally between them. Lovecraft emphasizes some of the influences that shaped his writing, but also gives a general sketch of his life. He declares that "any actual literary merit I may have is confined to tales of dream-life, strange shadow, and cosmic 'outsideness.' . . ." He also asserts that "I refuse to follow the mechanical conventions of popular fiction or fill my tales with stock characters and situations, but insist on reproducing real moods and impressions in the best way I can command."

22 McNelly, Willis E. "Bradbury Revisited," *CEA Critic*, 31 (March 1969), 4, 6.

Combines a sketch of Bradbury's personal beliefs and the characteristics of his fiction. He is "essentially a romantic" and an "exemplar of the Turner thesis about the frontier tradition," an opponent of the machine and of conformity. Suggests that "ultimately the religious theme is the end product of Bradbury's vision of man." Metaphor and ironic detachment characterize his work.

23 Moskowitz, Sam. *Seekers of Tomorrow: Masters of Modern Science Fiction*. Cleveland and New York: World, 1966. (See II, 205.)

24 O'Neil, Paul. "The Amazing Hugo Gernsback: Prophet of Science, Barnum of the Space Age," *Life*, 26 July 1963, pp. 62–64.

Sketch of Gernsback's career and personality, with much attention to his predictions as well as his founding of the sf magazines. Names *Ralph 124C 41+* as prototype; it was "whacked together as a vehicle for scientific prediction, and as such it is an astonishing performance."

25 "Playboy Panel: 1984 and Beyond," *Playboy*, 13 (July 1963), 25–37; 13 (August 1963), 31–33.

Writers Anderson, Asimov, Blish, Bradbury, Budrys, Clarke, Heinlein, Pohl, Serling, Sturgeon, Tenn, and vanVogt talk about a range of topics from encounter with aliens to the present sexual revolution—"topics that have provided sf with many of its themes."

26 "Portrait of a Genius: Ray Bradbury," *Show*, 4 (December 1964), 102–104.

An interview in which many of Bradbury's ideas are repeated. There is no formula for writing sf or any other fiction. Machines amoral: "something in the very manner of their construction and the power locked in their frame inspires man to idiocy." Finds sf a "convenient short-hand symbolic way to write of our huge problems." Some biographical materials drawn upon for certain stories.

27 "Promethean Fire (an interview with Stanislaw Lem)," *Soviet Literature*, 11 (1968), 166–170.

Lem, described as vying with Wells as the most popular foreign sf writer known in the Soviet Union, was interviewed during a trip to Russia. He suggests that "art does not always portraitize, and its subjects, both fantastic and true-to-life, are always symbolic."

28 Shenker, Israel. "Michael Crichton (rhymes with frighten)," *New York Times Book Review*, 8 June 1969, pp. 5, 40.

A character sketch of Crichton accompanying the review of his *Andromeda Strain*. Good for biographical detail.

29 Smith, Godfrey. "Astounding Story! About a Science Fiction Writer," *New York Times Magazine*, 6 March 1966, pp. 28, 75–77.

Begins with a biographical sketch of Arthur C. Clarke, but concentrates upon *2001*, "conceived in epic proportions," and

Childhood's End, considered his best novel. Contains the remarks that anything which is theoretically possible will be achieved in practice and that the universe is "queerer than we *can* imagine."

30 Strugatsky, Arkadi and Boris. "Kobo Abé on Science Fiction," *Soviet Literature*, 11 (1968), 171–175.

Extracts from a three-hour interview. Kobo Abé insists that he is not an sf writer and that "fantasy should not be set apart as a special genre." He would emphasize the ability of sf/fantasy to speak of the problems of the present.

31 Tunley, Roul. "Unbelievable But True," *Saturday Evening Post*, 8 October 1960, pp. 30, 90–92.

A sympathetic sketch of John W. Campbell as the pioneer of modern sf who "killed off the hackneyed type of tales dealing with bug-eyed monsters and such," who developed the story "that has a plausible scientific basis," and who edited "the most influential publication in its field." It presents many of the incidents which have come to characterize Campbell, from the Cartmill A-bomb story to his interest in psionics and the Norman Dean incident.

32 "Unreal Estates: On Science Fiction," *Encounter*, 24 (March 1965), 61-65.

Reprint of the Amis and Aldiss interview with C. S. Lewis originally published in *SF Horizons* (1964).

33 "Voices," *Colloquy*, 4 (May 1971), 2–9.

Lead article in the issue devoted exclusively to sf. Sprague deCamp, Gordon Dickson, Harlan Ellison, Damon Knight, and Ursula LeGuin answer three questions: "What is science fiction, why do you write science fiction, what is the future of science fiction?"

34 Vonnegut, Kurt, Jr. "Science Fiction," in *Page 2: The Best of 'Speaking of Books' from the New York Times Book Review*, ed. Francis Brown. New York: Holt, Rinehart, and Winston, 1970, pp. 117–120. (See II, 291.)

35 Warner, Harry J. *All Our Yesterdays*. Chicago: Advent, 1969.

An informal, nostalgic history of "fandom" through the 1940's. Shows what an in-group the sf community can be; but the "outsider" should at least sample it in order to realize the intense enthusiasm of the fans. Also excellent for showing the close relationship between audience and writers-editors, with the resultant influence upon the magazines. Contains valuable bits of information that would otherwise have been lost.

36 Williamson, Jack. "As I Knew Hugo," *Extrapolation*, 11 (May 1970), 53–55. (See VII, 26.)

37 Wollheim, Donald A. *The Universe Makers: Science Fiction Today*. New York: Harper & Row, 1971. (See II, 303.)

Author Index of Entries

(Anonymous articles are cited by title.)

Abernethy, Francis E., I, 1
Adams, J. Donald, I, 2; III, 1
Adams, Phoebe, III, 2
Adams, Robert M., III, 3
Agel, Jerome, IV, 1
Alden, Robert C., V, 1
Aldiss, Brian, II, 1, 2, 3; IV, 2; IX, 1
Allen, D. C., II, 4
Allen, Dick, II, 5, 6; III, 4; V, 2
Allot, Kenneth, II, 7
Alpert, Hollis, IV, 3, 4
Amis, Kingsley, II, 8, 9, 10; III, 5, 6
Amory, Cleveland, IV, 5
Anderson, Howard A., IV, 6
Andrews, Carolyn, VIII, 1
Andreyev, Kirill, III, 7
"Apes in Heaven," III, 8
Appel, Alfred, Jr., II, 11
Appel, Benjamin, I, 3
Armytage, W. H. G., V, 3, 4, 5, 6
Arnold, John E., VI, 1
"Arthur C. Clarke: he's so far out, he's in," IX, 2
Ascher, M., I, 4

Ash, Lee, IX, 3
Ashmead, Laurence P., VII, 1
Asimov, Isaac, I, 5, 6, 7; II, 12, 13; IV, 7; V, 7; VI, 2, 3; VII, 2, 3, 4, 5
Atheling, William, Jr., II, 14, 15. See also Blish, James
Atkins, John, V, 8
Atwood, Margaret, II, 16
"Avoid 'Typhoid Mary,' Editors Warned," VII, 6

Bacon, Leonard, III, 9
Bailey, J. O., II, 17, 18, 19, 20
Baker, Robert H., III, 10
Ballard, J. G., IX, 4
Balliett, Whitney, III, 11
Banks, William H., Jr., VI, 4
Baring-Gould, William S., II, 21
Barron, A. S., I, 8
Barron, R. Neil, VI, 5
Barthell, Robert J., II, 22
Bass, Ralph, II, 23
Baxter, John, IV, 8
Beck, Clyde F., II, 24
Becker, Mary Lamberton, II, 25

Beja, Morris, IV, 9
"Beneath the Surface," III, 12
Bennett, Michael Alan, II, 26
Bergonzi, Bernard, II, 27, 28, 29, 30
Berkvist, Robert, III, 13
Bernabeu, Ednita, I, 9
Bernstein, Jeremy, IX, 5
Bester, Alfred, II, 31
Billam, E. R., II, 32
Birchby, Sid., II, 33
Bishop, Claire Huchet, I, 10
Black, Elfred, VI, 57
Blank, E. W., II, 34
Bleiler, Everett F., VIII, 2
Blish, James, II, 35, 36, 37, 38. See also Atheling, William, Jr.
Bloomfield, Paul, V, 9
Boggs, W. Arthur, II, 40
Boone, Andrew R., IV, 10
Boucher, Anthony, II, 41, 42; III, 14, 15
Bowen, John, II, 43
Bowers, Dorothy W., VI, 6
Bradbury, Ray, II, 44, 45; IX, 6, 7
Bradley, Marion Zimmer, II, 46
Brady, Charles A., II, 47
Brague, Paul E., VI, 7
Brandis, Eugeni, II, 48
Bretnor, Reginald, II, 49, 50
Brien, Alan, II, 51
Brody, Alan, IV, 11
Brophy, Brigid, III, 16
Brophy, Liam, II, 52
Brown, Harcourt, II, 53
Brunner, John, II, 54; IX, 8

Brutenhuis, Peter, III, 17
Bryan, C. B. D., II, 55
Brynes, Asher, III, 18
Bufkin, E. C., II, 56
Bulman, Learned T., VI, 8
Burgess, Anthony, III, 19; V, 10
Burgum, Edwin Berry, II, 57
Burroughs, William, IX, 9
Butor, Michael, II, 58, 59

Callahan, Patrick J., II, 60
Cameron, Alastair, VIII, 3
Campbell, John W., Jr., I, 11, 12; II, 61, 62; VII, 7, 8
Cantril, Hadley, IV, 12
Carey, Graham, III, 20
Carter, Everett, II, 63
Cerf, Bennett, II, 64
Chalker, Jack L., VIII, 29
Chambers, John, II, 65
Christopher, John, VII, 9
Churchill, R. C., V, 11
Clarens, Carlos, IV, 13
Clareson, Thomas D., II, 66, 67, 68, 69, 70, 71, 72, 73; III, 21, 22, 23; IV, 14; VIII, 1, 4, 5, 6
Clarke, Arthur C., I, 13, 14
Clarke, I. F., II, 74, 75, 76, 77, 78, 79; V, 12; VIII, 7
Cochell, Shirley, VI, 9
Cockcroft, T. G. L., VIII, 8
Coffey, Warren, III, 24
Cole, Walter P., VIII, 9
Collins, Christopher, II, 80
Colquitt, Betsy Feagan, II, 81
Conklin, Groff, I, 15; II, 82

Conquest, Robert, II, 83, 84, 85
"Controversy over Soviet SF,"
II, 86
Cooper, Jean E., VI, 10
Cosman, Max, III, 25
Cox, Arthur Jean, II, 87
Crawford, Joseph H., Jr., VIII, 10
Crichton, J. Michael, II, 88
Crispin, Edmund, II, 89; III, 26
Crowther, Bosley, IV, 15
Cruse, Amy, II, 90

Dahlberg, Edward, III, 48
Dane, Clemence, II, 91
Darrach, Brad, VII, 10
Davenport, Basil, II, 92, 93; III,
48
Davies, H. Neville, II, 94
Day, Bradford M., VIII, 11, 12,
13
Day, Donald B., VIII, 14
Deasy, Philip, I, 16
deCamp, L. Sprague, I, 17, 18; II,
95
deFord, Miriam Allen, I, 19
DeForest, Lee, II, 243
Deisch, Noel, II, 96
Delany, Samuel R., II, 97, 98
Dempelwolff, Richard F., IV, 16,
17
Dennis, Nigel, III, 27
Denney, Reuel, II, 99
Derleth, August, II, 100; IX, 11,
12
Devoe, Alan, II, 101
DeVoto, Bernard, I, 20

deWohl, Louis, I, 21
Dmitrevsky, Vladimir, II, 48
Dodd, Alan L., VI, 11
Doherty, G. H., II, 102
Donovan, R. M., VI, 12
Donovan, Richard, II, 103
Dovey, Irma, VI, 13
Doyno, Victor A., IV, 18
DuBois, William, III, 28
Ducharme, Edward, II, 104
Dunn, Linwood, IV, 6

Edelstein, J. M., III, 29
Egoff, Sheila A., I, 22
Ellik, Ron, II, 106
Elliott, Robert C., V, 13
Ellis, H. F., II, 107
Emmons, Winfred S., Jr., II, 108;
VIII, 15
Erisman, Robert O., III, 30
Eschelbach, Claire John, VIII, 16
Eshbach, Floyd, VII, 11
Estrada, Jackie, VII, 12
Etchison, Dennis, IX, 13
Evans, Bill, II, 106
"Evolution and Ideation," IX, 14

Fadiman, Clifton, II, 109, 110
"Fantastica," III, 31
Fenichel, Robert R., IV, 19
Fenton, Robert W., II, 111
"Fiction," III, 32, 33, 34, 35
Fiedler, Leslie A., II, 112
Field, Ruth R., VI, 14
Finer, S. E., I, 23
Finkelstein, Sidney, I, 24

Fishwick, Marshall, II, 113
Fison, Peter, II, 114
Forbes, Allyn B., II, 115
Fox, Dorothea M., VI, 15
Frank, Stanley, II, 116
Franklin, H. Bruce, I, 25; II, 117, 118
Franson, Donald, VIII, 17, 40
Fraser, G. S., III, 36
Fremont-Smith, Eliot, III, 37
"From Icarus to Arthur Clarke," II, 119
Frye, Northrop, V, 14
Fuller, Florence, I, 26
Fuller, Richard, IV, 20
Fungesten, Peter, I, 46
Fuson, Ben W., II, 120, 121
"Future Indefinite," II, 122

"Gadgets From Hollywood," IV, 21
Gallant, Joseph, II, 123
Gardner, Martin, II, 124
Gehman, Richard B., II, 125
Gerber, Richard, V, 15
Gernsback, Hugo, VIII, 18
Gerson, Villiers, III, 48, 49
Gibbs, Angelica, II, 126
Giffin, S. F., I, 27
Gilmore, Maeve, II, 127
Glass, Bentley, I, 28
Glicksberg, Charles I., V, 16
Glicksohn, Susan, II, 128
Golding, William, II, 129, 130, 131
Goldsmith, Maurice, II, 132

Goodstone, Tony, IV, 22
Gorer, Geoffrey, III, 38
Gove, Philip Babcock, II, 133
Granin, Daniel, V, 17
Grant, Allan, IV, 23
Green, Martin, II, 134, 135, 136; III, 39
Green, Roger Lancelyn, II, 137
Grennan, Margaret R., II, 138
Grigorescu, Dan, IV, 24
Grimsley, Juliet, VI, 17
Gross, Elizabeth H., VI, 18
Grunwald, Henry Anatole, V, 18
Gulbin, Suzanne, VI, 19
Gunn, James, IV, 25

Haight, Gordon, II, 139
Hall, H. W., VI, 20; VIII, 19, 20
Hamburger, Philip, IV, 26
Hamilton, John B., II, 140
Hanlon, Mercedes, VI, 21
Harrison, Harry, II, 141, 142; VII, 13
Hart, Lyn, II, 143
Hartley, Margaret L., I, 29
Hatch, Robert, III, 40
Hauser, Frank, IV, 27
Hayakawa, S. I., III, 41
Heinlein, Robert, II, 144
Heins, Henry Hardy, VIII, 21
Henighan, Tom, II, 145
Hicks, Granville, II, 146
Highet, Gilbert, I, 30, 31
Hillegas, Mark, I, 32, 33, 34; II, 148, 149, 150, 151, 152, 153;

III, 42, 43; V, 19; VI, 22; VIII, 22, 23, 24, 25
Hilton-Young, Wayland, II, 154
Hipolito, Jane, II, 155
Hirsch, Walter, I, 35, 36
Hobana, Ion, II, 156
Hoch, David G., IV, 28
Hodgens, Richard M., IV, 29
Holcomb, Claire, II, 157
Holland, Norman N., IV, 30
"Hollywood Builds Flying Saucers," IV, 31
"Hollywood Goes to Mars," IV, 32
Holmes, H. H., III, 44, 45
Hopkins, D. F., III, 46
Howe, Irving, II, 158
Hudson, Derek, IX, 16
Hughes, David Y., II, 159
Hulme, Hilda M., II, 160
Hurley, Neil P., I, 37
Hurley, Richard J., VI, 23, 24
Huxley, Aldous, I, 38
Huxley, Julian, IX, 17

"I Sing the Body Electric," III, 47
"In the Realm of the Spacemen," III, 48, 49
"Inspirational Value of Science Fiction," V, 20
"Interplanetary Cop," IV, 33
"Interplanetary Frolics," III, 50
Iosefescu, Silvian, II, 161
Irwin, Martha, VI, 51

Janes, Adrian, II, 162
Jenkinson, Karl, VI, 25

Johnson, William B., I, 39
Jones, W. M., II, 163
Josselson, Diana, III, 51

Kagarlitski, Julius, II, 164, 165, 166
Kagle, Steven Earl, II, 167
Kauffman, Stanley, VII, 14
Kaufman, V. Milo, II, 168
Kelly, R. Gordon, I, 40
Kenkel, William F., I, 41
Kennebeck, Edwin, III, 52
Kent, George, IX, 18
Ketterer, David A., II, 169
Kilpatrick, Clayton E., III, 53
Kivu, Dinu, IV, 34
Klein, Marcus, III, 54
Knepper, B. G., II, 170
Knight, Damon, II, 171; VI, 26
Knox, George, V, 22
Koestler, Arthur, II, 172
Kontaratos, A. N., IX, 19
Kostolefsky, Joseph, II, 173
Krim, Seymour, III, 55
Krueger, John R., II, 174, 175
"Kurt Vonnegut, Jr.: A Symposium," II, 176
Kuttner, Henry, II, 177; VII, 15, 16
Kyle, Richard, II, 178

LaFleur, Laurence J., II, 179
Lambert, P. C., II, 180
Lantero, Erminie Huntress, I, 42
Lardner, Rex, III, 56
Lauterbach, Edward S., VIII, 6
Leahy, Jack Thomas, II, 181

Lear, John, I, 43
Lederer, Richard, VI, 27
Leeper, Geoffrey, V, 23
LeFranc, Bolivar, IX, 20
Leiber, Fritz, III, 57, 58
Leighton, Peter, II, 183
Leinster, Murray, VII, 17
Lemire, Eugene D., II, 184
"Let Imagination Soar," III, 59
Levin, A., VI, 28
Levin, Martin, III, 60, 61, 62, 63
Lewis, Arthur O., Jr., VIII, 26
Lewis, C. S., II, 185
Ley, Willy, I, 17; III, 64
"Little Hmān, What Hnau?" III, 65
Livingston, Dennis, V, 24, 25, 26, 27; VI, 29, 30, 31
Lokke, Virgil L., V, 28
Lovecraft, Howard Phillips, II, 186; IX, 21
Lovell, A. C. B., II, 187
Loveman, Amy, II, 188
Luckiesh, M., I, 44
Lundwall, Sam J., II, 189
Lupoff, Richard A., II, 190; VII, 18

McCauley, Virginia C., VI, 32
McComas, J. Francis, VII, 19
McConnell, Frank, IV, 35
McCreight, Cathryn, VI, 33
McCusker, Lauretta G., VI, 34
McDonnell, Thomas P., I, 45
McNelly, Willis E., II, 191, 192; IX, 22

Maddison, Michael, V, 29
Maddocks, Melvin, III, 66
Madsen, Alan L., VI, 35
"Making Up a Mind," III, 67
Malec, Alexander B., VII, 20
Malone, Nancy, IV, 36
Mandel, Siegfried, I, 46
Manser, A. R., I, 47
Mansfield, Roger, VI, 40
Manson, Margaret, VIII, 27
Marple, Allen, I, 48
Marshak, Alexander, I, 49; II, 194; VI, 36
Marshall, David F., VI, 37
Mascall, E. L., III, 68
Medd, H. J., I, 50
"Media Information," II, 195, 196; VII, 21
Meek, Captain S. P., VII, 22
Menzel, Donald H., I, 51
Menzies, Ian S., I, 52
Mercer, Derwent, I, 53
Merril, Judith, II, 198
Methold, Kenneth, II, 199
Michaelson, L. W., I, 54, 55, 56
Miesel, Sandra, II, 200, 201
Mitchell, Stephen O., II, 202
"Mixed Fiction," III, 69
"Monkey's Pa, The," III, 137
"Monster of the Month: *Outer Limits*," IV, 37
Mooney, Ernest W., Jr., VI, 38
Moore, Robert E., VI, 39
Moorman, Charles, II, 203
Morgan, Edwin, III, 70
Morgan, W. John, III, 71

Morgenstern, Joseph, IV, 38
Morsberger, Robert E., IV, 39
Morton, A. L., V, 30
Moskowitz, Sam, II, 204, 205, 206, 207
Mullen, Richard D., II, 208, 209, 210, 211
Muller, Herbert J., I, 57, 58
Murphy, Carol, I, 59
Murray, Tony, VI, 40
"Mystery—Detective—Suspense," III, 72

Naipail, V. S., III, 73
Negley, Glenn R., V, 32; VIII, 28
Neill, Sam, II, 212
"Never Too Old to Dream," III, 74
"New Novels," III, 75
Newman, James R., III, 76
Nicolson, Marjorie, II, 213, 214, 215, 216
"Nightmares and Realities," III, 77
Norman, H. L., II, 217
Norton, Andre, I, 60
Norwood, W. D., II, 218, 219
"Novels of the Week," III, 78

O'Brien, Robert C., I, 61
O'Connor, Gerard, II, 220
Olney, Clark, II, 221
O'Neil, Paul, IX, 24
"Overtaking the Future," VII, 23
Owings, Mark, VIII, 29

Panshin, Alexei, II, 222, 223, 224, 225, 226, 227, 228, 229, 230, 231, 232, 233; VI, 41, 42, 43, 44
Paris, Bernard J., II, 234
Parkinson, Robert C., II, 235
Parrington, Vernon Lewis, Jr., V, 33
Patrick, J. Max, V, 34
Patrouch, Joseph, I, 62
Penzoldt, Peter, II, 236
Perry, Nick, II, 237
Peterson, Clell T., II, 238
Phelan, J. M., I, 63
Philmus, Robert M., II, 239, 240
Pierce, John R., I, 64
Pilgrim, John, I, 65
Plank, Robert, I, 66, 67, 68, 69, 70, 71, 72; II, 241, 242; IV, 40, 41; V, 35
"*Playboy* Panel: 1984 and Beyond," IX, 25
Pohl, Fred, I, 73
Poore, Charles, III, 79
"Pop Theology: Those Gods From Outer Space," I, 74
Porges, I., VI, 45
"Portrait of a Genius: Ray Bradbury," IX, 26
Post, Jeremiah B., VIII, 30, 31
"Potpourri," III, 80
Pratt, Fletcher, II, 243; III, 49, 81, 82, 83, 84, 85, 86, 87, 88, 89, 90, 91, 92, 93
Prescott, Orville, III, 94

Prescott, Peter S., III, 95
"Pretty Gentlemen and Betafied
    Lady," III, 96
Priestley, J. B., I, 75; II, 244
Pritchett, V. S., II, 245
"Promeathean Fire," IX, 27
Pulvertaft, Thomas B., II, 246
Purdom, Tom, VII, 24

"Questing Characters," III, 97

Raddatz, Leslie, IV, 42
"Rape of the Future," IV, 43
Reilly, Robert, II, 247
Rhodes, Carolyn H., I, 76
Richardson, Maurice, III, 98, 99
"Rifts in the Moonscape," III, 100
Riley, Robert B., I, 77
Robinson, Guy S., I, 78
Roemer, Kenneth M., VIII, 32
Rogers, Alva, II, 249
Rogers, Ivor, II, 250; IV, 44
Rogers, Robert, IV, 45
Rojas, Billy, V, 36, 37
Rongione, Louis A., I, 79
Rose, Carl, I, 80
Rose, Lois, I, 81
Rose, Stephen, I, 81
Rosenfeld, Albert, IV, 46
Rottensteiner, Franz, II, 251
Rowland, Stanley J., III, 101
Russ, Joanna, II, 252; VI, 46

Sackett, Samuel J., II, 253
Samuels, Charles Thomas, III, 102
Sanz, Jose, IV, 47

Sapiro, Leland, II, 254, 255
Sargeant, Winthrop, IV, 48
Scarborough, Dorothy, II, 256
Schickel, Richard, III, 103
Schmerl, Rudolf B., II, 257, 258,
    259
Scholes, Robert, II, 260, 261
Scholl, Ralph, VIII, 33
Schott, Webster, III, 104
Schwartz, Sheila, II, 262
"Science Fiction for Young
    Adults," VI, 48
"Science Fiction Presents a Strange
    Picture of Science," I, 82; III,
    105
"Science Fiction Rockets into the
    Big Time in Entertainment,"
    VII, 25
"Science in Science Fiction," I, 83
Scobie, Steven, IV, 50
Scoggins, Margaret C., VI, 49
Scott, Alan, VI, 50
Scott, J. D., III, 106
Searles, A. Langley, II, 264
Searls, Hank, I, 84
Seelye, John, IV, 51
Sewell, Margaret, VI, 51
Shackleton, C. C., II, 265, 266
Shaftel, Oscar, I, 85
Shanks, Edward, II, 267
Shatnoff, Judith, IV, 52
Shayon, Richard Lewis, IV, 53
Shenker, Israel, IX, 28
Sheppard, R. Z., II, 268
Shober, Joyce Lee, VIII, 16
Shuldiner, Herbert, IV, 54

Sieman, Frederick, VIII, 34
Silverberg, Robert, II, 269
Simak, Clifford, II, 270
Simon, Frank, I, 86
Simpson, D. J., VI, 52
Sisario, Peter, II, 271
Sister Mary Bennett, VI, 53
Skeels, Dell R., II, 272
Slate, Tom, II, 273
Slater, Joseph, II, 274
Smith, Charles C., VI, 54
Smith, Curtis C., II, 275
Smith, Godfrey, IX, 29
Solomon, Eric, II, 276
Solomon, Stanley, VI, 55
Solon, Ben, II, 277
Sontag, Susan, IV, 55
Southern, Terry, III, 107
"Space Ahoy," III, 108
"*Space Patrol* Conquers Kids,"
    IV, 56
Spacks, Patricia Meyer, II, 278
Speer, Diane Parkin, II, 279
Spencer, Theodore, III, 109
Spinrad, Norman, II, 280
Stacy, Paul, IV, 58
Staggers, Anthony, II, 281
Stevenson, Lionel, II, 282, 283
Stockton, H. G., VI, 56
Stone, Graham, VIII, 35
Strauss, Erwin S., VIII, 36
Strugatski, Arkadi, IX, 30
Strugatski, Boris, IX, 30
Stumpf, Edna, I, 87
Sturgeon, Theodore, III, 110, 111,
    112, 113, 114, 115, 116, 117,

118, 119, 120, 121, 122, 123,
124, 125, 126, 127, 128, 129,
130, 131, 132, 133, 134, 135
"Sums and Scrubbers," III, 136
Sussman, Herbert L., I, 88
Sutton, Marilyn, I, 89
Sutton, Thomas C., I, 89
Suvin, Darko, II, 284, 285, 286
Sweetzer, Wesley D., VIII, 37

Takeo, Okuno, II, 287
Teitler, Stuart A., VIII, 38
Tenn, William, II, 288
Thale, Jerome, II, 289
"Theological Thriller," III, 138
Tomlin, R. J., I, 90
Trevor, William, III, 139
Tuck, Donald H., VIII, 39
Tunley, Roul, IX, 31

Ulanov, Barry, II, 290
"Unreal Estates," IX, 32
"Utopias You Wouldn't Like," V,
    38

Vandenberg, Stephen C., I, 91
Van Horne, Harriet, IV, 59
Velikovich, A., VI, 28
Viggiano, Michael, VIII, 40
"Voices," IX, 33
Vonnegut, Kurt, Jr., II, 291; IX,
    34

Walbridge, Earle F., III, 140
Walsh, Chad, III, 141; V, 39, 40
Walton, Harry, IV, 60

218

Warner, Harry J., IX, 35
Weales, Gerald, III, 142
Weaver, Edward K., VI, 57
Webb, Honor A., V, 41
Weinkauf, Mary, II, 292; V, 42
Weiss, Miriam Strauss, V, 43
Wells, Lester G., VI, 58
West, Anthony, II, 293, 294
West, Richard C., VIII, 41, 42
West, Robert H., I, 92
Westheimer, Joseph, IV, 6
Whiteside, Thomas O., IV, 61
Whitfield, Stephen E., IV, 62
Wilkie, Roy, II, 237
Wilkins, A. N., II, 296
Williams, Pat, II, 297
Williams, Paul, VI, 59

Williams, W. T., I, 93
Williamson, Jack, II, 299; VI, 60, 61; VII, 26
Wilson, Colin, II, 300
Wilson, Robert H., II, 301
Winandy, Andre, II, 302
Wollheim, Donald A., II, 303
Woodcock, George, V, 44
Woolever, John D., VI, 62
Wright, James W., IV, 63

Yaffe, James, III, 143, 144, 145
Yershov, Peter, II, 304
Young, B. A., III, 146

Zamyatin, Yevgeny, II, 305
Zaniello, Thomas, II, 306

Index of Authors Mentioned

Abbot, E. A., II, 250
Abé, Kobo, II, 287; IX, 30
Aderca, Felix, II, 156
Aldiss, Brian W., II, 15, 35, 54, 300; III, 12, 44, 139; VIII, 27; IX, 1, 20
Anderson, Poul, I, 29, 200; III, 30, 45, 120; IX, 25
Amis, Kingsley, I, 65; II, 36, 129; III, 40, 76, 113, 143
Arnold, Matthew, II, 271
Asimov, Isaac, II, 49, 128, 167; III, 92, 113; V, 41; VI, 34, 46; IX, 4
Atterley, Joseph, VI, 58
Auden, W. H., II, 5

Bailey, J. O., II, 25, 125; VI, 12
Balchin, Nigel, I, 50
Ballantyne, R. M., II, 134
Ballard, J. G., II, 3, 73, 122, 237; III, 35, 46, 63, 70, 136, 146; IX, 4, 8
Barker, P. A., III, 46
Barth, Donald, II, 260
Barthelme, Donald, II, 260

Bates, Harry, II, 87, 249
Bellamy, Edward, II, 40, 52, 121; V, 28
Belyayev, Alexander, II, 132
Beowulf, II, 65, 273
Bester, Alfred, II, 93; VII, 6
Bierce, Ambrose, II, 73
Biggle, Lloyd, III, 128
Blackwood, Algernon, II, 236, 283; III, 48; IX, 16
Blish, James, I, 42, 89; II, 192, 209, 300; III, 23, 50, 58; IX, 25
Bloch, Robert, II, 93
Bond, Nelson, I, 74; III, 49, 108
Borges, Jorges Luis, II, 306; III, 4
Boswell, James, II, 271
Boulle, Pierre, III, 2, 8, 137
Bowen, Elizabeth, IX, 4
Boyd, John, II, 155, 192
Bradbury, Ray, I, 2, 24, 29, 48, 63, 74; II, 32, 35, 41, 45, 99, 101, 103, 113, 114, 129, 173, 247, 271, 290; III, 7, 44, 47, 56, 83, 140; VI, 6, 17; VII, 14, 17; IX, 3, 6, 7, 22, 25, 26
Brecht, Bertolt, II, 284

219

Bretnor, Reginald, III, 1, 55
Brown, Frederic, I, 29; II, 99, 173
Brunner, John, II, 54, 192, 280, 284; V, 27; IX, 8
Budrys, Algis, IX, 25
Bulwer-Lytton, II, 34, 52, 170
Burgess, Anthony, III, 17, 51; V, 42
Burroughs, Edgar Rice, II, 111, 123, 126, 137, 145, 153, 175, 178, 190, 207, 210, 211, 273; VIII, 21
Burroughs, William, IX, 9
Butler, Samuel, I, 88

Campanella, Tommaso, V, 18
Campbell, John W., Jr., II, 49, 132, 249; III, 132; VI, 14; VII, 11, 12; IX, 31
Capek, Karl, III, 60
Capote, Truman, III, 66
Capuana, Luigi, II, 217
Carlyle, Thomas, I, 88
Cartmill, Steve, II, 62, 116
Castle, Jeffrey Lloyd, III, 98
Cervantes, II, 57
Chambers, Robert, II, 46
Chesney, Sir George Tomkyns, II, 30, 276
Chesterton, G. K., V, 30; VIII, 26
Christopher, John, I, 22; III, 26; VII, 9
Clarke, Arthur C., I, 2, 89; II, 12, 119, 167, 196, 205; III, 13, 18, 26, 28, 57, 80, 87, 114; V, 20; VI, 6, 14, 39, 46; IX, 2, 5, 25, 29
Clarke, I. F., III, 21, 37
Clement, Hal, I, 60
Cohen, Morton H., III, 142
Cole, Cyrus, II, 121
Cole, W. P., III, 121
Collier, John, II, 185
Conquest, Robert, III, 113
Conrad, Joseph, II, 239; III, 136
Costa, Richard H., III, 3
Crichton, Michael, III, 66, 95, 104; IX, 28
Crowcroft, Peter, III, 98

Dail, C. C., II, 121
Davenport, Basil, III, 59
Davies, Hugh Sykes, III, 29, 71, 97
Day, Bradford, III, 88
deBergerac, Cyrano, II, 204
deCamp, L. Sprague, II, 36, 114, 124; III, 48; VII, 11; IX, 33
Defoe, Daniel, II, 83
DeForest, William, II, 63
De la Mare, Walter, II, 236
Delany, Samuel, II, 73, 201, 268; VI, 41, 46; IX, 8
delRey, Lester, I, 74
Dexter, William, III, 98
Dick, Philip, IX, 8
Dickens, Charles, I, 88
Dickson, Gordon, IX, 33
Dickson, Lovat, III, 19
Disch, Thomas, II, 284; IX, 8

Donne, John, II, 214
Donne, J. W., II, 250
Donnelly, Ignatius, II, 40
Dostoyevsky, Fyodor, II, 80
Doyle, Sir Arthur Conan, III, 14,
  66; V, 14
DuMaurier, George, II, 90

Eberhart, Richard, II, 5
Eddison, E. R., II, 283
Ehrlich, Max, VII, 14
Eliot, George, II, 160, 234
Ellison, Harlan, III, 127, 130; IX,
  14, 33
Eustace, Robert, II, 90

Farmer, Jose, I, 74; III, 119
Fast, Julius, II, 167
Fields, Edward, II, 5
Fitzgibbon, Constantine C., III, 54
Forster, E. M., II, 150
Franklin, H. Bruce, II, 69; III, 15,
  42, 125
Fort, Charles, II, 100
Fuller, Alvarado, II, 121

Gernsback, Hugo, I, 43; II, 126,
  228, 229, 243, 246, 254; V, 38;
  VII, 21, 26; VIII, 18; IX, 24
Gilbert, Stephen, III, 95
Goldwin, Francis, II, 96, 240
Graves, Robert, III, 58; V, 8, 11
Greene, Graham, III, 52, 136
Greene, Thomas, II, 4

Haber, Hans, III, 10

Haggard, Sir H. Rider, II, 16, 90,
  178; III, 142; VIII, 38
Haldane, V, 9
Harrison, Harry, VII, 12
Hartley, L. P., III, 25, 73, 96; V,
  10, 42
Hawthorne, Nathaniel, I, 25, 117,
  290; IV, 35
Heard, Gerald, II, 101; V, 41
Heinlein, Robert, I, 43, 45, 48,
  60, 63, 65; II, 12, 93, 100, 191,
  222, 223, 268, 279; III, 13,
  74, 94, 111, 116, 120, 124, 128;
  V, 29; VI, 6, 8, 32, 34, 39;
  VII, 11; IX, 25
Heller, Joseph, II, 57
Herbert, Frank, I, 89; II, 167,
  235, 268
Hersey, John, I, 76
Hertzka, Theodore, V, 9
Heuer, Kenneth, III, 10
Hillegas, Mark, III, 6
Hilton, James, VI, 14
Hirsch, Walter, III, 105
Hodgson, W. H., II, 33
Holmes, Oliver Wendell, II, 63
Howard, Robert E., II, 202
Howells, William Dean, II, 40, 63
Hoyle, Fred, III, 36, 50, 128
Hubbard, L. Ron, I, 66, 116; III,
  41
Hudson, W. H., 145
Hughes, Richard, II, 283
Huxley, Aldous, I, 29, 58; II, 41,
  67, 113, 150, 157, 163, 257,
  283; III, 25, 38, 60, 79, 141; V,

9, 10, 15, 16, 18, 23, 30, 42, 44; VI, 14, 40; VIII, 1, 16; IX, 17

James, Henry, II, 27, 239, 290; IV, 35
James, M. R., 236, 283
Jameson, Malcolm, I, 60
Jones, Raymond, I, 60, 66; IV, 10

Kafka, Franz, II, 57, 122, 289
Katayev, III, 43
Kazantsev, A., II, 132
Kepler, Johan, II, 47, 180, 213, 214, 216
Keyes, Daniel, III, 67
Kipling, Rudyard, I, 88; II, 90; VIII, 26
Kirk, Russell, III, 115
Knight, Damon, II, 36, 113; IX, 33
Kornbluth, C. M., II, 93; V, 27
Kuttner, Henry, III, 98

LaSpina, Greye, III, 45
Lasswitz, Kurd, II, 148, 153, 251
Lawrence, D. H., IV, 35; V, 4
Leavis, F. R., I, 38
LeFanu, Joseph, II, 236
LeGuin, Ursula, II, 284; III, 135; IX, 33
Leiber, Fritz, III, 112, 118, 120
Leinster, Murray, II, 124, 126; III, 74
Lem, Stanislaw, II, 165; IX, 27
Lewis, C. S., I, 16, 21, 22, 29, 63, 74; II, 60, 101, 137, 138, 150, 152, 153, 154, 203, 215, 218, 219, 278; III, 9, 20, 65, 68, 78, 109, 138; IX, 9, 32
Lewis, Sinclair, I, 28, 64; II, 34
Ley, Willy, III, 85
Lindsay, David, II, 252; III, 5, 16, 31, 34
London, Jack, II, 40, 73, 123, 238
Lovecraft, Howard Phillips, II, 46, 108, 125, 277, 300; III, 72; VIII, 8, 15; IX, 11, 12, 21
Lovell, Sir Bernard, III, 57
Lowell, Percival, II, 153, 211
Lowell, Robert, II, 5
Lucian, I, 3; II, 65, 96, 116, 137, 213; VI, 58
Lucie-Smith, Edward, III, 4

Machen, Arthur, II, 34, 46, 283; VIII, 37
M'Intosh, J. T., I, 76
Madden, Samuel, II, 30, 276
Magidorf, Robert, III, 119
Malcolm, Donald, II, 3
Malinovski, Alexander, II, 132
Martinson, Harry, III, 117
Matheson, Richard, II, 290
Meade, L. T., II, 90
Merle, Robert, III, 95
Merril, Judith, II, 41; III, 45, 84, 100, 131
Merritt, A., II, 41, 202; VII, 14
Miller, Walter M., Jr., II, 26, 104; III, 11, 52, 54, 60, 67, 69, 99, 101, 144

Mitchell, John A., IV, 14
Moore, C. L., V, 42
Moore, Patrick, III, 10
Moore, Ward, II, 41
More, Thomas, II, 13; V, 13, 14, 18, 30, 43
Morris, William, I, 88; II, 40; V, 30
Moskowitz, Sam, II, 36; III, 21, 126, 129; VII, 21
Murdoch, Iris, II, 283

Nabakov, Vladimir, II, 11
Nearing, Kenneth, III, 92
Newcomb, Simon, II, 96
Norris, Frank, III, 84
Norton, Andre, III, 13; VI, 32
Noyes, Alfred, II, 52

Orwell, George, I, 29, 58; II, 41, 81, 113, 150, 158, 208, 257, 274; 283, 289; III, 25, 82, 139; V, 8, 10, 11, 16, 18, 23, 27, 30, 44; VI, 14, 19
Ouspensky, P. D., II, 250

Padgett, Lewis, II, 124
Paltock, Robert, II, 296
Pangborn, Edgar, III, 98, 118, 127
Pater, Walter, II, 83
Paxton, William, II, 120
Peake, Mervyn, II, 127
Piper, H. Beam, III, 13
Poe, Edgar Allan, II, 11, 20, 46, 47, 96, 117, 204, 217, 221; III, 136; VI, 58; VII, 17

Pohl, Fred, II, 290; V, 27; VI, 14; VII, 12; IX, 14, 25
Powell, Anthony, II, 89
Priestley, J. B., II, 250; III, 27; VI, 14

Read, Herbert, V, 30
"Reign of George VI, The" (anon.), V, 12
Rose, Lois and Stephen, III, 22
Roshwald, Mordecai, III, 54
Rousseau, Victor, I, 76; II, 208
Ruskin, John, I, 88

Scholes, Robert, I, 87
Seaborn, Adam, II, 17, 20, 94
Seabrook, William, VI, 15
Seicho, Komatsu, II, 287
Serling, Rod, IX, 25
Serviss, Garrett P., II, 180, 264
Shanks, Edward, II, 25
Shakespeare, William, I, 72; II, 1, 163; IV, 39
Shaver, Richard, II, 21
Shaw, George Bernard, V, 4, 9
Sherrif, R. C., II, 34
Sheckley, Robert, II, 290
Shiel, M. P., II, 283; III, 16, 31
Shelley, Mary, V, 14; VII, 17
Shloovsky, Victor, II, 284
Shinicki, Hoshi, II, 287
Shute, Nevil, III, 52, 54; V, 11
Sillitoe, Alan, III, 29; VI, 40
Silverberg, Robert, II, 73, 192; III, 134; IX, 14

Simak, Clifford, II, 73; III, 10, 116; VI, 14
Singer, Isaac, III, 4
Skinner, B. F., I, 58; II, 189; V, 43
Smith, Cordwainer, III, 122, 123; VII, 9; IX, 8
Smith, E. E. "Doc," II, 106, 205; VII, 11
Smollett, Tobias, II, 279
Snow, C. P., I, 38, 50; II, 134
Spinrad, Norman, II, 284; III, 128
Stahl, Henri, II, 156
Stapledon, Olaf, I, 14; II, 128, 157, 204, 275; III, 82; V, 8
Stevenson, Robert Louis, V, 14
Stewart, George, II, 123
Strugatsky, Arkadi and Boris, II, 86
Sturgeon, Theodore, II, 12, 41, 173; III, 49, 75, 92, 98; VII, 6; IX, 25
Sullivan, Walter, III, 121
Swift, Jonathan, II, 13, 138, 216, 271; III, 2, 137; IV, 50
Symmes, John Cleves, See Adam Seaborn
Szilard, Leo, III, 33, 145

Taine, John, II, 300; VII, 11
Tenn, William, II, 124; III, 116; IX, 25
Thomas, D. M., II, 5
Tolkien, J. R. R., II, 152, 189, 220; III, 122; VIII, 41, 42
Tsiolkovsky, Konstantin, III, 32

Tracy, Louis, II, 276
Tremaine, Orlin, II, 249, 255
Tucker, Wilson, III, 92
Twain, Mark, II, 23, 63, 117; III, 118

vanVogt, A. E., II, 209, 300; III, 74; V, 8; VII, 11; IX, 25
Verne, Jules, I, 10, 44, 49; II, 7, 9, 11, 34, 47, 53, 130, 149, 157, 183, 204, 214, 217, 246, 302, 303; III, 1, 2, 32, 46, 66, 74, 100; VI, 39, 58; VIII, 22, 23; IX, 18, 19
Visiak, E. H., III, 16, 31
Voltaire, II, 66; III, 115
Vonnegut, Kurt, Jr., I, 48, 76; II, 55, 88, 112, 176, 260, 261, 290; III, 24, 62, 101, 102, 103, 107; V, 11
Vosnensky, Andrei, II, 5

Wallace, F. L., II, 142
Waugh, Evelyn, III, 79; V, 42
Weinbaum, Stanley G., II, 204; III, 74
Weiss, Miriam Strauss, III, 22
Wellard, James, V, 9
Wells, H. G., I, 28, 33, 49, 58, 76, 88; II, 9, 11, 18, 19, 27, 28, 29, 35, 40, 47, 52, 73, 80, 90, 125, 137, 139, 148, 150, 151, 153, 157, 159, 164, 166, 179, 184, 208, 214, 217, 239, 240, 245, 246, 256, 264, 282, 283, 293, 294, 303, 305; III, 1, 3, 6,

19, 25, 32, 46, 68, 74, 78, 81,
95, 106, 109; V, 4, 9, 10, 23,
30, 38, 43; VI, 14, 58; VII, 9,
16, VIII, 7
Werfel, Franx, I, 21
West, Anthony, III, 83
West, Rebecca, III, 19
White, E. B., VI, 27
White, T. H., II, 283
Whitman, Walt, IV, 35
Wilkins, John, II, 213, 296
Williams, Christopher, III, 61
Williams, Charles, I, 21; II, 152
Williamson, Jack, II, 2; VII, 11,
26

Wollheim, Donald, VII, 14
Wright, Lan, II, 3
Wyndham, John, I, 22; III, 36,
50, 67, 77, 106; IV, 40; VII, 9

Yeats, William Butler, IV, 9
Yefremov, Ivan, II, 48, 132, 194
Young, Michael, I, 76; VI, 40
Yukio, Mishima, II, 287

Zelazny, Roger, VI, 41; VII, 9
Zamyatin, Eugeny, II, 80, 150,
304; III, 43; V, 42, 44